Taming Randomized Contr‹ Trials in Education

CW01083090

There is a recent surge in the use of randomized controlled trials (RCTs) within education globally, with disproportionate claims being made about what they show, 'what works', and what constitutes the best 'evidence'. Drawing on up-to-date scholarship from across the world, *Taming Randomized Controlled Trials in Education* critically addresses the increased use of RCTs in education, exploring their benefits, limits and cautions, and ultimately questioning the prominence given to them.

While acknowledging that randomized controlled trials do have some place in education, the book nevertheless argues that this place should be limited. Drawing together all arguments for and against RCTs in a comprehensive and easily accessible single volume, the book also adds new perspectives and insights to the conversation; crucially, the book considers the limits of their usefulness and applicability in education, raising a range of largely unexplored concerns about their use. Chapters include discussions on:

- The impact of complexity theory and chaos theory.
- Design issues and sampling in randomized controlled trials.
- Learning from clinical trials.
- Data analysis in randomized controlled trials.
- Reporting, evaluating and generalizing from randomized controlled trials.

Considering key issues in understanding and interrogating research evidence, this book is ideal reading for all students on Research Methods modules, as well as those interested in undertaking and reviewing research in the field of education.

Keith Morrison is Professor of Education and Vice-rector at the University of Saint Joseph, Macao, China.

Taming Randomized Controlled Trials in Education

Exploring Key Claims, Issues and Debates

Keith Morrison

 Routledge
Taylor & Francis Group

LONDON AND NEW YORK

First published 2021
by Routledge
2 Park Square, Milton Park, Abingdon, Oxon OX14 4RN

and by Routledge
52 Vanderbilt Avenue, New York, NY 10017

Routledge is an imprint of the Taylor & Francis Group, an informa business

British Library Cataloguing-in-Publication Data
A catalogue record for this book is available from the British Library

Library of Congress Cataloging-in-Publication Data
A catalog record has been requested for this book

ISBN: 978-0-367-48651-8 (hbk)
ISBN: 978-0-367-48652-5 (pbk)
ISBN: 978-1-003-04211-2 (ebk)

Typeset in Goudy
by Taylor & Francis Books

For Fun Hei: a non-random happiness

Contents

Illustrations

Figures

Tables

Acknowledgements

I am very grateful to the three reviewers of the manuscript of this book, for their wise, positive and helpful feedback; thank you. I am very grateful to Sarah Tuckwell and Lucy Stewart from Routledge, for their help and support in the preparation of this book. Thanks are due to the following publishers and authors for permission to use materials in the text:

Alliance for Useful Evidence (Nesta), for material from: Puttick, R. (2018) *Mapping the Standards of Evidence Used in UK Social Policy*. London: Alliance for Useful Evidence (Nesta); Gough, D., Oliver S., and Thomas J. (2013) *Learning from Research: Systematic Reviews for Informing Policy Decisions: A Quick Guide. A paper for the Alliance for Useful Evidence*. London: Nesta. *Cass School of Education and Communities*, University of East London, for material from Menter, I. (2013) From interesting times to critical times? Teacher education and educational research in England, *Research in Teacher Education*, 3 (1), 38–40. *Elsevier*, for material from Deaton, A. and Cartwright, N. (2018) Understanding and misunderstanding randomized controlled trials. *Social Science and Medicine*, 208 (1), 2–21. Gene Glass, for material from Glass, G. V. (2000) *Meta-analysis at 25*. Available from: http://glass.ed.asu.edu/gene/ papers/meta25.html. *Informa UK Ltd*, for Kvernbekk, T. (2018) Evidence-based educational practice. In *Oxford Research Encyclopedia of Education*. doi:10.1093/acrefore/ 9780190264093.013.187. *James Sheldon*, for material from Sheldon, J. (2016) 'What Works' doesn't work: the problem with the call for evidence based practices in the classroom. Paper Badass Teachers Association White Paper Collection, 1 (2). *John Wiley & Sons*, for words from Norman, G. (2003) RCT = results confounded and trivial: the perils of grand educational experiments. *Medical Education*, 37 (7), 582–584. *Sage Publications Inc.*, for material from Robinson, D. H. (2004) An interview with Gene V. Glass. *Educational Researcher*, 33 (3), 26–30. *Taylor and Francis*, for material from: Cohen, L., Manion, L. and Morrison, K. R. B. (2018) *Research Methods in Education* (8th edition). Abingdon, UK: Routledge; Morrison, K. R. B. (2001) Randomised controlled trials for evidence-based education: some problems in judging 'what works'. *Evaluation and Research in Education*, 15 (2), 1–15. doi:10.1080/ 09500790108666984; Morrison, K. R. B. (2012) Searching for causality in the wrong places. *International Journal of Social Research Methodology*, 15 (1), 15–30. doi:10.1080/13645579.2011.594293; Morrison, K. R. B. and van der Werf, M. (2017) Discourses of diversity in evidence-based educational research and policy making. *Educational Research and Evaluation*, 23 (3&4), 75–77. doi:10.1080/13803611.2017.1400158; Simpson, A. (2019) The evidential basis of "evidence-based education": an introduction to the special issue. *Educational Research and Evaluation*, 25 (1&2), 1–6. doi:10/1080/13803611.2019.1617979; Wiliam, D. (2019) Some reflections on the role of evidence in improving education. *Educational Research and Evaluation*, 25 (1&2), 127–139. doi: 10.1080/13803611.2019.1617993. *US Department of Education* (2018) *Reporting Guide for Study Authors: Group Design Studies*. Washington, DC: US Department of Education, Institute of Education Sciences, National Center for Education Evaluation and Regional Assistance, What Works Clearinghouse.

Introduction

Understanding and interpreting randomized controlled trials (RCTs) in education can be seductive, taking superficial evidence to declaim that something 'works'. If only it were that simple, but it is not. Not only is the 'what works' agenda replete with challenges and concerns, but RCTs, as part of 'what works', have challenges, criticisms, problems as well as promises and benefits.

It would take courage, even foolhardiness, to suggest that best practices in education should not be informed by evidence, or that RCTs have no place in evidence-based education. Rather, more fitting questions ask what kind of evidence is acceptable and what place RCTs have in the panoply of evidence-based education respectively. Both of these questions raise concerns about validity, reliability, generalizability, utility, acceptability of RCTs in evidence-based research in education, and, in turn, these expose concerns and challenges surrounding RCTs in education.

To address concerns in RCTs and evidence, this volume falls into two main sections. Part I sets RCTs in educational research in the context of evidence-based education and the 'what works' agenda. It argues that 'what works', whilst appealing in its simplicity, begs very many important questions. A key feature here is the issue of causality, as it features in terms of what users of research need to know, together with transferability and generalizability. Part One includes a chapter on causality, to show its complexity and to lay the ground for discussing causality within the context of RCTs in Part II, in which, whilst RCTs claim to be able to show that a particular intervention causes a particular outcome, this, in fact, is fraught with problems. RCTs are weak at showing mechanisms of causality and factors which, singly and in combination, bring about a particular outcome, and how these operate in a specific situation. Whilst one should not judge an RCT by what it does not purport to be able to do, *viz.* to show the detailed mechanisms of causality, nevertheless this is a weak spot for RCTs, as their inability to handle causality sufficiently undermines their generalizability and utility.

Having set the context of RCTs within the wider field of 'what works' in evidence-based education, Part II turns to RCTs *per* se. It introduces onto-logical and epistemological principles and challenges facing RCTs in educa-tion. Further, it strives to set a more fitting place for RCTs in educational research than the present supremacy that they currently command in the eyes of some policy makers, decision makers, researchers and practitioners. Taking the requirements of fitness for purpose, the book argues that, whilst RCTs in education are fit for some purposes, actually (a) these purposes are very limited, and (b) the demands for quality in RCTs renders suspect many existing RCTs in education.

This book is not anti-RCTs. Far from it. Rather, it advocates a much more sober assessment than often currently exists of what they have to offer educa-tionists. It suggests that, if they are to be fit for purpose, then they must improve their quality, recognize their limitations, and adopt much more modest claims for what they show about 'what works'. Whilst their appeal to simplicity may be attractive, they neglect many important considerations which education and the 'what works' agenda require. In other words, they have a place in educational research, but a higher bar than currently obtains should be set for their quality and a much more tempered view should be adopted of what they really show, do not show and contribute to education. They don't show much.

This book draws together over two decades of discourse, research in, and practice of, RCTs in education and catches current concerns surrounding them. It reports the landscape of RCTs in education and their challenges, widely referenced and clearly argued.

This book opens up issues to argue for a necessary fuller, more inclusive debate to take place on 'what works' and 'how we know'. It adopts a delib-erately sceptical view of 'what works', and it calls out policy makers, researchers, decision takers and educationists to justify the judgement that something does or does not 'work'. It draws together in a single volume the several arguments and issues raised in the voluminous material on 'what works', what counts as evidence, and what should be included in the debate, both *per* se and with particular regard to RCTs in education.

This book introduces key issues in understanding and interrogating research evidence and its potential contribution to the 'what works' agenda, focusing on RCTs in education. Whilst RCTs have their place in educational research, fitness for purpose dictates that its place is not all-conquering, and, indeed, is considerably more modest than its protagonists might claim.

Part I

Setting the scene for randomized controlled trials in education

Part I sets the context for considering RCTs in education, locating them within the evidence-based movement and the 'what works' agenda that has been sweeping across the world for over two decades, i.e. sufficient time for its wrinkles, conditions and problems to be identified and addressed. The argument presented is that, when considering the value of RCTs in education, we should rid ourselves of the belief that 'what works' is straightforward and unproblematic. Rather, the opposite is the case. 'What works' is not only a matter of empirical demonstration; it is a deliberative, value-laden, value-rich, value-saturated matter, and it is unlikely that all parties involved will agree as to whether something 'works' or does not 'work'. Indeed, the very definitions of 'works' and 'evidence' are contested and unclear.

Chapter 1 opens up the field by raising an initial set of questions in considering what constitutes acceptable evidence and what constitutes 'works' in the 'what works' debate. These indicate that 'what works' contains important sub-questions and sub-issues, and that, even if satisfactory answers can be provided to these questions, this is still insufficient, as predictability, transferability, generalizability and trustworthiness are questionable.

Chapter 2 identifies definitional problems in 'what works', what is 'evidence', what exactly is the 'what' in 'what works', how do we 'know' or judge if something 'works' or does not 'work', and what constitutes acceptable evidence. The chapter argues that evidence is not neutral; rather it is that which is brought forward to make a case beyond a reasonable doubt. The chapter draws on legal analogies in presenting evidence, and sets out demanding criteria for evidence that can be applied to 'evidence' in education. This, it is argued, enables rigour to be demonstrated in judging 'what works' and what are appropriate indicators of this. In turn, this raises challenges for educators trying to disentangle 'what works' in a complex, multivariate, multidimensional world, and assessing and evaluating 'what works' in a way that is faithful to such complexity. The problem is compounded because almost anything has been shown by research evidence to 'work', so the user of 'evidence' has to be able to discriminate between different quality in, and uses of, research findings. This returns to issues raised in Chapter 1, of the need to address many questions in deciding whether something 'works', as there is no single, universal yardstick for objective measures. Whether something 'works' depends on who is judging and on whose evidence, in what circumstances and conditions, and so on; it is a human activity, not a mechanistic formula. Whilst the power and integrity of evidence are important, the chapter opens up a vast array of questions and concerns about a wider range of topics and elements concerning research evidence.

Chapter 3 sets the context for discussions of causality in RCTs, and, in doing so, makes a case for requiring a much more nuanced, complex, cautious and less naïve approach to understanding causality than RCTs provide. To the argument that the strength of RCTs is precisely because they show causality, other factors having been controlled out or simply over-ridden, the chapter argues that this claim is not as simple as RCTs would have it be, and that causality as espoused in RCTs is much more problematic and uncertain, not least in mistaking as 'noise' what is, in fact, part of the 'signal'.

Having set the scene for considerations of 'evidence' and its limitations, 'what works' and questions against its apparent simplicity, and the importance of attending to causality, Part II moves specifically to RCTs in education.

Chapter 1

Questioning evidence of 'what works' in educational research

Introduction and overview

This chapter argues that:

- Findings concerning 'what works' are equivocal rather than certain, often lacking predictability and generalizability.
- RCTs are only one of a vast range of types, methodologies and methods of research in education, and that to elevate them above others is misconceived when one applies the 'fitness for purpose' criterion.
- Defining 'evidence', 'what works', what is the 'what' in 'what works', and what 'works' means, is open to very different interpretations.
- Understanding these different interpretations raises many questions that call out all-too-easy definitions and answers.
- A sober, critical, sceptical view of 'evidence' and 'what works' is a caution against over-simplistic assertions of what research shows and what can be taken from research in education.

This lays the ground for interrogating the appeal of RCTs in Part II.

The limits of what 'research shows'

'The research said that this would work. I tried it. It didn't.'

It would be hard to justify not having evidence inform what we do in education. We may think that what we do is the best way, but relying on intuition and experience may be insufficient; we may be recycling poor practice whilst earnestly believing that it is good practice because we have been doing it for years. As Cain (2019) remarks, reliable research is better than alternatives such as trial and error, or, indeed personal hunches (p. 10). In a climate of accountability, practices should be informed by evidence rather than its lack. Indeed, Didau (2015), Gorard et al. (2018) and Major and Higgins (2019) note that many practices are not informed by evidence and continue in spite of evidence of their ineffectiveness and harm.

The move towards evidence-based education in judging 'what works' appears unstoppable. However, what constitutes evidence, and evidence of 'what' is not always clear. There is no 'one size fits all' in considering what kind of evidence is important, nor how it is gained and used. It may come from a survey, a test, an observation, an RCT, from the views and wisdom of acknowledged experts, and so on. Fitness for purpose is paramount, and evidence must be actionable and useful. This book, whilst applauding the moves made towards promoting evidence-informed education in principle, argues that, in the 'what works' agenda, considerable caution must be exercised in considering the nature and trustworthiness of the evidence, in making the connection between 'evidence' and 'what works', and in moving from evidence to practice. And evidence is only one element in the 'what works' agenda, nor does it provide conclusive, eternal and incontestable truths, but it helps. Research-informed decision making, practice and policy are surely better than their non-informed counterparts.

We have to give the lie to the emphasis placed on large-scale, putatively disinterested and objective 'evidence' and the privileging of RCTs as fitting 'evidence' for 'what works' as the sole or main path to salvation in improving education. This book calls out those whose preoccupation with certain kinds of 'evidence' renders them partially sighted or blind to the benefits of other kinds of evidence in yielding truths in a complex world or whose all-too-easy dismissal of values-based teaching and the professional wisdom of experienced practitioners is accompanied by a reliance on 'evidence' whose basis is shaky, non-generalizable and subject to personal, selective preference. For sure, RCTs have their place, but there is no reason why they should sit alone on the throne of what is considered to be suitable evidence.

Moves towards a 'what works' agenda in education, which is intended to be evidence-based and/or evidence-informed, has been sweeping across the world almost without hindrance. It is the new orthodoxy, not least as it serves so many agendas. It purports to have a benevolent intent, improving education and avoiding relying on untried interventions in education; it furthers outcomes-based approaches, accountability and performance metrics; and it seeks to draw on 'best evidence' and research. Evidence-informed practice uses the best evidence to achieve desired goals or outcomes and, indeed, to prevent undesirable outcomes.

This immediately opens up the debate, as the term 'best' is not an empirical matter; it is a normative, moral and ethical matter, requiring judgement, statements of values and deliberation. It moves beyond pragmatics.

That education should be informed by cumulative and progressive research is surely beyond question. Like medicine, the ongoing accumulation of research evidence can make great strides forward in improving practice. On the other hand, evidence-based practice has received criticism for: misrepresenting the nature of the debate on what schools and educational institutions *should* be doing; neglecting the inclusion of values in, purposes of, and justifications for education and its decision making; narrowing the curriculum to that which is tested; making contestable assumptions about transferability; and over-simplifying what is, essentially, a highly complex, variable-dense, multi-faceted, multi-layered and multifactorial situation in classrooms and schools. Evidence-based practice has been criticized for its amoral, pragmatist approach to education, for over-simplifying educational discourses on how to improve education, for adopting too narrow, even singular, an approach to what constitutes 'evidence', for accepting all too easily what count as research findings, for overstating the generalizability of research findings, and for excluding a multitude of factors in addressing the 'what works' agenda. It has done little to close the gap between research and practice, and between research and policy making.

Whilst it would be difficult to support the view that educational practice should not be evidence-informed, and whilst 'what works' should be a worthy goal of education, it is the brand or type of 'what works' and 'evidence' that is often considered to be important. High quality research and evidence are essential – of the essence – if we are to ensure that the often once-in-a-lifetime experience of education is to be maximized. But 'evidence' is a slippery term, as it includes more than empirical data and Shakespeare's 'ocular proof' of observed phenomena; rather it engages issues of worth, values, morals, purposes, justifications, opinions, judgements, contestation and questioning, and emanating from many sources. It requires the status, credibility, rigour, scope, worth and applicability of 'evidence' and 'what works' to be interrogated. 'What works' is as much a matter of values and judgement as it is of empirical outcomes; it is a normative, not simply an empirical matter (Sanderson, 2010).

Even though the agendas and time frames of researchers and policy makers often collide rather than coincide, or research bears little direct relation or relevance to policy formation and decision making, nevertheless policy should be expertly informed. Governments and policy makers are charged with the responsibility of examining issues in depth. In an age of evidence-based everything, educationists have a right to have policy decisions informed by more than ideology. Answers to questions such as 'what evidence?', 'evidence of what?' and 'whose evidence?' are essential. The claim that evidence shows such-and-such is almost always questionable, as it is not always clear what, exactly, the evidence is 'evidence of', and this raises issues of validity and fairness. Solution-focused and strategic policy making, in all areas of educational policy making, should be informed by the best evidence available. Ask yourselves: 'is it happening?'

Best practice in education should be informed by evidence. Research evidence is a key means of updating and benchmarking practice, improving practice, for practitioners of all types and persuasions, not simply for a coterie of academics or like-minded educationists. High quality research should make a difference; it should open minds. As with policy making, educational practice should be informed by the best evidence available. Again, ask yourselves: 'is it happening?'

The reader wishing to find out 'what works' is all-too-easily swamped by materials from a range of organizations with a benevolent intent in helping educationists and practitioners in many spheres of education to use 'evidence' in promoting best practice; a worthy intention. For example: the What Works Clearinghouse; the Education Endowment Foundation together with its Teaching and Learning Toolkit; the Campbell Collaboration; the Evidence for Policy and Practice Information and Co-ordinating Centre (EPPI-Centre); the Comprehensive School Reform Quality Center; the Best Evidence Encyclopedia; the Coalition for Evidence-Based Policy; the What Works initiative and What Works Centres; the Evidence Based Education organization; the York University Centre for Reviews and Dissemination; the Alliance for Useful Evidence (Nesta); the Centre for Evidence Informed Policy and Practice; and countless systematic reviews, research syntheses and meta-analyses, some of which date back well before the advent of the 'what works' movement (e.g. the journal *Review of Educational Research*).

However, as Nesta (2016) remarks: evidence 'rarely speaks for itself' (p. 4); it is mediated and aggregated through a host of sources, parties and affiliations. Hence this book is cautionary. We risk all too easily slipping into simplistic, if attractive, conclusions about 'what works' and what constitutes usable 'evidence'. Rather than rushing headlong into accepting 'evidence' as indicating 'what works', it is important, for safeguarding high quality education, to address a range of questions, and the list is long, for example:

Definitions

1 What does 'works' mean?
2 What is the 'what' in 'what works'?
3 What constitutes 'evidence'?
4 Whose evidence?
5 Is an opinion 'evidence', and, if so whose opinions count?
6 What is 'good evidence' for 'what works'?
7 Compared with what do we judge if something 'works'? Is it any better or worse than other 'treatments'/methods?

Validity and reliability

1 Evidence of what, exactly?
2 Given that 'what works' should be judged in terms of the stated purposes of a project or intervention, how sensible or possible is it to separate out those purposes from the whole gamut of purposes of education, intended or not, that are served by a particular intervention?
3 How to address the complexity, multi-dimensionality and multi-valency of constituents of defining 'what works'?
4 How can we be *sure* that something works every time or most of the time?

5 When is evidence enough to be deemed secure?

6 Is evidence, *per se* enough on which to base decisions about what to do?

7 What to do with research that shows that something 'works' sometimes but not always?

8 How secure are the findings? Have they been corroborated?

9 Over how many occasions and contexts must something 'work' for it to be claimed that it 'works' (e.g. a joke works well once but dies if repeated; a student may obtain a fluke high or low score once)? When is 'enough' really enough?

10 When does something 'work', and for how long must it work before it is deemed to be successful?

11 After how long must something 'work'?

12 When to assess whether something 'works' (assessing in too short a time or too long a time can bring unreliability or invalidity)?

13 What variables and factors were not included in the research, hence were not controlled (e.g. teacher enthusiasm and expertise)?

14 What do the terms used in research mean to different participants and readers (e.g. 'direct instruction', 'collaborative learning', 'cognitive demand'), often being very general in nature?

15 What significance is accorded to the concepts and practices in question, as these vary from culture to culture and context to context ('significance' is not the same as 'presence', e.g. the 'Big Five' personality traits may be important in one culture but may be unimportant in another culture, even if they are present)?

16 How acceptable, useful or naïve is it to reduce the dynamic interpersonal complexity of teaching and learning to a single number (e.g. effect size) and to invest so much in a single figure or a 'yes' or 'no' ('yes, it works'; 'no, it doesn't')?

17 How valid and reliable are proxy variables for matters which are not directly observable (e.g. intelligence; understanding; learning)?

18 What kinds of data and methodologies are required to understand 'what works'?

19 What are the limits and possibilities of different methodologies and methods in providing useful research evidence of 'what works'?

Judgements and conditionality

1 Under what conditions does something 'work', 'not work' etc.?

2 In whose terms is 'what works' being judged ('what works' in one person's eyes does not work in another person's eyes)? There is no one version or judgement of 'what works'.

3 How to take account of the point that 'what works' is a matter of judgement rather than data, and that this judgement is imbued with moral, values-related and ethical concerns?

4   What 'works' for whom, and under what conditions?
5   Why does something 'work' for some people and not for others, and which parts 'work' and do not 'work' for whom, and why?
6   Against what and whose criteria is 'what works' judged?
7   Who decides if something does or does not 'work'?
8   How do we know when something has 'worked'?
9   At what point is it decided that something does or does not 'work', or partially 'works'?
10 Why categorize in absolute, binary terms 'what works' or does not 'work'?
11 Should 'what works' be an absolute or a graded category; should 'what works' and 'success' be on a scale rather than a category?
12 What is the minimum level needed to show that something 'works'?
13 At what cost/benefit is 'what works' being judged?

Consequences

1   What is the negative fallout of 'what works', and on whom?
2   How much does 'what works' actually matter?
3   How far does 'what works' risk short-termism?
4   What happens when teachers and policy makers get hold of research?
5   How much research evidence do we need in order to justify a policy decision?
6   How selective is the reading of 'evidence' and what it means?
7   How does externally imposed 'evidence' cede the professional wisdom and autonomy of teachers to political powers and decision makers if handed-down recipes become the order of the day?

Moving from description to judgement to prescription is seductive but commits a fundamental category mistake in moving so lightly from an 'is' to an 'ought', and, whilst 'what works' is a neat slogan, it can conceal and mis-represent, rather than clarify, educational practices, decision making and the rigour which must be exercised in interrogating research 'evidence'. All too easily the evidence-based movement can be hijacked by political agendas (Biesta, 2010; Bjerre and Reimer, 2014; Wiberg, 2014). Indeed, Greenhalgh et al. (2014, p. 1) note that a similar problem exists in the medical field, with which RCTs in education have often been compared (Chapter 6), where industries producing drugs and medical devices increasingly set research agendas and define what is to count as a disease, i.e. vested interests are at play.

Further, evidence underdetermines what teachers do in considering and deciding what to do in their own classrooms; other factors and considera-tions (e.g. aims, cultural purposes, values, environmental and contextual matters (Rømer, 2014)) come into play in the theatre of teaching and learning (Kvernbekk, 2011). Education should not simply submit to the yoke of evidence-based research or render invisible those matters of education which are not visible in evidence-based research (Rømer, 2014).

The simple label 'what works' risks overlooking questions such as 'compared to what?' and 'at what point does one decide whether something has worked, not worked, worked not very well, worked very well, and so on?'.

SPORTS INTERVIEWER: 'How good is your tennis?'
TENNIS PLAYER: 'Compared to what?'

How many times do surveys ask such questions, without any indication of criteria, standards for making judgements, and reference groups for comparisons? My tennis is fantastic, compared to a monkey's, but hopeless and risible when compared to a Wimbledon champion. The point is this: in the 'what works' agenda we need comparison standards and reference groups, and we need criteria and threshold statements to decide if and when something can be judged to be 'working', 'not working', 'working a little', 'working a lot' and so on. RCTs claim to address both of these requirements in having control groups/counterfactuals for comparison and measures of effect size respectively. How far this is acceptable is investigated throughout this book.

Further, the speed with which authors claim that 'research shows that ...' is disarming. Typically, the first response to such a claim should be 'no it doesn't'. The often outrageous claim that 'research has shown' should be replaced by certain 'if and only if' (iff) requirements:

> this piece of research, with such and such a sample, in such and such a context, subject to such and such a set of conditions, constraints, contingencies, boundaries and limitations, mindful of such-and-such a set of alternative explanations, *suggests* that ... whilst other studies suggest that ..., and that whilst it might 'work' for some areas it also has negative outcomes.

Just because research has shown that such-and-such might 'work' in a such-and-such a research setting, be it contrived or naturalistic, this is no reason to believe that it will work in a different temporal, locational, contextual setting (the transferability and generalizability issue), or even the same setting, a second time. A joke told once is funny; a joke re-told a second time is boring, even annoying. What works with Form A is a disaster with the parallel Form B, even with the same teacher, the same curriculum, the same pedagogy, the same timing, the same resources and similar, but not identical, students. The same teaching works wonders with student A's learning, but for his partner sitting next to him in the same class there is little or no learning taking place. If only there were simple recipes, but there are not. To think otherwise is an exercise in self-deception. And, indeed, custom might stale the infinite variety of classrooms.

What has happened may be a poor predictor of what might happen; not only are there inbuilt limits of induction but in an emergent, nonlinear world in which theories of complexity and chaos show sensitivity to initial conditions and the ongoing interplay of a vast array of variables and factors in our 'normal' lives, there are massive, unpredicted and unpredictable changes, tipping points and phase changes (new worlds).

Cartwright (2009) suggests that inferring from efficacy (e.g. applicability to an ideal, specific group in question) to effectiveness, e.g. applicability to wider, 'real world' and different populations, is 'induction on a wing and a prayer' (p. 203). Further, she argues that to be able to decide on whether efficacy can be turned into effectiveness, the two being different, requires theory without which there is 'zero evidentiary power' for such a move (p. 204). RCT's require an extraneous underpinning theory, without which evidence is meaningless (Cartwright, 2009, pp. 204–205).

Morrison and van der Werf (2018, p. 1) comment that thesis supervisors routinely castigate their students for using the phrase 'research has shown'. Indeed, they frequently delight in showing (off) that, in fact, research has *not* shown such-and-such. Novice or enthusiastic researchers make claims for what research shows when, in reality, it simply doesn't show it. Whether a piece of research really 'shows' what it claims to show is an important and worthwhile question, as many claims do not stand up in the face of external validity – generalizability and wider applicability – and of internal validity, i.e. whether the research design, together with the evidence and analysis provided, actually support the claims being made.

The problem of 'what works' goes further: just because something 'works' in one research setting is no guarantee that it will 'work' in other contexts and situations, and something might 'work' for one party whilst 'not working' for another party. We delude ourselves if we really believe that what 'works' in one world will 'work' straightforwardly in another; the limits of transferability and applicability are legion, such that it is simply the optimism of naivety to think that what works here will work somewhere else. There is a difference between finding a result and using a result, between finding a cause and using a cause (Kvernbekk, 2018).

Different parties want different things from research evidence and make different cases for how research is used. For example, policy makers may want a popular 'quick fix'; researchers want evidence of causality; teachers want evidence of what will work in classrooms. Teachers who read research will almost automatically ask themselves 'that's all very well, but will this work with the students in my class?', 'what will I need to do to make it work here?', and 'what can I take from this research for my own work with these students?'. Biesta (2007, 2010), Oancea and Pring (2008) and Sheldon (2016) make a powerful case for teachers being the final arbiters of what 'what works' and what is usable in classrooms. As Sheldon (2016) writes: 'researchers should *not presume* to tell teachers how to deal with the situations they face' (p. 3). He argues that, as teachers:

we read literature, we take courses, we attend professional conferences, we reflect on our practice, we dialogue with colleagues; we do use what works for us, and we need to push back against those who seek to devalue this knowledge, whether they are a researcher, an administrator, a policy maker, or even fellow teachers.

(Sheldon, 2016, p. 5)

Teachers are not simply carrying out prescribed recipes; rather, Biesta (2007, 2010) suggests, the professional expertise, experience and judgement of teachers have a significant part to play here, otherwise democratic decisions and deliberation on the uptake of evidence-based practices in relation to aims and ends of education are under threat if professionals have to accept received decisions (Biesta, 2010, p. 493).

People take the results of research evidence and do something with it and to it; they have the sense to realize that it cannot simply be imported lock, stock and barrel without modification, and that to accept it without question is almost a guarantee that it won't work. To suggest that RCTs provide a recipe or a cookbook of what to do is not only to assume mistakenly that teaching is simply a technical delivery service – the application of handed-down procedures to formatted technicians – but it is to misrepresent what teachers actually do in classrooms, in which tacit knowledge (implicit learning and that which is often not formally taught or even verbalized; Sternberg, 1995, p. 321) and experience have a profound influence on how teaching and learning takes place.

Evidence-based methods, as Wiberg (2014) avers, risk becoming sole 'authoritative knowledge', thereby undermining the professional judgement of educators and turning it into 'conforming judgement' that is subject to an 'authoritarian structure of guidance' (p. 51). Indeed, she notes that educators find it impossible not to exercise their judgement (p. 60). She alerts educators to the dangers of having politicians and administrators tell educators to use evidence-based methods, i.e. making choice behalf of professionals (p. 61), breeding conformity and the neglect of professionally contextualized practices. Educators, she avers, should avoid being seduced by the 'authoritative label' of being 'evidence-based' (p. 62). Similarly, Albrechtsen and Qvortrup (2014) caution again the degrading 'technological fantasy' of 'what works' as externally imposed requirements in the face of teacher professionalism (p. 74).

We don't have, and never will have, enough evidence to say unequivocally that something 'works', as it is far too simplistic a question. Even if we accept that 'what works' is, at best, probabilistic, we have to interrogate the 'evidence' and the case that the 'evidence' makes. What 'works', e.g. what makes a positive difference, or what serves a purpose, or what helps to achieve a goal, or what is successful, is fundamentally contentious. This problem is compounded by the nature, quality, scope and trustworthiness of the 'evidence' adduced. 'What works' depends in part on the question being asked and addressed (Hammersley, 2013, p. 13).

Conclusion

This entire book argues that we are still a long way from having sufficient trustworthy 'evidence', and that knowing with any certainty – even if it is probabilistic and constrained – is not only a chimera but it is asking the wrong question. Whilst we can easily create a hierarchy of evidence, this does not mean that the evidence is sufficiently safe for universal, local or even individual application. 'What works' should come with a government health warning to indicate the limits of its applicability, its negative as well as positive effects, the limits on what can and cannot be safely concluded from the evidence, the conditions under which it might or might not 'work', and a covering statement to say that, actually, to avoid the ecological fallacy, it might not 'work' in specific contexts. As the Association of Teachers and Lecturers (now the National Education Union) remarked in 2013: 'what works' is 'an oversimplified concept on which to base research and policy' (Association of Teachers and Lecturers, 2013, p. 1). We simply don't have enough evidence, other than in an unrefined or over-simplistic way, to suggest that something 'works'; indeed, this is too simplistic a question, and one to which only a highly conditional, simplistic answer can be given. Instead of 'what works', much more sensitive questions are required: 'what works, for whom, in the presence of which factors and conditions and in the absence of which factors and conditions, singly or in combination, in what ways and with what side effects, following what causal chains, how successfully, based on what and whose evidence and criteria, compared with what, with what level of trustworthiness, in whose eyes, and with what fallout?' This is by no means the entire question but simply an indicator of the complexity involved in understanding 'what works'.

We need a much more critical and rigorous interrogation of research 'evidence' and a healthier dose of doubt than current obtains, before accepting what research 'evidence' shows, and how credible and applicable it is.

Chapter 2

Understanding 'what works' and what constitutes 'evidence'

Introduction and overview

This chapter argues that:

- Simplistic notions of 'what works' are dangerous and misleading, and it is necessary to define terms: what is the 'what' in 'what works'; what does 'works' mean; what does 'evidence' mean, and what it means to 'know' and judge that something does or does not 'work'.
- Even when we might have clarified these meanings, this only moves us a small distance along the road to discovering 'what works', as it is necessary to examine and hold up to critical, sceptical interrogation the research studies that purport to provide 'evidence'.
- There are many challenges in deciding 'what works'.
- An initial checklist of questions can be asked not only of each piece of research evidence but of combined and collected research studies in meta-analysis, meta-meta-analyses and systematic reviews.

Having introduced this checklist, the chapter introduces areas in which judgements must be reached in deciding whether or not the research evidence passes muster in indicating whether or not something 'works'.

Definitional challenges

The question of what constitutes 'evidence' is important. 'Evidence' is not the same as 'data'; evidence concerns what is taken from data, and for what purposes. There are many definitions of 'evidence', and these have a wide embrace. The *Oxford English Dictionary*'s definition of 'evidence' is 'the available body of facts or information indicating whether a belief or proposition is true or valid'. Evidence is that which supports, confirms or disconfirms a claim or hypothesis, providing a reason or reasons to believe that something is, is not, may be in part or in whole, true or false (Kvernbekk, 2018); evidence-based practice comprises 'interventions to bring about desirable outcomes for one or more clients and prevent undesirable outcomes, guided by evidence of how well they work' (p. 4). In doing so, it requires decisions to be taken on what constitutes and counts as 'evidence'. This is immediately problematical, as it suggests that some evidence is stronger than others, that there is a hierarchy of evidence (e.g. the evidence from professional expertise and experience might not weigh as heavily as that from certain kinds of research; Oancea and Pring, 2008).

RCTs, with claims to indicate causality, are currently at the top of the ladder, whilst case studies and qualitative research are at the bottom (Alliance for Useful Evidence, 2016, p. 31). Pawson (2006, p. 49) comments that a hierarchy of evidence places RCTs at the top, followed, *seriatim*, by quasi-experimental studies; before-and-after comparisons; cross-sectional, random sample studies; process evaluation, formative studies and action research; qualitative case studies and ethnographies; descriptive examples of good practice; professional and expert opinion; and, at the bottom of the pile, user opinion. 'Evidence' has been moving inexorably towards that derived from RCTs, second to which are often correlational studies that derive from pre-tests and post-tests, warranted by an underpinning of robust theory (e.g. Slavin, 2016; See, 2018). Such rankings, privileging some kinds of evidence over others, violate concerns for fitness for purpose.

Placing RCTs at the top of an imaginary hierarchy is as ridiculous as saying that we should use only surveys to provide evidence, or only use naturalistic research; it is a nonsense. There is no universally privileged position for RCTs to be at the top of a hierarchy (Morrison and van der Werf, 2019). Indeed, if there were to be a hierarchy, RCTs should not be at the top, as they offer so little. The question of evidence is one of fitness for purpose, be the research experimental or non-experimental (Schwandt, 2009, p. 198). Jadad and Enkin (2007) note that to place RCTs at the top of a hierarchy of evidence is 'fundamentally wrong', as is a hierarchy itself (p. 106). Using hierarchies is little more than importing the 'baggage' of a limited, naïve view of scientific methodology (Rømer, 2014, pp. 110–111).

We have to consider what evidence is for (Kvernbekk, 2011, 2018). Is it, for example, to prove beyond a reasonable doubt, i.e. that there is a good reason to believe that something is true, recognizing that it might be fallible (Kvernbekk, 2011, p. 519), to support, to challenge, to confirm, to disconfirm to contribute to a claim? Many different kinds and sources can provide evidentiary support for a claim; in the context of 'what works' this is often taken to be empirical evidence from RCTs. However, that only goes a small distance in answering questions of 'evidence', as, for example, if it is to disconfirm or confirm that something is or is not possible, then only one piece of evidence might be required (Kvernbekk, 2018), whereas if we want to argue for generalizability then much more evidence may be needed. If we want to argue that intervention X is more effective than intervention Y, then we need to have evidence from comparative data, and this raise challenges of (a) establishing similar or identical conditions of causality, contexts and evidentiary sources and types and (b) establishing the trustworthiness and relative strength and power of the evidence (Chapter 5).

Schwandt (2009) argues that reliable evidence should answer three important questions; 'What happened here? What does that mean? Why did that happen?' Further, adopting the analogy of a law court, we make judgements of evidence based on the principle of 'innocent until proven guilty': for the sake of safety, risk reduction, safeguarding and protection of learners, teachers, educationists, learning, teaching and education, we start with the assumption that the research does *not* show that something 'works' or does not 'work', and then we proceed to demonstrate 'beyond a reasonable doubt' that something 'works' or does not 'work', after possible competing causes, judgements or explanations have been eliminated. In determining causality for example, as in RCTs, the legal 'but for' clause is invoked, that such-and-such would not have occurred *but for* the presence or action of such-and-such, e.g. 'but for' the defendant's negligent conduct, the plaintiff would not have been injured.

In law, evidence is attested to support a claim or a judgement, to support or contest a case. Here the burden of providing proof is on those who bring forward the evidence, and different kinds of evidence require different burdens of proof (Spencer and Spencer, 2013, p. 9), leading to a conclusion on the balance of probabilities (p. 13). This involves asking awkward questions to get at what might be construed to be the 'truth' of 'what works'. As Bickman and Reich (2009 p. 71) comment, to judge the quality of evidence, it is essential to know which questions were asked about such-and-such a topic, and of whom, why, how, in what form and under what conditions, i.e. to provide a warrant for credibility (see also Schwandt, 2009, p. 199; Major and Higgins, 2019, p. xi). Credibility is a subjective as well as an objective matter; it does not reside within the information itself but how people judge it; different people judge the same 'evidence' differently in the same and different conditions.

We can extend the analogy further. In a court of law what constitutes 'evidence' is carefully defined as 'any material which has the potential to change the state of a fact-finder's belief with respect to any factual proposition which is to be decided and which is in dispute' (Murphy and Glover, 2011, p. 1). Evidence must be relevant, sufficient and true (Thomas, 2004, p. 5). Scriven (2009) notes that, in a court of law, eyewitness testimony and observational evidence are important, subject to standards of credibility and trustworthiness. Similarly, Schwandt (2009) notes that historical evidence looks to speeches, documents, memoranda etc. Experimental evidence holds no privileged position in the evidential enterprise. Indeed the European Evaluation Society (2007), whilst noting that RCTs may be useful for some purposes, 'deplores' the view that RCTs are 'the best or only rigorous and scientific way' of conducting evaluation (quoted in Donaldson, 2009, p. 246), as they are rarely suitable for complex situations, limited in generalizability and in examining emerging and unintended outcomes, and that other approaches might be more suited to identify what works for whom and under what circumstances (p. 247).

There should be no hierarchies of evidence (Schwandt, 2009, p. 207). Data may be subjective, objective, personal, general, measures, meanings etc. (e.g. evidence from Upshur et al.'s (2001) conceptual taxonomy of evidence (quoted in Schwandt, 2009, p. 206)). Methods of data collection alone do not determine the validity, credibility, trustworthiness, believability and reliability of the evidence (Schwandt, 2009, p. 209); there is more to evidence than this, involving the judgements made of the evidence, and by whom.

Spencer and Spencer (2013) writing specifically about legal evidence, note that 'evidence' must abide by many criteria; it must be:

- admissible;
- ethically, legally, fairly and properly obtained;
- relevant (enabling a finding to make more or less probable that it would have been if the evidence had not been included), and logically defensible for the case in point;
- fair, i.e. not prejudiced or misleading;
- factual (rather than circumstantial);
- sufficient to be convincing;
- worthwhile ('evidential worth');
- of sufficient weight to warrant inclusion (salience and importance);
- open to challenge and interrogation;
- at a high standard of proof;
- clear on its presumptions and assumptions, and that these are defensible;
- reliable, trustworthy, valid and believable;
- suitably cogent and compelling;
- true (the truth, the whole truth and nothing but the truth, with no errors of commission or omission);
- unprejudiced and disinterested: objective;
- clear on its type and status (e.g. hearsay, fact, opinion, first-hand, oral, written etc.);
- provided by suitably competent people/sources (raising the question of 'who is the expert?');
- verifiable and able to be corroborated;
- consistent;
- trustworthy;
- presented in a suitable, appropriate form;
- available for public disclosure.

These many facets provide a standard of rigour which can be applied to the 'evidence' in judging 'what works'. For example, Mathison (2009) notes that 'good' evidence requires 'relevance, verisimilitude, coherence, justifiability, and contextuality' (p. 182). Julnes and Rog (2009) comment that for evidence to be useful it must be 'actionable' (p. 96), and that stakeholders have different needs and agendas and operate under different constraints and conditions (p. 125). Rallis (2009) notes that a requirement of evidence is probity ('goodness and absolute moral correctness, in determining what constitutes credible evidence in evaluation and applied research') (p. 169), and that this, in turn, recognizes that there are many ways of obtaining an understanding of a particular phenomenon. Without such probity, we hold to an impoverished view of humans and education (Mathison (2009) comments that credible evidence is not the province of one or two methods only). Schwandt (2009) notes that the inferential force of evidence needs to be judged as to how strongly it points to the claims made from it or to the hypotheses under consideration (p. 201). He gives a clear example of the need for careful consideration of the claims that are made from evidence: just because your dog worships you does not mean that you are wonderful (p. 201)!

The analogy of the court of law also raises the question of what is the equivalent court of appeal for deciding whether somethings 'works' or does not 'work' in education. Who are the experts, the decision makers, and the participants in coming to a decision? What if decision makers disagree? Whose view prevails?

Further, what, actually, is the 'what' in 'what works'? What we might think is a statement of the obvious is not so obvious. We might think that we have a clear definition of an intervention or a practice, but it may not be so clear to participants and readers of research. A teacher might think that she is using collaborative learning positively but her students might think that it is an exercise in dereliction of her duty as a teacher. A researcher in the United Kingdom and in China might accept the definition of higher order thinking as it appears in Bloom's taxonomy, but their interpretation of what it means in practice might be poles apart. One person's definition of, for example, direct instruction is another person's definition of a lecture or another person's definition of teacher-led question-and-answer, or another person's definition of the classroom-based elements of the flipped classroom, and so on. You call it 'collaborative learning'; I call it 'asking my friend when I get stuck'. I might think that I am conforming to the rubrics of an experiment only to find that another teacher is doing something completely different when abiding by the same rubrics.

What something actually is and what we think it is are not the same; an ontological and epistemological difference. We think, for example, that we are using a valid proxy for something called 'learning', i.e. which is often not directly observable, whereas the indicator that we are using is about performing without learning. We think we are measuring a student's understanding and knowledge in a test, but in fact we are measuring the student's test-taking, test-grooming and test-practice skills.

The same words mean different things. The English language is replete with contronyms and ambiguities, and even conceptual and definitional analysis may not solve the problem of different interpretations of what words-in-use mean to their users. The same practice (e.g. in an intervention) does not 'work' the same in different circles: Cartwright and Hardie (2012) give the example of an intervention to provide nutrition to young children, which worked successfully in Tamil Nadu but exactly the same intervention failed in Bangladesh because of differences in the social situation of mothers. Simpson (2018b) gives the example of the word 'tea' (p. 899), which can be used to denote the drink of infused leaves or a full meal eaten in the early evening; the two differ so greatly that to use them both in a single meta-analysis of RCTs makes little sense.

This problem is compounded when the data collection instruments use proxy indicators which may have limited validity or which may differ in application, meaning, instruments, agendas, timing, interpretation, connotation and significance across contexts, age groups, genders, classrooms, abilities, interests, locations, ethnicities, teachers, students, cultures and so on. In short, what we think we might be measuring may not be what we are actually measuring: we may think we are measuring student interaction and collaboration, but what we might actually be measuring could be student motivation, boredom or desperation, or teacher enthusiasm, expertise and coercion.

The problem is that, in a lot of educational research we are involved in what is a complex, dynamic, evolving, emergent, human-centred situation over time and with minds and behaviours at different stages of maturity. Yet what do we do: we use a single measure, or a 'before and after' assessment, or a few interviews, or a survey or two, and then we extrapolate from a simple statistic or proxy indicator to a vast field of human experience, relegating so much of what constitutes human behaviour to peripheral 'noise'. How demeaning, how belittling, how simplistic is that! Little wonder that teachers are suspicious of 'what research shows'. The failure of research to catch the behaviour, aspirations, intentions, conceptions and constructions of the world, views, experiences, interpretations, motivations, actions and what people deem to be important, is breath-taking.

The attribution of what 'works' means (e.g. 'success') is problematic. Different parties have different conceptions of success and 'what works', and different criteria and standards for judging it; what constitutes success in one person's eyes might be deemed less successful, or positively unsuccessful in another person's or party's eyes; this depends in part on the values and agendas of the person or party making the judgement, on whether the benefit of the intervention or practice is worth the cost, and on the negative fallout of the intervention. As Puttick (2018) notes: standards of evidence frequently differ for 'practical reasons' which may reflect the goals of the organization, and, indeed, different organizations come to different conclusions on the same intervention, *viz.*, some organizations judged it to have worked well, whilst other are less convinced, raising the questions of which party is correct and whether the intervention has 'worked' or not 'worked' (p. 5)

Why are the views, opinions and decisions of some people and parties concerning 'what works' privileged whilst those of others are downgraded, side-lined or simply ignored? For example, Rallis (2009) notes that a study of a federally funded summer program to improve the performance of young adolescents with emotional problems (p. 168) encountered challenges when the funders wanted 'externally defined outcome measures' whereas the evaluators wanted to know what participation in the program had meant to the teenagers involved (p. 169).

Do researchers really have more knowledge than teachers and less knowledge than policy makers? Is there a pecking order of credibility and legitimacy? Whose criteria and standards are being used here, and why (Didau, 2015, pp. 107–137)? Are the views of experts sufficient to endorse something as 'working'; after all, as Hirsch (1997) remarked, it is 'almost impossible' to find any piece of policy that has not been supported by research somewhere and by somebody (Hirsch, 1997). Oakley (2007) cites the example of research results which found that day care had adverse effects on children whilst other research found the opposite (p. 95). Similarly, Wiliam (2019) notes that 'almost anything works somewhere, and nothing works everywhere' (p. 137), such that asking 'what works' is the wrong question, and it should be replaced by 'under what circumstances does this work' (*ibid.*), thereby attesting to the conditional and contextual nature of success.

It is important to ask 'what works', for whom, where, under what conditions, constraints and contingencies, with what consequences – anticipated and unanticipated – and how to judge whether a practice or intervention is really 'working' and/or 'working' as intended. The answers that we receive to the question of 'what works' may depend on what is being asked and how it is being asked. Further, if something 'works' once or in one piece of research, does this constitute a sufficient criterion for saying that it 'works', and, if not, how many times, in how many contexts and in how many pieces of research must it occur, and who decides? And let us say that the research is rigorous, valid and secure; so what? How does that show 'what works' for me and for you; the two statements – 'what works' and 'for you/for me' – are synthetic, not analytic; it is a leap of faith to believe otherwise.

Whilst meta-analysis and research syntheses might be of assistance here, what if, in the examples of research included in them, there are different time scales and duration of the research studies, different research designs, methodologies, sample sizes and sampling strategies, instrumentation, age groups, ability groups, cultures and contexts, and what if the quality of one piece of research is weaker or stronger than others (Chapter 12)? What if not all the studies agree that something has 'worked', or if different degrees of success have been found, or, indeed, contradictory evidence is provided (and this includes, for example the problem of publication bias in which there is a tendency to publish only those studies which show success rather than failure or limited success; e.g. Cheung and Slavin, 2016; Connolly et al., 2017, p.162), or if the researcher 'cherry picks' which studies or parts of studies to use to support a claim? Cheung and Slavin (2016) note that papers reporting statistically significant findings were up to twice as likely to be published than those without such significance, even if the research designs used were the same.

There is no universally agreed objective yardstick against which to judge 'what works', despite indicators such as effect size or the widely discredited statistical significance. Judgement is a human activity, not simply cranking out a 'yes', 'no', 'partially' or whatever terminology one uses. In the face of this, human subjective judgement is not only important but, entirely correctly, open to question and potential criticism, not only on grounds of bias but on grounds of lack of expertise, failure to include such-and-such, unsubstantiated or unjustified personal definitions and so on.

'What works' is in part normative, a human judgement which involves values, opinions, worth, consideration of morals and ethics, purposes and intentions, i.e. non-observable but key elements of the human make-up, yet so much 'evidence' is reduced to the empirical and the instrumental (Sanderson, 2010), taking too little account of what other stakeholders might consider to be necessary and important (Julnes and Rog, 2009, p. 120). As Julnes and Rog contend, evidence is not credible in an abstract or universal sense, but, rather, might be credible under some conditions and not credible under other conditions (p. 120). Evidence also concerns what *has* happened – the past, however recent – rather than what will or might happen.

What power in terms of evidence is given to opinions, the opinions of experts and experienced professionals, the deliberative aspect of decision making in deciding 'what works'? Whilst evidence might include opinions and views canvassed, overall, evidence is a tool, not the end or sole tool, in deciding 'what works'. Evidence is the servant, not the 'master', in deciding 'what works' (Kvernbekk, 2016, p. 13); it might provide us with support or backing rather than universalizable proof of a claim, or indeed it might disconfirm a belief in 'what works'. As Kvernbeck (2016) remarks, 'evidence is *made*, not *found*' (p. 18).

Why is it, then, that empirical evidence, i.e. that which is verified, verifiable and falsifiable by observation and experience rather than by reflection, moral debate, ethical analysis, logic or theory, holds sway in the court of 'evidence'? Who decides which evidence is legitimate, which has more or less status, and which should or should not be included? Is the aggregation of many pieces of empirical research worth more or less than the deliberative approach to decision making? This is not to say that 'evidence' should not be empirical; far from it. It is to reiterate that evidence is not as neutral and disinterested as empiricists might argue; it is always incomplete, located within paradigms and open to abuse.

How many research studies constitute a minimum satisfactory number, over how many contexts, times, situations, cultures, groups, locations and so on? This is only one aspect of 'what works'; as Kvernbekk (2018) argues, we need to know the causal *strength*, the causal *frequency*, and the causal *tendency* of an intervention or practice. Whilst effect size may indicate the causal strength of an intervention (though this is questionable; see Chapter 10), this leaves unaddressed the issue of frequency (regularity) or tendency (the scope of the findings: over how many groups, contexts and situations).

Further, over how long must an intervention and its effects remain for it to be judged effective or efficacious? When should the assessment of effectiveness take place? Chapter 3 indicates that the effects of a cause might take years to manifest themselves, and that short-term effects may be little guide to 'what works' in the longer term.

What if a majority of studies showed a positive effect of such-and-such an intervention but each of these studies: (a) was small scale; (b) was of short duration; (c) was of a single, one-off incidence of the intended positive outcome; (c) included some contradictory evidence; (d) did not provide any counterfactual evidence (i.e. if A had not happened then B would not have happened); (e) provided no evidence of the sustainability of the effects of the intervention or practice (e.g. if this was not built into the research), thereby risking the Hawthorne effect? Does this mean that only large-scale studies or meta-studies can count as 'evidence'? Further, what if studies showed negative side-effects? How is account taken of these? How do benefits outweigh costs? What are the opportunity costs?

Should one indicate that such-and-such an intervention 'works' on a simple majority vote on a given number of research studies or studies which have a particular cut-off point in terms of effect size? What if only one or two studies are included as 'evidence? And what if, in the interests of triangulation, a case study, an ethnographic study, a phenomenological study and an experimental study are conducted on the same topic but yield different and conflicting results: the findings differ according to the lenses used (e.g. Julnes and Rog, 2009)? Taking a legalistic turn, what is the minimum evidence required to show that a claim that such-and-such 'works' from a given number of studies is beyond reasonable doubt? What is the level of certainty or probability that is required? How is this decided, and by whom? And why these people and not others? Are the labels of 'what works' and 'what does not work' discrete and categorical or are they, for example on a sliding scale, and, if so, what are the cut-off points, and why these? At what point does one judge that something has 'worked', and what if it has 'worked' but not as much as predicted or desired? Further, it is not only the quantity of evidence that is important, it is its quality. Here we engage the need for rigour in research, and Chapter 11 discusses this. Suffice it to remark here that criteria need to be developed for evaluating the research evidence and that judgements and decisions on 'what works' are essentially, integrally human matters; they are not self-evident or unequivocal but, rather, emanate from people.

How do we really 'know' what works? How can we *claim* to know, when, even in the face of thousands of research papers published every year, it remains the case that our knowledge is imperfect, incomplete and inductive? Do we decide by majority vote, from an incomplete sample of papers or people? Who decides? Do we adopt a Bayesian probability approach in factoring in doubts and negative cases? And how do we *decide* whether something 'works', how many research papers do we need, and what happens if just one of them challenges other findings (Russell's (1959) acknowledgement of the limits of induction and inference is powerful here: suddenly finding a black swan demolishes the assertion that all swans are white). Induction also houses further dangers; not only is it predicated on the best evidence to date, but its reliability depends on the context to which it refers. Russell's sad story of the inductivist chicken signals the dangers of misreading the context of the situation: social, gastronomic, economic, dietary, intentional and so on. The chicken, having had day after day of being well fed by the farmer, concludes that this will continue, only to have its neck wrung by the same man one day. The chicken paid the price of having too small and superficial a frame of reference, focusing on surface behaviours and factors inductively, whilst the farmer's frame of reference was that of a man living in particular, underlying socio-economic conditions and contexts. Induction on its own can be lethal.

So, here we have a situation in which the 'what' and the 'works' in 'what works', coupled with questions about what constitutes valid and reliable evidence, are potentially ambiguous, abstruse, open to those with the loudest voice and the biggest share of power on the highest rungs of a pre-determined ladder of status, with the classroom teacher – the very person who has the greatest understanding of her or his students – at the bottom of the heap. And, anyway how do we really 'know' something? Claims to really know 'what works' are at best tentative, conjectural, context-bound, and seriously incomplete, as, for example, such claims should abide by principles of being universal, necessary, sufficient, probable, frequent and causally powerful (Cartwright and Hardie, 2012, p. 48).

This is not to advocate a counsel of despair or to state that research has little value. On the contrary, rigorous research evidence which states its boundaries clearly must replace the unsupported whims, personal preferences, politically expedient, untried interventions and agendas of decision makers and policy makers who are only there because they happen to have a modicum of power or a political appointment. As Slavin (2016) remarks disarmingly: education policy is informed less by evidence than it is by politics, money, personalities, even by myths (p. 1). Without evidence, there is a gross elision, wherein the slide from an 'is' to an 'ought' becomes almost invisible. As the philosopher Habermas suggested, the power of the argument must trump the positional power of the person making it. And it is to say that, just as 'what works' must be weighed, challenged, disputed, interrogated and judged, so must the evidence which feeds into it, and judges and judgements are open to scrutiny, interrogation and challenge. Though this is a statement of the obvious, its routine violation gives cause for concern, not least when research findings are abused and misused.

What, then, do producers and users of 'evidence' need in order to plan, ensure, interrogate and evaluate evidence presented or to be presented? This is a hefty challenge, for it engages several issues in judging the quality of the evidence and its match to specific agendas in deciding the 'what' and the 'works' in the 'what works' agenda.

An initial excursus here might be the stuff of evaluating research evidence, as, for example in a research paper. Going along this track is dangerous, with potholes, barriers and obstacles every step of the way. Consider, for example, the questions below in evaluating whether a piece of research evidence is useful in addressing the 'what works' agenda. These are introductory only, and several of these matters are addressed further in subsequent chapters; their inclusion here signals clearly that judging 'what works' from research evidence is not a walk in the woods (Morrison and van der Werf, 2018).

There is a clear and present danger that, in ensuring the rigour and suitability of research evidence, one descends into interminable checklists, many of whose items are a matter of opinion and which, anyway, are largely unused or underused. Hence, whilst the list below indicates the spread of concerns to be faced in coming to a judgement of whether a piece of research provides robust evidence of 'what works', it exacts its price in its length, complexity and, with it, the risk of being technicist, mechanistic, and, indeed, largely ignored because it is simply too long and too complex (Gorard et al., 2017, p. 48). Like it or not, a careful filtering system for judging the quality of research evidence by experts is a useful rule-of-thumb. For example, journal editors and reviewers, research funding reviewers, experts in the relevant field might be as good as it gets, imperfect but 'good enough'.

Foundations of the research

In judging whether something 'works', many questions are engaged. Some of these are set out below.

1   *Background*:

   a   How clear is the statement of the context/problem and what has given rise to the research?

2   *Purposes*:

   a   How clearly stated are the purposes of the research?
   b   How clear is the statement of what the research seeks to do, to 'deliver', to find out?

    c   How clear and defensible are the statements of what the paper does, what it argues, what it shows, what it concludes?

3   *Type of research:*

    a   How clear is the statement of whether and how the research seeks to test a theory or hypothesis, to develop a theory, to investigate and explore, to understand, to describe, to develop specific practices, to evaluate, to investigate?

4   *Significance of the research:*

    a   The 'so what' question: why is the research important?
    b   Is there a statement of the significance, importance and originality of the research?
    c   Is there a statement of the contribution of the research to the field, to knowledge, the justification for, and significance of this?

5   *Assumptions made in the research:*

    a   How complete, clear fair and defensible are the assumptions made and the justification provided for these?
    b   How acceptable is it to apply the *ceteris paribus* condition (e.g. all other things being equal)?

Literature review, warrants and theoretical underpinnings

1   *Utility and warrants:*

    a   How useful and appropriate is the literature review: to identify where the originality of the research might be, how the research is similar to and different from, other relevant research in the field, how the literature informs the present research, i.e. how it is a springboard into the present research rather than being an inert summary of other people's research, i.e. how the argument for the present research is developed through the literature?

2   *Scope and validity:*

    a   Is the literature review more than a list of topics and authors; does it synthesize and integrate material from different kinds of source into an argument that leads into and informs the present research, that demonstrates the validity and credibility of the present research and the terms in which the research operates?

3   *Theoretical underpinning:*

    a   Does the research state the theory underpinning the research, and provide a defensible justification for the selection of theory used?

   b   Does the research provide a statement of the warrants provided to link evidence to conclusions and to link key concepts and items?

Design, planning and implementation

1   *Scope and purpose:*

   a   How wide/narrow is the scope of the research, and how is this justified and fit for purpose in addressing the 'what works' agenda in question?

   b   How manageable is the research, given its scope, and how is this addressed?

   c   How clearly stated are the purposes of the research and how well do they fit the 'what works' agenda in question?

   d   How 'achievable' are the purposes and 'deliverables' of the research (e.g. is the research being too ambitious, given the resources available)?

2   *Research questions and hypotheses:*

   a   How fair, clear and adequate is the operationalization of the research purposes into research questions?

   b   How clear, defensible and relevant to providing 'evidence' for the matter in hand is/are the research question(s)?

   c   How comprehensive are the research questions, and how defensible is their scope?

   d   How acceptable is/are the hypothesis/es to be tested?

   e   How significant and fit for purpose is/are the hypothesis/es being tested (i.e. beyond the commonplace or obvious)?

   f   Who decides the intended and actual outcomes; where do outcomes come from?

3   *Methodologies and paradigms:*

   a   How suitable/fit for purpose are the methodology/ies and paradigm(s) on which the research is built (e.g. surveys, experiments, ethnographic, naturalistic research, tests, action research, case studies)?

   b   How well do the methodologies and paradigms fit the research purposes and the nature of the phenomena under investigation?

   c   Does the research really do justice to the complexity of the issue and to the context in which the research takes place – the richness and mire of human activity?

4   *Validity and reliability:*

   a   What steps has the research taken to ensure reliability and validity, and what kinds of reliability and validity?

b   How clear, defensible, and suitable are the steps taken to address validity and reliability in the conceptualization, planning, methodology, instrumentation, data analysis, discussion, the drawing of conclusions, and reporting?

c   How sufficiently and acceptably have reliability and validity been addressed?

d   What are the limits of validity and reliability here, and how much do these compromise the research?

5   *Context*:

a   How clear, sufficiently comprehensive and justifiable are the statements of the boundaries, contexts, contingencies, limitations, constraints on the research and a justification of these?

b   How appropriately and sufficiently have the context of the research and contextual factors been included and excluded in the research? How has sufficient account been taken of contextual factors, and how acceptably and defensibly has this been addressed?

c   How has 'noise' in the research been addressed and separated from the 'signal'?

d   How acceptable, defensible and sufficient is the inclusion and/or exclusion of contextual features, contingencies, conditions and constraints in the research?

6   *Variables and factors*:

a   How acceptable, sufficient and defensible are the indication, definition and selection of variables and factors to be included and excluded?

b   How acceptable and defensible are the proxy variables and indicators used for unobservable factors?

c   How appropriate and defensible is the identification of independent and dependent variables, and a sufficient, tenable justification for which are independent and which are dependent?

7   *Controls and counterfactuals*:

a   How acceptable, sufficient and defensible are the controls which are and are not included in the research and how these are handled, with justifications?

b   What counterfactuals are included in the research (e.g. comparison with groups who have not been exposed to a particular intervention)? How acceptable and defensible are these?

c   How acceptable and defensible is the exclusion of counterfactuals in the research?

8   *Time factors*:

   a   How acceptable and defensible are the time scales and timing used in the pre-test/baseline assessment (where relevant), the duration of the intervention, the data collection period, the post-test (where relevant)?

   b   How long after the intervention does the post-intervention data collection take place, why and with what issues raised and addressed?

9   *Sampling*:

   a   How clear, acceptable, relevant and useful is the sample: appropriateness; nature; fitness for purpose; size; scope; access; inclusion of sufficiently large subgroups; representativeness (and of whom/what); sampling strategy (e.g. probability and non-probability sampling, random sampling, opportunity sampling)?

   b   How have sampling bias and sampling error been addressed?

   c   What are the limits of the sample, and how sufficiently have these been stated?

10   *Data and instrumentation*:

   a   What data collection instruments are being used, and how appropriate and fit for purpose are these? How justified and defensible are the instrument for data collection?

   b   What are the limits of the data collection instruments, and have these been acknowledged and addressed?

   c   How suitable, fit for purpose and appropriate are the data sources, data types and data collection instruments, and how defensible is the justification provided for these? How do these constrain, limit and bound the research and what can be derived from the research?

   d   What limitations are there in the data sources, types and uses, and how clearly have these been stated?

   e   How acceptable, sufficient, defensible, suitable, appropriate and fit for purpose are the data collection, processing, analysis and verification techniques?

11   *Ethics*:

   a   What ethical principles have been addressed and how acceptable and complete are these?

   b   Has sufficient attention been given to the ethics of the research?

   c   What negative side effects have been looked for and/or found?

   d   Who are the researchers? Do they have any vested interests and if so, how have these been addressed? What is the positionality of the researchers?

12 *Coherence*:

   a How internally coherent is the overall research design and its con-
      tributing elements?
   b How have any conflicting elements been addressed?

Data analysis and findings

1   *Data processing and analysis*:

   a What data processing and analysis strategies, techniques and pro-
      cedures have been used in the research, and how are they defen-
      sibly fit for purpose, appropriate, fair, adequate and correctly
      conducted?
   b What limitations, strengths and weaknesses of the data analysis
      have been disclosed, and how do these affect the credibility of the
      research and the conclusions drawn from it?
   c How has bias been overcome?

2   *Fitness with agendas*:

   a How suitable, appropriate and fit for the 'what works' purposes of
      the research is the data analysis?

3   *Credibility*:

   a How secure are the findings, given the research design, the scale of
      the research, attrition and incomplete data, data quality, and other
      threats.

Discussion and conclusions

1   *Claims*:

   a What are the security of, warrants for, and validity of, the conclu-
      sions drawn and claims made from the data and the research?
   b On what grounds are the claims of the conclusions made, and how
      acceptable are these?
   c Do the conclusions and claims really follow from the data?
   d Are claims made for the research fair, over-stated, unsupported (what
      is claimed and what it is legitimate to claim are very different)?
   e Is there genuine discussion of the data and what they really show?

 f Have possible alternative explanations for and interpretations of the findings been provided, together with the justification for the explanation/interpretation chosen, i.e. not merely a repetition of the findings?

2 *Limitations*:

 a How sufficiently, adequately and appropriately are the limitations of the data acknowledged?

 b What side effects have been found, positive and/or negative?

3 *Relevance*:

 a How relevant are the data, their analysis and findings for the research purposes, research questions/hypotheses and the 'what works' agenda in question?

 b Are there clear answers to the research questions, hypotheses and research purposes?

4 *Conclusiveness*:

 a Do the conclusions really conclude, i.e. weigh the evidence and come to a final decision/statement rather than simply summarizing?

5 *Impact*:

 a Are there statements of the potential impact of the research, with justification?

 b What implications are presented in the research, and do they follow from the data, findings and conclusions?

Generalizability

1 *Validity*:

 a How valid are the generalizations drawn from the data and the research, and on what grounds?

 b Are claims for generalizability suitably cautious?

2 *Scope*:

 a How generalizable are and are not the findings of the research, to whom, on what grounds and with what justification?

 b What are the limits of generalizability of the findings, on what grounds, and have these been acknowledged in the research?

Evaluation

1   *Strengths, weaknesses and limitations:*

    a   Has the research acknowledged its strengths, weaknesses limitations, and are these correct, fair, understated or overstated, included or omitted?

    b   How serious are the weaknesses and limitations? How far do they undermine the credibility and trust that can be placed in the research findings?

    c   Has the research been published? If so where, and with what review procedures (e.g. blind peer review)?

To this somewhat formidable introductory checklist must be added the point that this is in respect of a single piece of research. When one considers that to judge fairly 'what works' from research evidence typically requires evidence to be drawn from multiple studies, replication studies and a broad evidential base (and Makel and Plucker (2014) note the dearth of replication studies: only 0.13 per cent of articles on education appearing in the top 100 journals were replication studies). In turn this raises issues that are familiar to meta-analysis, systematic reviews and research syntheses (e.g. Suri, 2018):

1   *Selection of research studies:*

    a   Making clear the criteria and protocols for the eligibility for selection and the subsequent inclusion of research studies and the inclusion of diverse studies which may or may not have been intended to serve the present 'what works' research purposes, agenda and scope, i.e. their relevance to the topic or issue in question;

2   *Differences between studies:*

    a   Overcoming challenges posed by differing samples and sample sizes, scope, timing and duration, contexts, cultures and locations, and the strength of the impact of all of these on the research;

    b   Taking account of differences in constraints and contingencies in the research sites;

    c   Addressing differences in the quality of the research papers used (e.g. between poor quality and high quality research: methodological rigour);

    d   Engaging differences in the strengths and magnitude of the effects founds;

    e   Accounting for outliers and disconfirming findings;

    f   Taking cognizance of differences in what counts as appropriate and acceptable data (e.g. 'hard' and 'soft' data; opinions; 'facts'; observable, empirical and non-empirical data);

3   *Combining studies:*

   a   Combining and using primary and/or secondary data;
   b   Combining, integrating and drawing from studies with differing styles, types, paradigms, ontologies, epistemologies, methodologies, instrumentation, data types, data sources, data analyses, mixed methods etc.;

4   *Audience and readership needs:*

   a   Meeting the needs of different readership and audience requirements;

5   *Validity, reliability and commonality:*

   a   Overcoming publication bias (the proclivity to publish 'successes');
   b   Moving beyond the focus on aggregates and averages rather than sub-groups;
   c   Avoiding Type I errors (false positives) and Type II errors (false negatives);
   d   Taking account of different reliability indices and other approaches to reliability;
   e   Over-simplifying findings in the search for commonality;
   f   Over-reliance on simple statistical treatments (e.g. effect size);
   g   How to cope with replication studies that produce different results (Bal et al., 2002).

Bal et al. (2002) note that differences between studies render the synthesizing of studies potentially dangerous, as they may not be fairly comparable, unable to be fairly combined in meta-analyses, and the variables at work in different studies may not be sufficiently similar to warrant being combined (p. 132). As they argue, a trade-off is necessary between having acceptable results, perhaps using the *ceteris paribus* clause, and over-simplifying a complex real environment (p. 136). This book pays further attention to *ceteris paribus* clauses in Chapters 3 and 9, and to meta-analysis and meta-meta-analysis in Chapter 12.

Even if all these requirements have been met, the question remains of the trust that can be put in the findings when applied to the hurly-burly, 'real' world learners and teachers. In order to do justice to the complexity, richness, emotion-imbued, personality-affected multi-dimensionality of the multiply real worlds of learners and teachers, we should adopt a perhaps sceptical approach to what 'research shows' (Jackson, 1968; Nuthall, 2007). Indeed, as Biesta (2010) avers, the attempt to reduce the complex world of many possible options for action as, for example, occurs in an RCT, concerns who is exerting power, such that reducing complexity should be taken as a 'political act' (p. 498).

What to expect from research evidence and what do we need to judge it?

If research evidence is to be used in the 'what works' agenda, then its users have an ethical and moral obligation to ensure that it clears a high bar of rigour and that the claims made from it are defensible. For example, Gorard et al. (2017, p. 37) suggest that, for descriptive research there should be: a robust research design which is fit for purpose, hopefully with comparison groups and counterfactual opportunities, able to suggest causal explanations, and whose research questions are aligned with the design; a large number of cases (overall and in each sub-group); minimal attrition and missing data, e.g. insufficient dropout to upset findings ('the number of counterfactual cases needed to disturb the finding'; p. 45): 'sensitivity analysis'; the use of high quality, reliable (replicable) data using standardized, pre-specified and independent data; and no evidence of conflicts of interest or vested interests; having too many possible outcomes such that the one being sought is impossible not to find; no threats to improper diffusion or disclosure of treatments; and the possibility of generalizability (pp. 37–48).

Gorard et al. are discussing particular kinds of research, e.g. large-scale, quantitative research that can suggest causality; whilst such research is patently useful, it risks regarding contextual factors as 'noise', and tries to separate these from the 'signal'. It rises above context. How far this is acceptable is questionable, not only because contextual factors may be influential in the situation but also because generalizability and transferability of the research finding from one case to another may be highly questionable where contexts differ. And, anyway, not all research is like that. Small-scale and qualitative research, e.g. case studies, ethnographies, naturalistic research, observational studies, may not fit the prescriptions of Gorard et al. but be no less valuable, being close to 'real life' and to the intensity of context, sensitive to the multiple factors operating in a human situation or setting, and doing justice to the agency and complexity of participants, even though this might limit generalizability and transferability.

As Thomas (2012) argues, science also focuses on, and is based on 'contextual, case-based research' (p. 36), and, indeed, he provides examples of how natural science has progressed on the basis of case studies, e.g. pulsars, palaeoanthropology (pp. 36–37). Such work catches imagination, curiosity, creativity, insights, the 'eureka' moment. Case studies can reveal insights; witness the studies by Piaget and the work on play therapy by Axline. In the face of such imagination, creativity, reflection, insight, contextuality, passion, deliberation and curiosity, RCTs play only a confirmatory role (Thomas, 2012, p. 40) and come a mean, poor 'also-ran'. Indeed, the logic of experimentation per se, let alone in RCTs, is called into question (Chapter 4).

How small-scale studies might scale up when used in combination, e.g. in meta-analyses, meta-meta-analyses and systematic reviews, is challenging and important (Chapter 12). However, the story does not rest there. The preceding argument indicated that attention must be given to a panoply of issues concerning: the foundations of the research; defensible warrants and theoretical underpinnings of the research; robust and internally coherent design, planning and implementation; the inclusion of the influence of contextual factors; appropriate and correct data analysis and what it shows; the provision of alternative explanations of the findings and the defensibility of the explanation chosen; the logic, fairness and reasonableness of the conclusions and claims made from the research; the acknowledgement of the limitations of the research; the suggestion of to whom the findings might and might not be generalizable; the overall evaluation of the research. Of particular concern here is the need to ensure that due weight is given to contextual variables and factors, their conditions, constraints, contingencies and limitations, controls involved in the analysis, and the defensibility of the warrants which underpin the research in establishing the legitimacy of claims made.

This applies to individual pieces of research. However, to this must be added the requirements of rigour, relevance, fitness for purpose set out earlier for combining, aggregating and integrating research studies in meta-analysis, meta-meta-analyses and systematic reviews (Chapter 12). A key concern here is the need to ensure that due attention is given to the perplexing question of how far the research examples selected for inclusion give a balanced, representative view of the field, including disconfirming cases, how far they really address the topic in hand (a validity matter), and how fairly and adequately differences between studies have been addressed.

Major problems exist in terms of *definitions, ontology* (what it is that we are researching), *epistemology* (how we know that we are really researching it and not something else; what constitutes 'knowing'), what *criteria* are being used to judge whether, in what ways, and how far something does or does not 'work', and *who* has the credibility, legitimacy, expertise and authority to make such judgements.

Even if all of these concerns have been adequately addressed, the point remains that 'evidence' is not neutral. Whilst *data* might be neutral (though not always), evidence is not; 'evidence' is what we do with the data. Imagine a court of law; here evidence is amassed to persuade a jury as to whether the defendant is or is not guilty beyond a reasonable doubt. In other words, an *argument* is assembled from data, to press home an agenda, and this is subject to verification, cross-examination, deliberation, interrogation, corroboration, challenge and weighing the evidence before coming to a judgement. The advocacy and adversarial system is a useful analogy of how research evidence can be used. Evidence is not self-evident in the 'what works' agenda; it feeds into a deliberative judgement, including questions of relevance, sufficiency, veracity, corroboration (Thomas, 2004), clarity, indisputability and certainty (Albrechtsen and Qvortrup, 2014, p. 72). The case is made for and against a proposal and this is weighed and then a judgement is made.

Kvernbekk (2016, 2019) indicates the place of evidence in the 'what works' agenda. Drawing on the work of Toulmin (2003) she argues that evidence is just one element in a range of considerations that apply in making a case. She notes, from Toulmin, that there is a difference between a claim and a conclusion, and that 'what works' is more of a claim (C) than a conclusion. To support a claim requires data (D) and that to move from data to a claim requires a warrant (W), the job of which is to 'register explicitly the legitimacy of the step involved' (Toulmin, 2003 p. 92, cited in Kvernbekk, 2016, p. 30), 'that which licenses the inference' (Kvernbekk, 2016, p. 34). Warrants are not data, but, as Kvernbekk indicates, are rules and justifications that entitle connections to be made between data and claims (p. 34). As warrants vary in their strength, they require qualifiers (Q) to denote their strength, and as they are open to question about their strength, a role is required for rebuttals (R) (e.g. by other evidence) and backing (B) for the warrant. Hence there is a spiral of argumentation (Kvernbekk, 2016, p. 30) which includes C, D, W, Q, R and B. This elegant analysis underlines the point that 'what works' is not self-evident but is subject to interrogation, with empirical data accompanied by theoretical support – what underpins the claims of what the evidence is evidence *for* (p. 32) – that data are but a starting point in securing the weight of evidence, such that it is beyond reasonable doubt so that we can have reasonable confidence in it, and that the security attributable to evidence comes at a high price of warrants, arguments, backing, surviving challenges and rebuttals, careful formulation of claims, and the strength of the qualifiers adduced.

The matter does not rest there. The points made so far are largely in relation to 'what works' in the research context – what works 'there'. However, this is only one side of the coin. The other side of the coin is what works in a different context – what works 'here' (Cartwright and Hardie, 2012). This engages a range of issues in relation to the new context, its contingencies and conditions, ways of working, people involved (e.g. teachers and students), local and cultural factors and so on, i.e. a myriad of new issues. This is the generalizability issue (Chapter 12). Data, in themselves, underdetermine 'what works'. At most, research evidence provides support for a claim or for a premise in a sub-argument about evidence, i.e. it plays an indirect role in the overall argument. The chapters in this book suggest that, for something to work, requires causal structures and chains to be operative together with 'support factors' (Chapter 3), contexts and conditions to be favourable and sufficiently similar to those that gave rise to the original research, and so on.

The several steps in moving from data to evidence to applying evidence in educational practice are set out in Figure 2.1. This is a vastly stripped-down model of how evidence features in the 'what works' agenda. However, it indicates that data alone are not the full story in judging 'what works', that deliberation and evaluation feature in every stage of moving from evidence to application in new settings, and that simply because evidence shows that

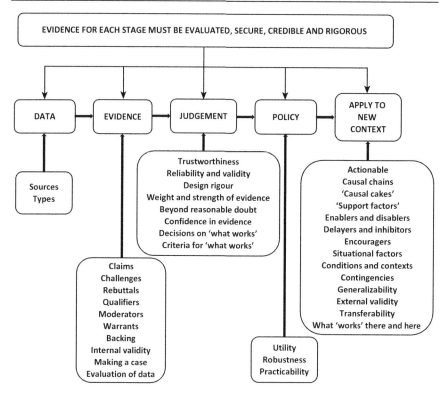

EVIDENCE FOR EACH STAGE MUST BE EVALUATED, SECURE, CREDIBLE AND RIGOROUS

DATA → EVIDENCE → JUDGEMENT → POLICY → APPLY TO NEW CONTEXT

Sources
Types

Trustworthiness
Reliability and validity
Design rigour
Weight and strength of evidence
Beyond reasonable doubt
Confidence in evidence
Decisions on 'what works'
Criteria for 'what works'

Actionable
Causal chains
'Causal cakes'
'Support factors'
Enablers and disablers
Delayers and inhibitors
Encouragers
Situational factors
Conditions and contexts
Contingencies
Generalizability
External validity
Transferability
What 'works' there and here

Claims
Challenges
Rebuttals
Qualifiers
Moderators
Warrants
Backing
Internal validity
Making a case
Evaluation of data

Utility
Robustness
Practicability

Figure 2.1 From data to evidence to judgement to policy to application

something 'works' in one location is no guarantee that it will 'work' elsewhere, i.e. its efficacy in one situation underdetermines its effectiveness more widely. Applying the evidence to new contexts, i.e. putting it into practice elsewhere, engages the vast sphere of managing change and innovation, and it is noticeable that the 'what works' agenda pays scant regard to this important factor.

Conclusion

Whilst avoiding an unreachable counsel of perfection, what constitutes 'good enough' research and evidence is contestable. Who decides? How safe is it to accept what researchers and experts say when their research takes just a slice out of the complexity of everyday life and where what we know is tentative, falsifiable, conjectural and looking to predict from an already-interpreted past to an unpredictable future which may or may not be research-informed, in which small changes and differences have massive effects, in which phase transitions and tipping points render any sense of certainty suspect?

Even if we draw on a vast range of research, we simply don't know for how long it will be relevant and valid, what its shelf-life will be, how enduring it will be, and where and when it will be worth applying. Where is the evidence, other than through historical analysis, that something has worked and/or worked over time and place and contexts, and, anyway, what is the relevance of history in an unpredictable future? Just because it worked then, why should it work now? Time is a powerful factor, and the past is often a poor predictor of the present or the future. Indeed, Major and Higgins (2019), strong advocates of the 'what works' agenda and meta-analyses, are careful to note that research may tell us what has worked in the past but that is no guarantee that it will work in the future (p. ix) (i.e. the limits of induction) and that 'what works' has the status of an induction of 'what works', and even that is subject to conditions being met. Yes, we should learn from the past right up to the present, but is that sufficient for the future or even the present? Is that 'good enough', even if it's all we have? How far is whether something 'works' tomorrow little more than a leap of faith?

Chapter 3

The search for causality

Introduction and overview

If users of research are to be able to use research findings in their own contexts, they need to know the causal mechanisms, processes, factors and interactions of these factors in producing the observed outcomes. Whilst RCTs claim to identify that a particular input, *ceteris paribus*, causes a particular outcome, what happens between this input and outcome is often opaque, and this is a problem which is only soluble, in part, by supplementary evidence in the RCT. The chapter unpacks key issues in understanding causality:

- 'Causal cakes' and 'causal webs' trump linear 'causal chains' and links in 'causal chains' in understanding causality.
- Causal factors operate *together* rather than in isolation, and they are context-specific.
- Demonstrating causality is assisted by identifying counterfactuals.
- Identifying when causes and effects begin is often unclear.
- Controlling variables in order to identify causality often misrepresents the importance of the interplay of variables at work in causality.
- Identifying causality must take account of necessary and sufficient conditions (INUS conditions), triggers of causal outcomes and combinations of causally related factors operating in a particular situation.
- The contextual specificity of much causality attenuates generalizability, as causal conditions, ingredients and 'support factors' must be similar, even identical (e.g. in their presence, relative weights of factors and how they work together) if transferability from one context to another is to be successful, i.e. to ensure that a particular intervention 'works' in a context different from its original.
- The *ceteris paribus* clause, widely invoked in causality, is highly questionable.

Whilst causality is an essential element in understanding whether something 'works' in a 'what works' agenda, it is often under-investigated and poorly understood. This is true of many kinds of research in education, including RCTs.

The importance of causality in educational research

Causal explanation is the 'holy grail' for much educational research. Why things happen in the way that they do, and establishing causality and the patterning of causality across cases and samples, are not straightforward. Success hinges on the ability, based on purported evidence, to infer the effects of causes and the causes of effects. Causality is frequently not observable in an ocular sense, but relies on probabilistic inference, induction, warrants, purported and indirect evidence, habituation in thinking, and not on the logically deduced, regular, 'constant' in Hume's 'constant conjunction' as a feature of causal thinking. In the empirical sciences, causality is synthetic and contingent, not analytic and deducible. It is an inductive, inferential and empirical matter rather than a solely logical, deductive matter.

Evidence-based practice is premised in large part on causality: we want to know that an intervention 'works' in terms of bringing about a desired goal, i.e. causes it. This is a powerful argument for RCTs, though even here causality can be disputed, as RCTs can be considered correlational with a suggestion, rather than a perfect proof, of causality, and there is no guarantee that if something 'works' once, it will 'work' again. We cannot be sure that it 'works' every time, and outcomes, like much of causality itself, are probabilistic rather than deterministic.

For educational practices to 'work' and to be transferable, it is important for research 'evidence' to understand 'what causes what', to determine the effects of causes and the causes of effects. However, this is not a straightforward enterprise, as causality is often not directly observable, it is conjectural; we infer on the basis of incomplete knowledge. It is impossible to predict with 100 per cent certainty that such-and-such will happen (an effect) on the basis of what we think is or are the cause or causes, and probabilistic causality assumes that we know all the relevant factors involved. As Major and Higgins (2019) comment, certainty is replaced with 'good bets' (p. xxii).

'Evidence' and 'evidence-based practice' are profoundly and unavoidably causal. For educational practices to 'work' and to be transferable, research 'evidence' must understand 'what causes what'. This is so that we can predict, with as much certainly as possible, what will 'work' in classrooms and in education more widely, and that 'what works' is as securely predictive as possible. In a climate of interventions purporting to show 'what works', i.e. looking for the effects of causes, it is noticeable that alternative ways of addressing causality, e.g. moving from observables to the identification of causes (inferring causes from effects), are under-represented in the 'what works' agenda.

Without understanding 'what causes what', the 'what works' agenda and what constitutes 'evidence' is impoverished to the point of uncertainty and blunt interventions: a shot in the dark based on the fact that a previous shot in the dark happened to work.

Causal chain, links, cakes and webs

What constitutes a cause and what constitutes an effect are problematic, as there are often sub-causes and sub-effects, causal processes, causal chains, webs and lines. The terms 'cause' and 'effect' are, in many cases a shorthand for many sub-causes, sub-processes and sub-effects. To infer simple causality is to misread many situations excepting those where massive single over-determining causality is clear, and it is useful to consider causal processes, causal chains, webs and lines. However, these present their own difficulties in establishing causality, as chains of causal events are difficult to disentangle and, indeed, there may be several acting and interacting simultaneously with each other. Rather, different 'webs' of causes (Morrison, 2012), akin to 'causal cakes' from Cartwright and Hardie (2012), operate at different stages of an intervention, e.g. its planning (antecedent factors), its implementation (transactional factors) and its outcomes, and it is important to understand the causal factors at work at each stage or in each area of an intervention or activity. As Mill (2006) remarks, to understand causation we have to include all the antecedent factors, i.e. the environment and all the conditions. A cause, he remarks 'is the sum total of the conditions positive and negative taken together'.

There is often more than a single cause at work in any effect and there may be more than one effect from a single cause: an obvious point but one with con-siderable significance, not least in judging 'what works', where and for whom it 'works' and does not 'work', and with what positive and negative processes and outcomes; this mitigates against simplistic attribution of causality.

The causal chain from cause to effect is convoluted and not simple to unravel or determine. Whilst a causal chain requires the presence of con-tiguous links in the chain, the journey from an initial cause to its putative effect (in the case of an intervention), or the journey from an effect back to a cause (in tracing a cause from an effect), is not straightforward, and it is uncommon to know the degrees of freedom involved. Further, every link in the causal chain has its own web of causes operating on that link; hence to think of cause and effect as a simple linear movement from cause to effect is to misrepresent what is really happening, which is that many causes acting simultaneously may bring about one or more effects (Morrison, 2012).

Cartwright's and Hardie's (2012) 'causal cakes' operate in a causal situation: imagine that we wish to make a pancake; the ingredients (the authors term these 'support factors') – flour, milk, egg, oil – must all be present to make the pan-cake, and without any one of these there is no pancake. Further, mixture, heat and cooking are also required. In other words, a particular cause or a single constellation of causes, separately or in combination, may be insufficient, on its own, to bring about an effect; all the 'support factors' (*ibid.*) must be present; this has important implications for policy makers and for managers of change and managers of interventions.

We can extend the analogy further: there may be more than one 'causal cake' present in any causal situation, mediating or moderating the causal sequence (Cartwright and Hardie, 2012). For example, some 'causal cakes' may act as enablers whilst others may act as inhibitors, delayers or disablers (negative 'causal cakes', which may outweigh the positive 'causal cakes'). And, indeed, enablers, encouragers, hasteners, disablers and inhibitors set off their own causal paths and causal chains, just as interventions set up different causal paths (Kvernbekk, 2016, p. 83).

Imagine a situation where an intervention is tried out to promote collaborative learning in classrooms, for example. An enabling 'causal cake' might be a classroom culture of mutual support, enjoyment of working together, a collectivist culture, interesting tasks, enthusiastic children, and tasks that can *only* be accomplished if children work together. A disabling 'causal cake' might be the presence of a competitive culture, free riders, imprecise guidance from the teacher, parental pressure for their child to be 'top of the class', and undemanding tasks that could be done equally well, if not better, by children working on their own. Here the intervention – the introduction of collaborative learning – works well in one situation, but is frustrated to the point of failure in another; the link from cause to effect – the causal chain – differs in the two situations, even though the initial cause remains the same. The 'causal cakes' – the conditions, 'support factors' and contexts – differ such that generalizability relies on the presence of similar or alternative enablers in moving from situation one to situation two, from 'there' to 'here' (Cartwright and Hardie, 2012).

More than one 'causal cake' may be involved in bringing about a particular effect (Cartwright and Hardie, 2012). Which are they and how do they work together, particularly in complex, variable-dense situations such as schools and classrooms? If 'what works' is to transfer successfully from one situation to another (from 'there' to 'here'), then the 'causal cakes' must be similar in the two locales and must play the same roles in both, hence an intelligence gathering exercise is required to see how far this condition obtains. Not to do this is to risk failure and 'tissue rejection', whereby a transplanted organ (an intervention) is rejected by a recipient's body if suitable preparations, e.g. suppressants and immune systems, have not been made (Hoyle, 1975). In an RCT, it is important to know what are the causal 'webs' and the 'causal cakes' operating in a situation, as the RCT might 'work' for one group with regard to its specific conditions, but may not be generalizable or effective overall for a wider population or under a wider set of conditions.

With regard to links in the causal chains, at link one there are specific conditions and causal factors operating; at link two a different set of conditions and causal factors operate; at link three, another set, and so on. This has major implications for generalizability (Chapter 12), for the conditions, causal factors and contingences operating on every link in the causal chain in one situation or location may not be the same, or be in the same sequence as those operating in another situation or location, thereby confounding attempts simply to transplant locale one into locale two.

Causes of effects operate in specific circumstances and situations, and account must be taken of these circumstances and conditions in understanding 'what works' as, without such knowledge, the level of certainty, i.e. 'beyond a reasonable doubt' (Chapter 2) is questionable. Further, effects may not be direct, linear functions of causes, and there may be few, many, increasing, reducing, unpredictable, i.e. nonlinear effects of causes (Chapter 5). It is hard to see how RCTs address this.

Understanding causality is not for the weak-hearted. Indeed, if we are to believe the suggestion that correlational analysis from big data trumps causal analysis (Ayres, 2007; Mayer-Schönberger and Cukier, 2013), then the role of causal analysis in understanding 'what works' is problematic (and RCTs seem to manage with an unsophisticated view of causality). As Mayer-Schönberger and Cukier (2013) contend: in a world of big data, being fixated on causality should give way to correlational analysis (p. 14).

Further, as Morrison (2009) notes, the absence of a cause may, itself constitute a cause (p. 46): not to give a plant some water may cause it to die. The relative strength of a cause may be unstable (see the discussion of 'dose–response' in Chapter 6), depending on the presence, strength, intensity or absence of other causes, or the point in time at which the cause is active or inactive, and the population in question (p. 42). The causal palette, then, is complex. It is difficult to see how RCTs address this complexity; rather, they tend to simply override it and to ride roughshod over mechanisms of causality.

Causality, causal explanation and data analysis

Researchers wishing to know 'what works', often seek to understand the relative strengths of relevant causes in specific contexts and circumstances. The relative strengths of causes depend on the presence or absence of other causes (e.g. enablers, inhibitors, preventers). In identifying the *relative* strength of causes, the problem is raised of which variables to include (i.e. 'what is relative to what'), as the exclusion of relevant variables in determining causality is a major difficulty in research (and this impacts on RCTs, as they seek to isolate and control variables). Causes, like effects, operate in conjunction with, rather than in isolation from, other causes, circumstances and conditions.

Contextuality – the conditions in which the cause and effect take place, and the theatre of causality – is a key factor in identifying causality. Taking a piece of evidence out of context undermines its significance, and context is required in order to provide the specific criteria by which the evidence is to be judged (Mathison, 2009, p. 182). Mathison provides the example of culturally different judgements made on the same evidence, suggesting that truth and credibility are judged, in part, by social conventions and within particular inquiry traditions, paradigms and epistemological traditions (p. 195). Here the challenge is to identify which contextual factors are important in arriving at causality and causal conclusions (Julnes and Rog, 2009, p. 97). Even if account is taken of which causal factors to include, how can their *relative* strengths – the strength of one cause compared to that of one of more other causes – be determined?

In quantitative data, statistical treatments such as multiple regression purport to identify the relative strengths of causes. However, this may not be the case, as: (a) such analysis is based on calculations of correlations, not causal warrants (I may find a strong correlation between rainfall and how much money I have, but the two are not causally related); (b) it assumes linear causal relationships, yet the world is nonlinear; (c) there is a risk of overlooking the inter-relatedness and interactions of multiple causes with each other, with multiple effects and with multiple interactions of multiple effects, hence causal 'webs' (Morrison, 2012), 'causal cakes' (Cartwright and Hardie, 2012), i.e. clusters of inter-related, multi-directional causes and factors, may be more fitting descriptions of causality than causal lines and causal chains; and (d) the calculations are based only on the variables that have been included, and, once other variables are included, these change the relative weights of causes. As Morrison (2009) remarks: using statistics to determine causation, even though widely practised, is open to question, as they beg the question: the statistics and analysis rely on assumptions, theories and warrants that pre-exist the statistics; without these, statistics risk simply reinforcing existing assumptions rather than really identifying causality (p. 206) (see also Cartwright, 2009).

Statistics alone do not prove causality; to believe that they do is to engage in circular thinking. Rather, it is the theoretical underpinnings, warrants and assumptions that embody causality, and statistics can support, challenge, extend and refine these underpinnings and assumptions. Behind statistics lie theories and models, and it is in the construct validity of these that causality lies. Further, it is the *mechanisms* of causality that should concern researchers, rather than solely numbers and statistical explanations. It is difficult to see how RCTs address such mechanisms and warrants; they often seem unconcerned with them.

Further, between independent and dependent variables of cause and effect respectively lie many causes, causal processes, and unknown degrees of freedom; these could be influencing the effect and, therefore, must be taken into account in any causal explanation, even if the transitivity argument applies. The argument supports micro-to-macro-analysis and explanation rather than macro-to-micro-analysis and explanation in what is often regarded as the opaque processes in a black-box, input-output model of causality such as in RCTs, even with classroom-based RCTs and process evaluations.

Working with quantitative methods in understanding causality risks committing the ecological fallacy – inferring an individual's causal behaviour from a general population's or sample's apparent causal behaviour. Conversely, extrapolating from individual studies to generality is dangerous. Individual and general levels often operate separately, and assuming cross-over might commit a category error. Causal explanations at the level of aggregate variables are incomplete, as behind them, and feeding into them, lie individuals' motives, values, goals, and circumstances, which might be exerting the causal influence; hence a theory of individual motives might be required in understanding and explaining causality. This argues for the importance of individual as well as collective, aggregate accounts, so action narratives are important in accounting for causality and effects. But if we go down the qualitative data path in establishing causality we encounter a different set of problems, as there are many action narratives and individual motivations, with multiple pathways of causality rather than simple input-output models. Little wonder, perhaps, that RCTs typically opt for quantitative measures rather than qualitative assessments, though this is changing to embrace qualitative process data in recent RCTs (e.g. Connolly et al., 2017, 2018).

For educational researchers, it is important to ascertain the causes of *why* something does or does not 'work'. Causality may be present but unobserved, not found, and, indeed, might be unobservable, particularly in the presence of stronger causes or impeding factors. Further, causality can apply in the situation of a non-change just as it applies in a situation of change; a cause can lower the likelihood of an effect rather than increase it, or even prevent a particular effect. RCTs risk overlooking such important nuances; they may wish to find 'what works' regardless of subtle causal factors and their interplay. But such interplay lies at the heart of what makes education educational.

One way of focusing a causal explanation is to examine regularities (e.g. purportedly in meta-analysis, see Chapter 12) and then to consider rival explanations, rival hypotheses and the theories that underpin them. However, the observation of regularities and frequencies is not essential to an understanding of causality; that is only a matter of trends and correlations, not necessarily causality. The most robust causal explanation is that which: (a) is founded on, and draws from the most robust theory (e.g. that theory which embraces intentionality, agency, interaction as well as structure, i.e. micro- and macro-factors); (b) explains all the elements of the phenomenon, i.e. that fits the *explanandum* and data more fully than rival theories; and (c) is tested in contexts and with data other than those that gave rise to the theory and causal explanation.

Quantitative data might be useful for identifying the 'what' of causality, whilst qualitative data might be useful for identifying the 'how' and 'why' of causality, though this is a crude distinction, even if applicable to RCTs. Qualitative data can accompany RCTs in education. Quantitative and qualitative *data* on their own, have no necessarily privileged position in understanding causality, as there still needs to be a theoretical warrant for causally connecting two events.

Causes, like effects, often operate in conjunction with other causes, circumstances and conditions, rather than in isolation. Causes are coincident with other causes. Contextuality is a key factor in identifying causality. Even if account is taken of which causal factors to include, how can their relative strengths – the strength of one cause compared to that of one of more other causes – be found? Striving to balance them out between control and treatment groups, as in randomization in RCTs, seems to miss the point that such factors are important in education. Indeed, there is an argument that searching for simple causality should be replaced by constructing *narratives* of what has happened and why (Thomas, 2012, pp. 42–43; Biesta, 2014).

Causality and counterfactuals

One distinguishing feature of causality is the significance of counterfactuals, i.e. the absence of X would have led to the absence of Y: without cause X then effect Y would not have happened. This is an argument used in RCTs, in which a control group is the counterfactual.

In an RCT, if we can isolate, control out, hold constant the effects of all the key factors or variables in both the control and experimental groups, except for the intervention given to the experimental group, and then show that there was a difference in outcome for the experimental group but not in the control group, then the suggestion is that the intervention had a causal influence on the outcome in the experimental group. Without counterfactual evidence, it is dangerous to assume that X causes Y; indeed, as argued below, one of the weaknesses of the *ceteris paribus* condition in many putative RCTs is their inability to provide or address counterfactuals.

However, the counterfactual argument is not clear. Morrison (2012) argues that:

> the counterfactual argument for causality ... states that if cause X had not happened then effect Y would not have happened; a cause is not a cause unless its counterfactual is true ... . In probabilistic causation, it is often difficult to meet the counterfactual requirement ... as there are instances where causality is present but where the counterfactual requirement is not met, e.g. in cases of over-determination and preemption (many causes acting on an effect such that, if one cause is removed, the effect still occurs), and when the effects of a cause are

masked – but not eliminated – by the presence of other causes or effects. A cause may be present but not raise or lower the likelihood of an effect … . A cause may be inhibited, prevented, reduced, facilitated, enabled, increased and otherwise affected by the presence of other causes. If the effect of cause A is cancelled out, equalled or reduced by another cause, does it cease to be a cause? Not at all. A cause is not the same as its manifestation.

(Morrison, 2012, p. 18)

RCTs are designed to include counterfactuals and comparison groups, which case studies and other forms of qualitative studies often do not possess (Cook, 2001). This implies that, if we wish to establish a cause, we need a carefully specified counterfactual in order to make sense of the cause. But this is unclear. In the familiar example of smoking causing cancer, what is the appropriate counterfactual for smoking? Is it, for example, smoking 10 cigarettes a day for 20 years, or smoking 50 cigarettes a day for 2 years, or not smoking at all? And why restrict the establishment of causality to the requirement of a counterfactual?

Causes and effects may only reveal themselves over time (a childhood injury may only manifest its effects when a person is old; the pleasures of learning Latin or reading Dickens at school may only be experienced later in life). This influences the timing of the outcome measure. Further, whilst causes and effects can be regarded as states *and* events, there is a case for regarding them as ongoing processes, e.g. a smoker continues to smoke even when cancer has set in, and lung cancer may have started long before it is detected. Where a cause begins and ends, where an effect begins and ends, when and how causes and effects should be measured, evaluated, ascertained and assessed, are open questions, requiring educational researchers to clarify and justify their decisions on timings. For RCTs in education, the timing and duration of a pre-test, intervention and post-testing must be justified and defensible.

Causality and controls

An RCT strives to identify causality through controlling variables, holding them constant. It may hold variable Z constant/controlled and see that variable X exerts an effect on Y, but in fact this may be a false positive, i.e. in reality X exerts no influence on Y. For example, we may find that increased teacher vigilance at trouble spots in schools (cause X) reduces the incidence of bullying (effect Y), even when the intervening variable Z (the threat of expulsion) is held constant. However, it may be incorrect to say that X causes Y, for several reasons. For example, there might be no causality present at all – the reduction in bullying might be caused by a completely different factor that happened to occur at the same time as X and which was not one of the factors held constant because nobody was aware that it might be an important factor.

The problem of controls is challenging. Morrison (2012) gives an example:

> we may think that there is a causal connection between the variable 'government pressure on schools' and the variable 'students' performance', but when we control for a third variable, 'parental pressure', we find no clear connection between 'government pressure on schools' and 'students' performance'. So, can we assume that 'government pressure on schools' has no effect on 'students' performance'? No, because 'government pressure on schools' may exert a strong effect on a fourth variable, say 'low teacher morale', and this 'low teacher morale' may be strong enough to mask (not remove) the causal link between 'government pressure on schools' and 'students' achievement'.
>
> (Morrison, 2012, p. 19)

Determining a cause is problematic, involving decisions on how far to go back in the temporal causal chain and how wide or narrow to go in the causal space, even though Pearl (2009) suggests a methodology for screening off 'ancestors' (prior causes) and 'dependents' (subsequent causes). The benefits of screening off and controlling for variables (e.g. the presence of a third variable or several variables) are important, as in partial correlations, structural equation modelling and RCTs. However, there are difficulties in this, since identifying which factors to screen off from which implies that it is actually possible to *know* which factors to screen off from which, and, in the case of multiple causality or over-determination, this may not be possible. How RCTs address such complexity is difficult to discern; they seem to simply over-ride them, showing little concern for them.

Screening off requires the ability to separate out causes, causal chains and causal lines, and this may be difficult to the point of impossibility. Controlling for the effects of additional variables is advisable if true causality is sought between a putative causal variable and its effect. However, the strength of this is only as powerful as the causal assumptions, theories and warrants which underpin their modelling, and this occurs *before* the RCT takes place, i.e. they are essential but extraneous to the RCT (e.g. Cartwright, 2009; Joyce, 2019).

Selectivity in working with causes

Selectivity is often a problem in working with causality: we may make incorrect causal inferences if we conduct solely confirmatory rather than disconfirming tests, or only ask questions that confirm our hypothesis, or select our results to include only those which support our argument ('cherry-picking'), discounting those which argue against it (and publication bias exists in RCTs, where papers with negative results or weak effect sizes are more difficult to publish). Further, we may conduct a test with, say, three samples, and then, finding no support for our hypothesis, extend this to five samples, or seven, i.e. until we obtain a majority that support our hypothesis. We can extend this to the duration of a piece of research; for example, if we don't find the result that we are looking for in, say, three months, then we extend the research to six months, i.e. until it yields the data that support our case. This argues for RCTs in education, as in clinical trials, to pre-register the trial before it begins and to pre-specify the time scale, scope, sampling and outcome measures, i.e. their protocols (Jadad and Enkin, 2007, p. 37ff.) (as in the Education Endowment Foundation's requirements).

Necessary and sufficient conditions

To understand causality in understanding 'what works', it is important for an RCT to establish the necessary and sufficient conditions in which it is situated. For example, for a match to light up, several conditions are needed: a dry match, an abrasive surface, flammable materials, a strong striking action and sufficient oxygen. However, it is not sufficient to say that the act of striking is the cause; the striking of the match is a *description* of a cause, but the cause may lie in a compound of factors: the presence of oxygen, the dryness of the match, the speed and firmness of the strike, the abrasiveness of the striking surface, the easily flammable materials, without which it would not light up. The striking of the match is the trigger – the last cause in a causal chain – and this must be separated out from total causality and relevant conditions. Similarly, RCTs operate in a range of causal conditions, and these are important determinants of whether the RCT shows 'what works'.

This raises the question of what are the necessary and sufficient conditions for such-and-such to 'work'. Mackie's (1993) INUS condition is useful here (an Insufficient but Nonredundant part of an Unnecessary but Sufficient condition), a condition which applies to RCTs in education. This raises the question in an RCT: 'what were the necessary and sufficient conditions in the specific situation which made the RCT 'work'?'

Necessary and sufficient conditions are those that obtain in a specific set of circumstances (Mackie, 1993). Mackie's 'INUS' conditions for causality concern *necessary* and *sufficient* conditions for a cause to have an effect. He gives the example of a house fire. Forensic experts indicate that it is caused by an electrical short-circuit. However, the situation is more complicated than this. For example, the short-circuit, on its own, is not a *necessary* condition for the fire, there being other possible ways of starting the fire. Equally, the short-circuit is not a *sufficient* condition for the fire, as, on its own, it need not have started the fire (e.g. if the short-circuit had not caused a spark, or if there was an automatic sprinkler system in the house, or if there was no flammable material in the house, or there was insufficient oxygen in the house to sustain the fire).

The point here is that, taken together, there was a set of conditions present that were *sufficient* for the fire to occur, triggered by the short-circuit, and, in these conditions, the short-circuit was *necessary* to set the house alight, or, as Mackie writes (Mackie, 1993, p. 34): the short-circuit which is the cause of the fire is an indispensable part of a sufficient, though not necessary, condition of the fire. Here the cause is an *Insufficient* but *Necessary* part of a condition which is itself *Unnecessary* but *Sufficient* for the outcome.

Mackie's work breaks with regarding 'necessary' conditions as being universal and omnipresent, replacing them with the constellation and combination of conditions *in a particular situation*. The challenge is to identify and understand the significant condition or conditions (e.g. events or processes) in a *specific* situation, that create the effects observed, asking 'what were the relevant sufficient conditions at the time to cause the effect?' This has a direct impact on RCTs, which strive to control out contexts and conditions, and the point here is that this risks overlooking the very factors which make a difference to the outcome. Rather, the RCT should specify the necessary and sufficient conditions which enabled it to 'work' or, indeed, not to 'work', to work well or not so well, and this requires not only the inclusion of process data in the RCT but to show the causal influence of such process data, if users of the RCT are to make real sense of how it might apply to their own situation.

Cause X and the conditions obtaining in one situation might bring about effect Y, or they might not; they might prevent, disable, displace or obstruct effect Y, or they might contribute to effect Y, or render effect Y a direct or indirect outcome. Evidence-based and evidence-informed educational practice must take cognizance of all of this, as 'what works' causally in one situation might not in another; conditions might enable or disable causal effects. This impacts directly on how far transferability and generalizability of findings from an RCT in one context 'work' (or do not 'work') in another. Rather than accepting that something 'works', users of evidence should take account of the INUS conditions in which it 'worked', what enabled it to 'work', or, indeed, what disabled it from 'working'. This suggests the need to accompany RCTs in education with sufficiently rigorous qualitative data not only on conditions and contexts, contingencies and situational factors, but how these are causal, and, indeed, with what knock-on effects on the users, for example the teachers and the students.

Causality and context

As mentioned above, even if causality is demonstrated, it is causality in a particular set of circumstances or contexts. How far these obtain in a different situation – a different classroom, with different teachers and different students, where both parties exert their own agency and ways of working – is open to question, and it is not always guaranteed that something which 'works' there or somewhere, will 'work' here (Cartwright and Hardie, 2012;

Kvernbekk, 2018). Kvernbekk (2018) clarifies the difference between finding causes and using them, as contexts vary, and contexts may affect whether a particular intervention brings about the desired result. Identifying a cause is necessary but not sufficient in suggesting that something 'works'. Further, Goldthorpe (2007) cautions researchers against confusing contexts and causes; for example, 'gender' may not be a *causal* factor, but it might be the site or theatre in which the causal factors operate; gender may be a moderator rather than a cause (Joyce, 2019, p. 51) and it may have differential influences on effects. RCTs may be no more than the theatre in which causes exert their influence and play themselves out in bringing about 'what works'.

The English statistician Bradford Hill (1965), writing in the context of RCTs in epidemiology, set out nine criteria for judging whether causality is present, and these point to the importance of understanding the situatedness of RCTs in affecting the findings (see also Mill, 2006, pp. 390–402):

1   *Strength* of the association (e.g. effect sizes): the larger the association, the greater the likelihood of it being causal.
2   *Consistency*: Has it been repeatedly observed by different persons, in different places, circumstances and times? If so, then this strengthens the likelihood of it being causal.
3   *Specificity*: If the factor and the effect are found in a specific population, and no other factors or explanations are present, then the greater is the likelihood of it being causal.
4   *Temporality*: The cause must precede the effect, even if the effect is delayed.
5   *Biological gradient*: The dose–response; the greater or more frequent the incidence, the greater or more frequent the effect.
6   *Plausibility*: If the relation between cause and effect is plausible, e.g. there is an empirical possibility or theoretical warrant.
7   *Coherence*: the cause-and-effect interpretation of data should not seriously conflict with the generally known facts of the case.
8   *Experiment*: confirmation by experimental or 'semi-experimental' studies.
9   *Analogy*: The effects of similar factors and their effects can also be considered.

Bradford Hill (1965) adds a note of caution: 'any belief that the controlled trial is the only way would mean not that the pendulum had swung too far but that it had come right off its hook' (p. 108). A salutary message.

Generalizing from causal research

This section lays the ground for discussing generalizability of RCTs in education in Chapter 12. Here a central issue in judging research 'evidence' is whether, and how far, what is found in one context or set of circumstances or population will apply to another context or situation or population: generalizability/'external validity'. We cannot take it for granted that 'what works' in one context will work in another: rote learning and cramming for examinations in East Asia might produce high examination scores there but low examination scores elsewhere; strong teacher direction in a Chinese school may go down very badly in a Spanish school. As Kvernbekk (2016) comments, external validity, as in an RCT, can be 'a rare treat' (p. 109) (Chapter 12).

Facts from specific studies are insufficient alone to indicate generalizability, and more is needed by way of 'causal principles' (what connects two factors in a warranted causal theory), 'causal roles' (the way in which causes work in different contexts) and 'support factors' (what other factors must be in place for causal principles and roles to work; Cartwright and Hardie, 2012, p. 50; see also Norman, 2003). Cartwright and Hardie (2012) note, however, that this is unlikely; 'causal roles', they aver, do not 'travel' well (p. 88) and 'support factors' and their relative strengths differ. For transferability, all of these factors must obtain, in their presence and in their relative strengths, as this affects the causality at work here. What is relevant 'here' (in one context) may be less relevant 'there' (in another context) as other conditions and 'local circumstances' are present (p. 41), so there is a need for findings to be 'evidentially relevant' to the context to which they are being applied (the 'there').

'Causal principles', 'causal roles', 'causal cakes' and 'support factors' may vary from one context to another; this frustrates easy attempts to assert 'what works' when applying findings from one study to another context, be it from an RCT or another kind of research. Teams of causes (Cartwright and Hardie, 2012, p. 52) differ and operate differently between one context and another, limiting generalizability. Further, if one identifies the context too specifically then the case becomes unique (Kvernbekk, 2016, p. 63); hence the challenge is to strike a balance between those studies which have high granularity – close-grained detail – and those with low granularity. Where the balance is struck is difficult to discern in the literature of RCTs and meta-analysis.

Morrison (2012) argues that 'webs of causality' – many factors and variables all inter-related – are more productive for thinking about causality than linear causality. There needs to be similarity in webs of causes between what operates 'here' and what operates 'there'. Not only should the presence of factors in a causal web be similar, but the salience and the location of each strand – the relative importance of each factor – should be similar for transferability and generalizability from 'here' to 'there'; such similarity is unlikely. Causals webs in one place are not the same as those in another: even if the same causes obtain in situation one and situation two, their relative strengths and influence may differ, causing something to 'work' in one situation but not another.

Cartwright and Hardie (2012) argue that causal principles (all the causes operating in a case, including their relative strengths and how they combine) (p. 43) must be similar for transferability, and that this is questionable in RCTs in education. What happens not only in a different location but at a different time may differ from that in another. Evidence is needed of a 'stable tendency' (p. 44), i.e. that the same findings, practices or interventions are stable across a wide variety of situations – locational, temporal, cultural, managerial, etc. This is a challenge for RCTs in education. Interventions may have negative outcomes in different circumstances and situations, and the strengths of the outcomes may differ across contexts. In this respect the 'evidence' to be provided must be 'relevant' (Chapter 2), and what is 'relevant' may differ across two or more contexts.

The matter is complex, for conditions, contingencies, constraints, and relevant factors 'there' may not be the same as those 'here'; populations, personalities, values, cultural practices may be similar but not sufficiently similar for something to work when moved from 'here' to 'there', even if the same causal factors are present in the two situations. How factors are combined might differ between 'here' and 'there'. Cartwright and Hardie (2012) note that 'similarity' is a vague term, and under its umbrella may be very disparate factors, some of which are included or excluded in the two situations. Even agreeing on what constitutes similarity may be impossible – who decides what is and is not to be included (indicators) in arriving at 'similarity' (p. 48). Indeed, 'similarity' is not sufficient here; rather, identifying the factors that lead to correct prediction is stronger (ibid.). Even if such factors are found, it is unlikely that they occur similarly in the target population or with the same intensity, strength, combination, weightings, causal impact and in the context of sufficiently similar enablers, qualifiers, inhibitors, causal chains, conditions, contingencies and side-effects (Kvernbekk, 2016, pp. 140–147). The user of evidence must determine whether these are sufficiently similar for the evidence to transfer securely. RCTs face this problem, to the extent that it might be invidious to infer generalizability.

The evidence that something can transfer easily and 'work' in new situations must be interrogated, as it may not 'work' well, if at all, or better, or the same, or it may have different outcomes, side-effects, positive and negative outcomes in another context. Where, then, is the evidence of generalizability? Is it simply in the number of RCTs? Surely not.

To compound the challenge, for a finding to travel well from one situation to another, requires a high degree of certainty, fidelity (to the original conduct of the study) and stability (persistence over time) (Kvernbekk, 2016, p. 111) in the original finding, and for the two sites to have similar ontologies in their systems, causal operations and dependencies (p. 109), e.g. logical contingencies, spatiotemporal contingencies and the comparative/commensurate strengths and weaknesses of these in both sites (p. 109). This features in claims for the generalizability of RCTs.

However, certainty is elusive, as we never have perfect knowledge, even if the knowledge purports to be objective. Fidelity to procedures, e.g. in an RCT, is unlikely unless questionable levels of prescription are insisted upon, and, anyway, practitioners operate interventions in their own ways. Stability depends on significant consistency across studies, with clarity in what does and does not change across studies. Kvernbekk (2016) notes that the importance of stability in enabling predictability is under-stated in the evidence-based literature. RCTs, she avers, rarely operate at high levels of detail in 'what to do' in the intervention (p. 124), thereby rendering fidelity problematic.

On the other hand, too much stability is restrictive and does little to build on the expertise and professionally variable judgement of the teacher. Kvernbekk argues (p. 167) that stability and fidelity must also be balanced with flexibility; she gives the example of a tightrope walker who has to follow rules of balance, which includes freedom to move her/his arms to secure such a balance. Without flexibility, a system – a tightrope walker in this instance – becomes unstable. How RCTs tread the fine line between fidelity to procedures yet flexibility is problematic, as too much flexibility might distort findings and their generalizability. Fidelity, albeit with appropriate flexibility, also requires fidelity to Cartwright's and Hardie's 'support structures', roles and contextual requirements, and these are often unlikely to be the same in a new situation in a different locale.

Nor does similarity of contexts and conditions tell the whole story. Causal processes and interactions vary in different situations. This raises questions such as 'what and where is the evidence of similarity of input and processes as well as of outcomes?' 'How is that evidence of similarity to be judged, and by whom?' This has implications for the standardization of operational procedures and protocols in RCTs in education.

For generalizability to be secure, several factors should be present, and this applies in RCTs, as in other forms of educational research:

- The contexts, conditions and contingencies, must be sufficiently similar such that differences between 'here' and 'there' are insufficient to bring about differences in outcomes.
- The 'causal principles', 'causal roles', 'causal cakes', 'support factors', causal processes, causal strengths, causal influences and their weighting, causal conditions, causal combinations and causal sequences must be sufficiently similar, such that differences between 'here' and 'there' are insufficient to bring about differences in outcomes.
- The ways in which the research is applied (e.g. what teachers and learners do; the protocols and procedures for an RCT to operate) must be sufficiently similar such that differences between 'here' and 'there' are insufficient to bring about differences in outcomes.

- The relevance accorded to the intervention or practice must be sufficiently similar such that differences between 'here' and 'there' are insufficient to bring about differences in outcomes.
- The research designs, contents, purposes, questions, methodologies, samples, methods, instrumentation, validity and reliability, conduct, data, data types, data analysis, findings and interpretation must be sufficiently similar in the RCT when it is applied elsewhere, such that differences between 'here' and 'there' are insufficient to bring about differences in outcomes.

However, even ensuring these does not guarantee success; they are based on 'similarity', and, as mentioned above, 'similarity' is a weak, ill-defined term. Having 'similarity' may not guarantee that 'what works' in one context will 'work' in another, as this is only one set of factors in a multi-factorial situation, which includes people and all their foibles, personalities, preferences, behaviours, ways of working, values, influences, and so on. By contrast, not having such similarities in place does not mean that something will not 'work', as there may be other factors that come into play which exert a strong influence for success and transferability, e.g. teacher enthusiasm, learner enthusiasm, parental pressure. In short, the presence of additional factors might cause something not to 'work' or, indeed, to 'work'.

The generalizability of research evidence also requires clarification of what it is, exactly, that is being generalized: a methodology, a practice, a content area, a selection from a bigger project, an entire or partial procedure, a recommendation, a design, a finding, an outcome, a way of doing things, an 'if X happens, then Y happens' statement, or whatever. This applies to RCTs, as to other forms of research in education.

In considering generalizability, who or what are the arbiters of success in deciding generalizability? At one level the answer is straightforward: this depends on the scope of the research evidence: collect as many examples of the same or similar practice 'working' in as many contexts and under as many conditions, situations, circumstances as possible, i.e. the accretion of multiple studies on the same topic from as wide as possible a sample (e.g. as in a meta-analysis and replication studies). This is exactly the advice from the US Department of Education (2003, p. 17) with regard to RCTs: 'the intervention should be demonstrated as effective, through well-designed randomized controlled trials, in more than one site of implementation; these sites should be typical school or community settings … ; the trials should demonstrate the intervention's effectiveness in school settings similar to yours' (p. 17). However, these requirements are unclear on what criteria 'similar' is to be judged, they understate the problems of transferability which reside in necessarily detailed causality (Kvernbekk, 2016, p. 99), they make too many assumptions that these few conditions will meet the requirements for transferability, and they take insufficient or no account of other necessary and sufficient (INUS) conditions and contexts present in both sites; hence generalizability is suspect here.

Just because something seems to 'work' in one or more contexts provides no guarantee that it will work in others, as the INUS conditions vary. The difference here is also between what the research finds and how these such findings are used; finding and using are two entirely different matters (Kvernbekk, 2016, p. 80). Transposition from one context to another encounters many complications.

At a second level, meta-analysis, replication studies, research syntheses and systematic reviews make a potentially useful contribution here, as they set their own protocols, e.g. the Evidence for Policy and Practice Information and Co-ordinating Centre (UK) (the EPPI-Centre: www.eppi.ioe.ac.uk), the Education Endowment Foundation, and Major and Higgins (2019).

At a third level, it may be the 'experts' who decide the generalizability of one or more pieces of 'evidence', though this opens a hornet's nest of who are the experts, how they warrant the sobriquet of 'expert', and experts in what exactly? And, anyway, what if experts disagree?

At a fourth level, it is the practitioners, the users, who decide if something 'works'; teachers rarely leave interventions or prescribed practices untouched; they do something with them, they use their informed professional judgement and experience in deciding 'what works' for them or the persons in their charge. In other words, they deliberate on generalizability, applicability and transferability in light of their own situation and those of the learners. Research evidence alone under-determines what practitioners do in their classroom with their students in their learning, curricula, time scales, conditions and contexts. Who would wish it to be otherwise? Just because for example, a large effect size is found, be it in a single study, meta-analysis or meta-meta-analysis, this does not present a self-evident case for the adoption of such-and-such an intervention in a particular situation.

At a fifth level, researchers build into their research the *ceteris paribus* clause, as this enables them to stipulate the conditions under which the research is believable and it strives to ride over the waves of contextual matters. It is to this that the next section turns.

Generalizability, then, may be chimerical, and 'context-sensitive case studies' (Elliott, 2007, p. 77) might not be as low down the hierarchy of evidence as suggested (Pawson, 2006), not least as teaching is a context-dense and variable-dense activity. Indeed, as Didau (2015) remarks, as long as teachers conduct research in their own schools and do not seek to generalize, then this is useful (p. 127).

The *ceteris paribus* clause

Researchers frequently tag onto their research the caveat of the *ceteris paribus* clause, and this is a feature of many RCTs. Random allocation to control and treatment groups, in an attempt to balance out the effect of many small variables, is an appeal to the *ceteris paribus* condition, but such an appeal is dangerous. Researchers may do this as a safeguard against criticism, or as part and parcel of the effects of the randomized selection and allocation processes in sampling, or as the next best thing to the *simpliciter* condition (unconditionality) in their attempt at generalizability. Causality, randomization and the *ceteris paribus* clause are intimately connected. The *ceteris paribus* clause in educational research, whilst being a commonplace assumption or requirement in some surveys and large-scale RCTs, is highly problematic, not least as chaos theory and complexity theory demonstrate that small differences in initial or emergent conditions respectively can have massive effects (Chapter 5). The *ceteris paribus* clause is frequently a vacuous or largely meaningless add-on, get-out clause.

In judging 'what works', educationists are faced with a problem which, although not necessarily spoken, suffuses discourses of 'evidence': the *ceteris paribus* clause (all other things being equal). The educationist is being asked to take on trust that a whole range of variables and factors are, in fact, equal or exert an equal influence. This is problematic. The *ceteris paribus* condition applies typically, though not exclusively, to quantitative studies, particularly surveys and RCTs, but, in judging 'what works', it undermines the confidence that can be placed in 'evidence', including claims made for RCTs in education.

At the outset, there is uncertainty about what *ceteris paribus* actually means. It can mean, for example, 'with other things the same', or 'all other things being equal or held constant', i.e. that no other factors might upset or interfere with the finding. Schurz (2010) comments that '"ceteris paribus" is a deeply *ambiguous* notion' (p. 75) (see also Bal et al., 2002, p. 132).

There are many examples of *ceteris paribus* clauses in educational research, e.g.: Bachan's and Reilly's (2003) study of gender effects in 70,000 students; Bachan's (2004) study of gender and nationality effects in 5,000 students; Arulampalam's et al.'s (2005) study of dropout probability in 724,000 students; Johnes's and McNabb's (2004) study of entry qualifications and subsequent success for 100,000 students; Houston's and Toma's (2003) studies of 115,000 students, reporting on home schooling; Rochat's and Demeulemeester's (2001) study of 641 freshmen in Belgian higher education; Smith's and Naylor's (2001) study of over 94,000 students, comparing home and international students' performance; Smith's and Naylor's (2001) study of qualifications and post-graduation employment of over 62,000 students; and Brutsaert's and Van Houtte's (2002) study of girls' and boys' sense of belonging in single-sex versus co-educational schools, with data from 6,327 students.

All of these examples are deliberately chosen to be: from large-scale studies; from a time frame that is not recent; from studies conducted in different countries; and from studies which deliberately use the *ceteris paribus* clause and the very words '*ceteris paribus*'. This raises many questions respectively:

- how acceptable it is to assume that, just because a sample is large, it is safe to assume the *ceteris paribus* clause (even if this is in the form of controls exerted in the conduct of the data analysis) and even in the face of claims that large-scale data move towards the *ceteris paribus* state;
- at what point in time a finding ceases to be relevant (Bal et al. (2002) argue that our 'understanding of phenomena (e.g. objects, subjects and conditions) can change – the *ceteris paribus* clause needs, therefore, to be considered in light of the current state of scientific developments' (p. 129) (and, as argued in Chapter 5, this is violated in RCTs in education);
- how far the results from one country, with its own set of contexts, can apply outside those countries; and
- how the *ceteris paribus* condition is being used, e.g. as a 'cover-all', 'get out' clause for self-protection, as an assumption rather than a proven reality, stipulatively (iff) or descriptively.

Todd and Wolpin (2003), using data from 9 studies of class size and achievement, comment that, in seeking to know what we can learn from experiments, an alternative to recourse to the *ceteris paribus* clause is to examine the non-*ceteris paribus* effects (p. F8). They note that experimental evidence, however, cannot generally be used to understand how the *ceteris paribus* clause changes the effect of class-size on achievement, as family and school variables change as a consequence of the experiment (*ibid.*).

Elgin and Sober (2010) remark that *ceteris paribus* is a 'get out' clause, a 'wish' or 'aspiration' whose claim to equality is not proven but assumed, and that it is arrogant to make such assumptions (p. 165). If the *ceteris paribus* clause is used stipulatively or as a 'cover-all' clause, then why should we believe that, empirically, it holds any water at all. Where is the evidence to support its valid use? On what empirical grounds is it acceptable? 'What works' is, in part, an empirical matter.

Bal et al. (2002) are sceptical of using the *ceteris paribus* condition, arguing that on many occasions, it is used as a 'kind of "wastebasket" to remove information contained in moderator variables that seem inapplicable in the study' (p. 130). Earman et al. (2010) comment that the *ceteris paribus* clause is only used because of laziness: though one *could* replace it with a precise, known conditional, lazy people choose not to do so. Further, Elgin and Sober (2010) comment that '*ceteris paribus* modifiers describe conditions that are almost never satisfied' (p. 165). What evidence do researchers provide for ensuring that the *ceteris paribus* condition is acceptable? How do they know? They simply assume, i.e. circularity abounds.

Mitchell (2009) suggests that, in seeking exceptionless laws of social behaviour (and this links, in part, to generalizability), the *ceteris paribus* clause is frequently invoked in the attempt to transform into universal laws what would otherwise be false claims to non-domain-restricted, exception-free universality. We simply don't know, she avers, what might interfere with this to question the 'all else being equal' clause (p. 140). In the social sciences, *ceteris paribus* laws are problematic since other things may not be equal, and asserting *ceteris paribus* may not be susceptible to being empirically tested (p. 141). Indeed, it is difficult to conceive of necessary counterfactual possibilities in *ceteris paribus* discourse, and that the 'cost of the *ceteris paribus* clause is high. First, although making a generalization universally true in this way can always be done, it is at the risk of vacuity' (p. 142), i.e. all other things are equal only when they are equal and are not equal when they are not equal e.g. smoking causes lung cancer unless it doesn't (Cartwright, 2019).

Woodward (2010) comments that *ceteris paribus* clauses are not only vacuous but that they are 'unacceptably circular'; if it means that something is true simply in those instances where no instances of it being breached can be found, then, strictly speaking, the *ceteris paribus* clause is no more than a tautology – it is true where it is true (p. 32). The *ceteris paribus* clause absolves the researcher from having to seek out any further evidence or make an admission of limits and constraints on the research. As Lange (2010) remarks, the *ceteris paribus* clause is little more than saying that something is true, other things being equal, unless something prevents it from being so or if other factors which might prevent it from being so, are absent (p. 131); it is capricious. Similarly, Spohn (2010) notes that *ceteris paribus* clauses require a standard of comparison which is usually left implicit and that 'the default standard' is provided by normal conditions, so that, in such cases, other things being equal simply means 'other things being normal' (p.111) (and Glymour (2010) notes that the meaning of 'normal' is, itself, unclear (p. 119)).

Earman et al. (2010) add that there appears to be to be no acceptable account of how *ceteris paribus* clauses or claims can be tested (p. 16) and that this is a major problem for them: there is no way of knowing if they are true of false (Glymour, 2010, p. 124).

The educationist, unable to find any tenable justification for the assumption of the *ceteris paribus* clause, faces a major challenge in accepting the validity and reliability of 'evidence' that appeals to the *ceteris paribus* condition, including that from RCTs. The *ceteris paribus* clause may be no more than a statistical article of faith or premise, rather than an empirical certainty, and it is constitutionally unable to catch the irreducible richness and evolving dynamics of the everyday world of the classroom, i.e. the central features of life in classrooms.

The *ceteris paribus* clause is problematic in that, if it is true (and we have no way of discerning this), then it is unclear how it takes account of context, and, if it is not true (and, again, we have no way of discerning this), then what effect context has on the findings. The educationist using RCT 'evidence' for judging 'what works', knowingly or not, is frequently faced with an assumption, declared or not, that the *ceteris paribus* clause applies, in that no conditionality or details of the constraints and limitations of context are provided. *Ceteris paribus* clauses ride roughshod over the very factors that make 'education' education: human agency, contexts, contingencies, differences, diversity, variety, variability, emergence, temporality, spontaneity, unpredictability, people, personalities etc. The assumption that it is possible, regardless of desirability, to hold factors constant, to remove behaviours from their contexts, might be superficially appealing in judging 'what works', but these, in fact, are the very stuff of 'what works'.

The appeal to the *ceteris paribus* clause is pernicious, as it renders claims to generalizability spurious, unfounded, or, at best, questionable. This raises serious questions against RCTs, with their implicit or explicit appeal to the *ceteris paribus* condition, e.g. in randomization. Users of research evidence in deciding 'what works' must be on their guard to detect where assumptions of the *ceteris paribus* clause have been made, what is the warrant for making such assumptions, and at what cost to the validity, reliability, believability and usability of the research evidence. Similarly, the drive for exceptionless, unconditional certainty and generalizability is a chimera, as diversity and difference rule; thank heaven.

Conclusion

Users of research must be able to detect the causal contexts, necessary and sufficient conditions, mechanisms, ingredients, 'causal cakes' and their interactions, triggers, counterfactuals and combinations of causal factors operating in a situation. RCTs are not strong in this respect, a point which is revisited in later chapters. These demands render problematic simple notions of generalizability and transferability of research from one context to another. Linear thinking – either in terms of combinations of causes, causal links, or single causes – is mistaken, as, in any situation, it is the *combination* of necessary and sufficient conditions and causes operating simultaneously, their interactions, relative weightings and processes, that brings about an effect. The chapter has argued for the need for RCTs to identify the INUS conditions operating in a situation, and if generalizability is sought, for these to be very similar in new contexts in which the RCT is to be applied; it has also suggested that such conditions might not obtain from one context to another.

Far from using *ceteris paribus* clauses to override or putatively balance out the myriad causal variables and factors, and their effects, operating in a situation, in fact it is the presence of these very small factors and variables that is essential in understanding causality, and this, in turn, renders counterfactual analysis – a central claim of RCTs – difficult, as the factors, variables and their interactions differ from case to case. A control group is an assumed, but not necessarily a true, counterfactual. The *ceteris* paribus clause is unhelpful, though widely used or tacitly appealed to in RCTs. Determining and disentangling causes and effects, the effects of causes and the causes of effects, is probabilistic, complex and often intractable. Controlling variables, a familiar and widely used element of research, misrepresents the importance of their ongoing presence, significance and interplay in bringing about an effect. The complexity of causality renders generalizability and transferability of findings from RCTs, and, indeed, other types of research, problematic. As will be seen in Part II of this book, RCTs have a clear difficulty in this respect.

Part II

Randomized controlled trials

Part I set the ground for considering randomized controlled trials (RCTs), locating them in the context of evidence-based education and the pursuit of 'what works' in education. Part II focuses on RCTs in particular.

Imagine that teachers of 6-year-olds in a primary school decide that they are going to conduct what they describe as an RCT in improving children's reading in English. Class A is the intervention group that tries out a synthetic phonics approach and Class B is the control group that continues with a 'mixed diet' of reading approaches. The children's English attainment levels in both classes are measured at the start of the RCT, using reading ages and a test of skills of decoding phonically regular words; the average score for each of the two classes is extremely close at this pre-test stage. The teacher of Class A is new and enthusiastic; the teacher of Class B is not. The new method is tried for one term and the children's attainment is measured at the end. Using averages, children in Class A's scores have advanced 9 months in terms of reading ages, whilst the children in Class B's have advanced only 3 months, and the children in Class A score 30 points higher than students in Class B. The school reports that the synthetic phonics approach has 'worked', that it has been tried and tested in what is widely termed the 'gold standard' of an RCT, and that henceforth it will be implemented across the school. The alleged comparison group/counterfactual is present, so that the question '"what works" compared to what?' is addressed, and the standards for deciding that the intervention has 'worked' are made clear: Class A obtained higher reading ages and scores on a decoding test than Class B.

Whilst this is a caricature, the claim that this is an RCT is entirely spurious, for several reasons:

- There was no randomized selection of students and no random allocation to each of the two classes, i.e. the 'randomized' in 'randomized controlled trials' was missing. The sampling was suspect.
- There were no controls apart from having a class whose similarity was in terms of age group and average score on a pre-test, e.g. there were

different teachers, different personalities, different scheduling, different class sizes, and different classroom organization, environment and ethos. Children in Class A spent more time on reading in class than children in Class B. Some children in Class B were absent through illness during the term, whilst those in Class A were not; some high-performing children in Class B left the school, whilst those in Class A did not. The 'controlled' in 'randomized controlled trials' was missing.

- At the start of the intervention, the parents of the students in Class A were given a full picture of the intervention, in order to give their informed consent; those in Class B were not.
- Some children in Class B were very challenging, a feature absent in Class A.
- Twenty children were in Class A and fifteen children were in Class B at the start.
- The putative claim to counterfactuals by using the control group (Class B) was illegitimate, as it differed in many respects from Class A.
- What was on 'trial' in this RCT could just as easily have been the teacher's enthusiasm and its effects on the children, rather than the synthetic phonics-based approach, or, indeed, both, i.e. there were problems of causality.
- Reading ages are a narrow and limited proxy for reading performance.
- The post-test measure favoured the testing of what the treatment groups had been exposed to and the control group had not, i.e. it was biased in favour of the treatment group.
- The children in Class A often played with children in Class B in school and out of school; and the teachers in the school often spoke with each other about what they were doing in the classroom, i.e. there was a high potential for 'contamination' in the putative RCT.
- The standard deviations of the scores in the two classes at the pre-test level were very different; for Class A they were small whilst for Class B they were large.
- The distribution of the pre-test scores for Class A were negatively skewed, whilst for Class B they were positively skewed.
- The rise in the average score of Class A at the post-test was because a small group of students obtained very high marks; the marks of a group of Class B students were low. The averages concealed differences.
- The results were attributed to the intervention, but there could have been a range of possible causes, which had not been controlled out.
- The results of a very small RCT were scaled up and generalized across the school, with no basis or warrant for secure generalization.
- Nobody placed the results 'on trial', i.e. interrogated the validity and reliability of the RCT and its outcomes.

What started out as an intended RCT fell very short of the care with which the RCT should have been planned and implemented, and what could be taken from this did not meet the requirements of 'randomized', 'controlled' or 'trials'.

The example raises many issues that the chapters in Part II address concerning RCTs. The analysis here is not to suggest that RCTs should not be conducted; rather it is to say that certain canons of rigour should be applied in RCTs and the conclusions drawn from them should be valid and reliable. Part II falls into several main areas in considering RCTs:

- The case for and against RCTs.
- Causality and controls.
- Contexts, scope, treatments and outcomes.
- Sampling in RCTs.
- Randomization and the *ceteris paribus* condition.
- Ethical issues.
- Timing and duration in RCTs.
- The limits of averages.
- The impact on RCTs of complexity theory and chaos theory.
- 'Medical models' of RCTs and their usefulness for education.
- Design issues and data analysis in RCTs.
- Reporting RCTs in education.
- Generalizability and external validity.
- RCTs and policy making.

These constitute an entrée into the contested domain of RCTs in education, with claims and counter-claims that are made for their place in educational research and the evidence-based movement in education. Each of these areas is problematic, as unpacked in this part.

After briefly tracing in the rise and prominence given to RCTs, Part II argues that such prominence is disproportionate and largely undeserved. RCTs claim to identify causality, but this is contentious. Claimed benefits of controls in RCTs, a key element of RCTs, are questionable, impractical and unreliable. RCTs' appeals to the advantages of building out 'local' contexts and conditions are called into question, as the very stuff of human behaviour and nature, and indeed social science more widely, should take these into account in educational research, i.e. rich, variable-dense human and environmental factors are central. These include, but are not limited to, agency, consciousness, creativity, spontaneity, (pro)activity rather than passivity, intentions, volitions, interactions, moral judgements, and the fecundity of human actions, together with the contexts, contingencies and conditions obtaining in any educational setting. These make educational research 'educational' (e.g. Pring, 2015; Cain, 2019), and it is essential to include them rather than dismissing them as contaminating factors in research; input/ output and would-be generalizable RCTs take insufficient account of these.

This is not to say that people do not behave agentically and in context in an RCT; it is to say that their agency is bounded, caged.

Cain (2019) remarks that teaching is far more than simply applying a given strategy; it is about interactions and human relationships, and these operate in complex situations with multiple interpretations of situations at work (p. 134). Similarly, Biesta (2014) comments that education is fundamentally an interaction between people, which varies and changes rather than being 'eternal' (p. 21).

Even though process evaluations and supporting qualitative data are increasing in RCTs (Connolly et al., 2018; Joyce, 2019, p. 48), these do not touch sufficiently the heart of many RCTs, which address the 'what' rather than the 'why', 'how', 'where' and 'so what for practice' that educators need to know if they are to improve and develop. RCTs are over-simplistic, over-reductionist and, despite their claims to causality, have little to say about the 'why' and 'how' of practices (Kvernbekk, 2019, p. 28). They fail to catch complex contexts, overriding the wealth of detailed variables at work in a situation (Wrigley, 2019; Wrigley and McCusker, 2019). What RCTs 'deliver' may not be what teachers and practitioners find useful in their own situations, *viz.* 'why' and 'how' something works. Recognizing the importance of including context in educational research and the significant role of context in attributing causality, there are limits to the generalizability of findings from RCTs.

Related to the importance of building in contextual factors and the 'human factor' in educational research, Part II argues that complexity theory and chaos theory call into question some of the 'scientific' premises of RCTs. Here it contends that to adopt approaches in educational research which insulate people from their contexts and conditions, and which isolate and control variables, is to engage in a misrepresentation of what educational research should be doing. This radically undermines RCTs. RCTs misrepresent the multi-directional, multi-factorial, nonlinear causal and networked connections between and within internal and external factors, and the dynamic emergence of ever-changing situations which RCTs vainly try to hold in temporal, causal, contextual and locational stasis.

Having set out some of the ontological concerns underpinning RCTs, Part II moves to epistemological and methodological, practical matters. Design issues are addressed and the nature and limitations of sampling are introduced, including sampling in addressing generalizability, together with randomization, random sampling and the *ceteris paribus* condition. Questions are raised of how far RCTs in education actually meet the claims made for and from randomization and random sampling and how achievable they are in practice. If they are not, and the suggestion is that this is likely, then this undermines the use of the already largely discredited null hypothesis significance testing. The widely used alternative – effect size – is also shown to be problematical and often misused.

Part II then turns to a defining element of RCTs: the use of averages. It argues that these are of limited value and that they often conceal what educationists really want to know, e.g. sub-group effects and for which groups an intervention might and might not 'work'. Part II draws on frequently alluded to 'medical models' of RCTs, and compares RCTs in clinical research and educational research. Though the premises on which RCTs in clinical research and educational research are based are very different, RCTs in education can gain great benefits from applying the rigour required in clinical trials.

Part II also raises issues of generalizability in and from RCTs, and shows that scalability and generalizability are problematical in RCTs. 'What works' in one educational context may not work in another.

Part II concludes on a cautionary note: whilst RCTs in education may be fit for some comparatively low-level or straightforward matters, they may not be fit for major features in the 'real' world of education, what makes 'education' education, and what makes 'educational research' educational. Whilst RCTs have their place in educational research, it is very much more limited than currently obtains. They don't tell us much, and at great cost.

RCTs in education beg several serious questions, and Part II calls out how far they really can provide useful evidence of 'what works'. RCTs can and, as a matter of ethical behaviour, should be improved; nevertheless, even if they are perfect – which is unlikely – they are still largely or often insufficient, on their own, to make research 'educational'. The final chapter includes fifty theses which draw together, in summary fashion, the arguments presented in the book.

Chapter 4

The rise of randomized controlled trials in evidence-based education

Introduction and overview

This chapter argues that:

- The increasing appeal of RCTs is considerable, but risky, and claims made for placing RCTs at the top of a hierarchy of 'evidence' are unacceptable.
- Even though RCTs are conducted in 'real world' settings, this does not render them reliable or valid, and reliability and validity in RCTs raise serious challenges to their utility.
- RCTs may be useful in some areas of educational research, but far fewer and of less significance than is claimed for them, and they are seldom fully used in policy making.
- RCTs adopt an impoverished and too-limited a view of 'science' and experimentation, and they neglect important paradigms of science.
- RCTs too easily dismiss other accepted ways of conducting research in education, be this in order to boost their own claims to supremacy or to identify limits of other methods.
- The case for RCTs in education is clear; the case against RCTs in education is powerful. Claims and counter-claims for RCTs in education are plentiful. RCTs in educational research are minimally useful and must take account of many features which are often missing in RCTs. There are serious limits to what RCTs in education can actually do and tell us; 'fitness for purpose' indicates such limits.
- There are key reservations about RCTs in education, and it is essential to address these.
- Causality and controls are problematic in RCTs, and appeals to counterfactual evidence and blinding – claimed as attractions in RCTs – are of questionable possibility in education. RCTs adopt a simplistic view of causality, and they have no privileged position in addressing causality, there being plentiful richer ways of determining causality that embrace 'causal cakes' and 'causal webs'. Whilst RCTs may not purport to

address complex causality – that is their claim to power – this results in a 'black box' approach to identifying links between input and output, and this undermines the usefulness of RCTs. Randomization in RCTs does not necessarily solve questions of causality. RCTs understate the causal power of human interventions, agency, intentionality and human-related factors, which are not solved by operating standardized protocols and procedures in RCTs, and, anyway, it is unlikely that intended standardized procedures actually operate in practice. RCTs' adoption of a linear view of causality is erroneous.

- Users of research need to know the 'why' and 'how' of 'what works', but RCTs under-address this.

Taking these points together, the chapter suggests that RCTs have a limited, occasionally mildly useful, place in educational research, occupying one position in the realm of fitness for purpose, but they must take their place alongside other forms of research which serve other, richer purposes in education.

The appeal to evidence

Much policy making in education has been marked by the comparatively slender evidence base on which it is built; policies are driven in by political will rather than evidence. The vehemence of expression against such practices can be witnessed in early statements such as those emanating from advocates of evidence-based education, e.g.: 'the ease with which politicians, policy makers – and even teachers – have been able to get away with implementing their prejudices without even token consideration of the evidence, let alone engaging in a serious and informed debate about its quality and importance is a disgrace' (Curriculum Evaluation and Management Centre, 2000a, p. 1).

However, there have been several recent moves to ensure that educational policy making is informed by evidence rather than political will. The empirical research base is increasing (e.g. Hattie, 2009; Gorard et al., 2017; Major and Higgins, 2019).

We should know whether something 'works' before we put it into policy. Further, as has been argued for decades (Curriculum Evaluation and Management Centre, 2000a, 2000b), we can often only know whether something works by 'trying it out'; practice should supersede political will (Tymms, 1999, pp. 82–95). For advocates of RCTs, the nature of evidence is of a particular kind only, and 'trying it out' is also only undertaken in particular ways: the RCT to ensure generalizability (e.g. Boruch, 1997; Tymms, 1999; Oakley, 1998, 2000; Mosteller and Boruch, 2002; Thomas and Pring, 2004; Torgerson and Torgerson, 2008; Donaldson et al., 2009; Hammersley, 2013; Pearce and Raman, 2014; Connolly et al., 2017, 2018; Gorard et al., 2017, 2018; Education Endowment Foundation, 2018; Major and Higgins, 2019).

Over the last two decades, RCTs have become more common and have been accorded the top position in the pecking order of evidence of 'what works'. The Education Endowment Foundation in the UK has given huge sums of money to the implementation and promotion of RCTs (opening in 2010, with a start-up government grant of 110 million pounds sterling). Many RCTs have been undertaken, and with vast numbers of teachers and students, e.g. at the time of writing, with RCTs involving a million students, over 13,000 schools, colleges and nurseries (Major and Higgins, 2019, p. x; Nevill, 2019), and a 'toolkit' of summaries of evidence on a range of topics on education of children from 5–16 (Education Endowment Foundation, 2019b). RCTs have moved out of the laboratory and into the classroom. As Connolly et al. (2017, 2018) note, teachers have been attracted by, and involved in, RCTs in large numbers, and have reacted positively to them. RCTs lay claim to being the fairest kind of test available, often working on teaching materials and methods, as these are concrete, relatively simple, straightforward, specific in their focus and easily measurable, i.e. relatively not complex. RCTs claim to give the lie to teachers knowing best by virtue of their experience or intuition.

The advance of RCTs in educational research seems unstoppable, rapidly achieving hegemonic status (Pearce and Raman, 2014). Their allure seems irresistible to governments and researchers alike; other forms of research are discouraged, not least by not being able to receive funding. The USA has the What Works Clearinghouse and its Institute of Education Sciences, and the non-profit Coalition for Evidence-based Policy. The UK's Education Endowment Foundation was established in 2011, initiating 59 RCTs involving 2,300 schools; at the time of writing it had initiated nearly 200 RCTs; the Behavioural Insights Team opened in 2012; and in 2013 the UK's Department for Education announced two major RCTs on (a) schools' attainment in mathematics and science and (b) child protection. Haynes et al. (2012), in a publication issuing from the Cabinet Office of the UK government, declared that RCTs are 'the best way of determining whether a policy is working' (p. 4). The What Works Network in the UK has seven independent What Works Centres and three affiliate members.

International organizations focus on RCTs (Bouguen and Gurgand (2012) reported twelve national RCTs in Europe), as do educational researchers in the evidence-based movement (e.g. Torgerson and Torgerson, 2001, 2003, 2008, 2013; Moore et al., 2003; Gorard and Torgerson, 2006; Donaldson et al., 2009; Hutchison and Styles, 2010; Goldacre, 2013; Pearce and Raman, 2014; Hassey, 2015; Connolly et al., 2017, 2018; Gorard et al., 2017, 2018; Education Endowment Foundation, 2018; Major and Higgins, 2019).

The highest quality RCT is the 'true' experimental design, with pre-test–post-test control and experimental groups and randomized allocation of participants to control and experimental groups. Of lesser quality are 'one group pre-test–post-test designs (where there is no control group), *ex post facto* designs (where the direction of causality may not be clear and the lack of controls may compromise reliability (Cohen et al., 2018)), and non-equivalent control group designs (where there are important differences between control and experimental groups). RCTs, their advocates argue, constitute the over-used phrase 'gold standard of evidence', and the aggregation of perhaps small-scale, published and unpublished experiments through meta-analysis yields a combined body of evidence whose collective weight is deemed to be important.

The parallels here are:

i The Cochrane Collaboration for evidence-based medicine (Sheldon and Chalmers, 1994; Maynard and Chalmers, 1997) where systematic reviews and documentation of well-controlled RCTs contribute to the accumulation of an evidential base that counters 'often untried and under-tested schemes that are injected into practice' (Cohen et al., 2018, p. 394). The Campbell Collaboration in education is seen as a 'younger sibling' (Coe et al., 2000, p. 2) of the Cochrane Collaboration.

ii Moves towards evidence-based policy and practice in health care and social work from the 1990s onwards (e.g. Boruch, 1997; Davies, 1999; MacDonald, 1997; Torgerson and Torgerson, 2008; Meinert, 2011) to which educational research has been likened (Chapter 6).

Deaton and Cartwright (2018) comment that RCTs claim to be largely exempt from many challenges faced in observational studies; they make few substantive assumptions, need little or no prior information; and are largely free of 'expert' knowledge which may be politically biased, manipulable, or 'otherwise suspect' (p. 2). A strong claim, but, as will be argued, whilst RCTs may be useful in some simple areas of education, in terms of their utility they are ontologically, epistemologically, methodologically and inferentially unsuited to many spheres of education. Whilst they may yield crude results concerning the 'what' of selected outcomes of certain interventions, they miss the 'why', 'how', 'where', worth, usability, transferability and implications of their outcomes for the practices of education. Kvernbekk (2019, p. 41) adds to this that evidence from RCTs rarely, if ever, answers counterfactual questions about individuals and 'what should I do?' (p. 41).

From the advocates of RCTs there is a clear argument:

• Policy making and practice should be based on 'what works' in education.
• 'What works' in education should be based on evidence of 'what works' in practice.
• The evidence should be derived from RCTs.
• The weight of evidence from RCTs can be ascertained through meta-analysis and meta-meta-analyses.

These are powerful claims which need to be examined (e.g. Gorard et al., 2017, 2018, Wrigley, 2018; Wrigley and McCusker, 2019). Many concerns about reliability, bias and validity are contained in Campbell and Stanley (1963), Jadad and Enkin (2007), Bickman and Reich (2009), Gersten and Hitchcock (2009), e.g. experimenter effects and allegiances; having volunteer teachers for the intervention group and non-volunteer teachers for the control group; having teachers select which students go into which group; history; maturation; non-equivalent groups; attrition and differential attrition in control and experimental groups; sampling and selection bias, such as volunteer samples from school and teachers (Cook and Payne, 2002, p. 165; Slavin and Smith, 2009); sample size; within- and between-group differences; questionable units/levels of analysis, e.g. using individual participants as the unit of analysis rather than more appropriate classroom and school cluster designs; demoralization in not being included in the treatment group and increased motivation by virtue of being in the treatment group; limited external validity; lack of design rigour; ethical problems; feasibility challenges; costs etc.

The early language of advocates of evidence-based education was loaded, for example: 'the *only* worthwhile kind of evidence about whether something works in a particular situation comes from trying it out. Arguments from theory are simply no match for something that has been tried and tested … . It is *only* by doing an experiment' that we know what works (Curriculum Evaluation and Management Centre, 2000b, p. 1); 'evidence *must* come from experiments in real contexts' (Curriculum Evaluation and Management Centre, 2000d, p. 1) (italics added); other approaches are 'pre-scientific' (Curriculum Evaluation and Management Centre, 2000a, p. 1); only RCTs provide the 'gold standard' of evidence (Curriculum Evaluation and Management Centre, 2000c, p. 1), and '*the* appropriate methodologies for finding things out, randomized controlled trials, are clear' (Tymms, 1999, p. 96) (italics added).

These were intemperate terms and, though perhaps legitimately raging against those aspects of public policy making which are ill-informed by evidence, they read like Messianic fervour rather than careful, sober argument. Their users can be charged with undermining alternative sources and kinds of evidence, e.g. survey, ethnography, naturalistic and qualitative research, case studies, observational methods, in order to elevate their own case. To claim that there is *only* one path to salvation is dangerous, doctrinaire, authoritarian and intolerant. As the Nobel Prize-winning physicist Wolfgang Pauli, in another context, was reputed to have said: 'This isn't right. This isn't even wrong.'

Further, the natural sciences, whose methodologies are invoked by advocates of RCTs, recognize the importance of observational studies and non-RCT experimentation. They are also turning to modes of understanding the world through complexity theory, i.e. methodologies which operate holistically at systems levels rather than in the fragmented, atomized, reductionist world of RCTs and, indeed through a plethora of 'scientific' approaches (e.g. Kaufmann, 1995; Waldrop 1992; Lewin, 1993; Cohen and Stewart, 1995; Morrison, 2008; Thomas, 2016; Wrigley, 2018, 2019).

Thomas (2012) notes Einstein's view that to be believe that there is only a single scientific method is a pretence (p. 29), that there is no 'correct method' and that a scientist must be an 'unscrupulous opportunist' (p. 29) who seeks to understand the world by 'whatever manner is suitable'. There is no 'privileged set of methods in science quarantined away from everyday thinking' (p. 29). Indeed, Thomas argues that, contrary to many critics of research on teaching as non-cumulative, in fact there is an 'accumulation of understandings rather than an accumulation of facts' over time (p. 30). He reminds readers that Einstein (1941), with remarkable prescience, noted that:

> when the number of factors coming into play in a phenomenological complex is too large, scientific method in most cases fails us. One need only think of the weather, in which case prediction even for a few days ahead is impossible.
>
> (Einstein 1941, para. 8, quoted in Thomas, 2012, p. 32)

Too easy dismissal of non-RCT methods undermines fitness for purpose; certain types of research are useful for certain purposes, whilst others (including RCTs) are not. It is unacceptable for the 'what works' agenda to hijack the notion of 'evidence' to be that which derives solely from RCTs; what constitutes 'evidence' is wider than that derived from RCTs. Even though the term 'evidence-based' derives in part from the Cochrane Collaboration in the world of medicine (www.cochrane.org), whose methods are RCTs and meta-analysis, nevertheless to import this into education as if it were unproblematic and the only type of reliable/valid evidence of 'what works' misrepresents what constitutes acceptable educational evidence.

The logic of randomized controlled trials

RCTs have a putative simple logic in which the design features are intended to deliver the conclusions. The logic is appealing in its simplicity:

a   have an idea about what might cause what and decide to run an RCT to test it;
b   randomly select the sample from the population;
c   randomly allocate the sample to control and experimental groups in order to have a counterfactual (the control group which does not receive the intervention) and in order to distribute evenly the many different variables at work, or, rather, their effects;
d   at the start, conduct a pre-test to see that the two groups do not differ from each other on measured variables;

e   then control for, i.e. control out, key (moderator) variables, holding them constant;
f   apply the intervention to the treatment group only;
g   then conduct a post-test to compare the performance of the two groups on the outcome measure – the post-test; and
h   hey presto, what you are left with is a clear line of causality in which the difference between the two groups at the end of the RCT is caused only by the intervention, because the groups were the same at the start and everything else was controlled out; it must be X that caused Y.

Input in; outcome out. Uncomplicated, undisputed causality: do this and you get that. Simple, elegant and watertight, isn't it? No.

Fundamentally worrying are the unspoken assumptions at work here, and this addresses (a) above. For example, what link the identified causes, variables to be controlled and conclusions drawn, do not derive from the RCT itself. Rather, they precede the RCT; they are not endogenous to it; what link independent and dependent variables are exogenous to the RCT; they derive from theoretical assumptions and warrants that link the variables, causes, pre-tests and post-tests in the RCT (Cartwright, 2009, 2019; Cartwright and Hardie, 2012; Joyce, 2019). Causal links are premised on theory, otherwise, like Hume's 'constant conjunction', they are fictive: an illusion, a wish. Without a theory that connects these variables causally, the RCT is no more than a confusion of correlation with cause. I can correlate the number of times that tourists wear sunhats in Spain with the incidence of pick-pocketing in Tokyo, but there is no theoretically warranted link. And where do theoretical links come from? From acute observation, precision-based investigation, longitudinal in-depth studies, the pursuit of exhaustive study of a specific phenomenon, detailed case studies, action research, ethnographies, and non-RCT experiments, from trying out ideas, reflection, creativity and imagination, 'blue skies' research, investigative research which give us grounds for thinking that such-and-such might 'work'. In other words, from a science that is many times richer than an RCT. In comparison to these, RCT are somewhat paltry in what they promise or deliver.

In the case of (b), it is unclear how the population is randomly sampled, or, indeed if it is possible to sample randomly (e.g. to avoid bias). In the case of (c), it is not always possible to randomly allocate the sample to one of two groups, and a control group is a questionably assumed rather than demonstrated, true counterfactual. In the case of (d), just because the two groups happen to be the same on the pre-test measure does not mean that they are the same in other respects or that randomization has really ensured that the effects of many small differences are evenly distributed between the two groups, sufficient to cancel out the effects of these differences. In the case of (e), it is impossible and unrealistic to even identify, let alone control out, all the variables at work in the situation – it may be possible in Fisher's agricultural model, but, with some exceptions, most people are not like vegetables or cereals. In the case of (f), the nature, contents and timing of outcome testing exerts an important influence on what is found. In the case of (g), the claim for causality, all other causes having been controlled out or their effects evenly distributed such that only the cause in question is the surviving, true cause, is simply a leap of faith in thinking that it is the only or main cause at work.

Cartwright (2019) notes that defining features of RCTs include: the assumption of orthogonality (the independence of two variables, i.e. minimal relationship to, or effect on, each other); calculating the average effect by subtracting the average of the control group from the average of the treatment group, standardizing this if desired; the unbiased estimation of the average treatment effect (e.g. through randomization) in the sample; adherence to procedures for random allocation and blinding. To these can be added adherence to: standard protocols for the trials (e.g. a document that states the research questions, rationale for the RCT, recruitment of participants, randomization, data collection and analysis, metrics and instrumentation), and procedures for the treatment and control groups ('treatment integrity' (Cook and Payne 2002, p. 164)); the isolation, control and manipulation of variables; random selection and allocation; and the pre-specification of outcome measures.

Gueron (2002, p. 19) note the importance of: making a case for RCTs as being the easiest way to ensure validity and reliability; addressing the right question, i.e. looking for net impact compared to counterfactuals, and recognizing that net impacts are normally smaller than overall outcomes and that the more rigorous and secure is the study, the smaller the net impact is likely to be (p. 40); ensuring that correct protocols (for each stage of the trial) and procedures ('treatments') operate and that training of researchers is provided; and ensuring that account is taken of the context of the results in reporting to policy makers and explaining variation in results according to contexts.

In education, however, other practices occur simultaneously in classrooms, or are introduced at some point in the RCT (Gueron, 2002; Weiss, 2002, p. 219) which might affect the RCT. Further, teachers exert a key influence on what is happening (e.g. Thomas, 2016), as do parents, thereby circumventing the effects of random assignment, and, given the variation in contexts, it is difficult to standardize treatments and controls across different locations.

The quality of the evidence

If trust is to be placed in evidence adduced for 'what works' then it is a *sine qua non* and an ethical responsibility for that research to be of the highest standards of rigour (and Cartwright (2019) argues that the conventional notion of 'rigour' in RCTs, e.g. randomization and blinding, is a very limited view of what 'rigour' requires). However, it is questionable how far even a limited view of 'rigour' as conformance to procedural standards of RCTs is occurring (Gorard et al., 2017; See, 2018).

Gorard et al. (2017) suggest that the most useful evidence is that from RCTs with large samples, careful controls, counterfactuals and a statement of how many counterfactual cases are required to call a finding into doubt (p. 42), clear and transparent research designs that are fit for purpose, low attrition, high quality data, appropriate data analysis, and which conclude fairly from the data and analysis. The authors provide a 'sieve' for estimating the 'trustworthiness' of the 'descriptive work' of the research (p. 37), with a hierarchy from (a) a 'strong design' for the research question (large group sizes), 'minimal attrition', standardized, pre-specified and independent data, and limited threats from 'diffusion or demands on the research' (p. 37), to (b), at the bottom: 'no consideration of design'; a 'trivial' scale of the study or unclear population and sample size; 'huge attrition', weak reliability, measures and too many outcomes; and 'no consideration of threats to validity' (p. 37).

Bagshaw and Bellomo (2008, p. 2) provide five levels of a hierarchy of evidence, with RCTs at the top:

Level 1 (highest level): Well conducted, suitably powered RCT
Level 2: Well conducted, but small and under-powered RCT
Level 3: Non-randomized observational studies
Level 4: Non-randomized study with historical controls
Level 5 (lowest level): Case studies without controls

In the National Endowment for Science, Technology and the Arts (Nesta) *Standards of Evidence* framework (Puttick and Ludlow, 2013) there are five levels in evaluating RCTs and their contribution to 'evidence'. Level 1 is the basic level, in which researchers describe logically, convincingly and coherently what they do and why it is important; Level 2 provides data indicating positive change but without attribution of causality; Level 3 shows causality by using a comparison or control group; Level 4 provides one piece of research and one replication study; Level 5 (highest level) provides systems and procedures, with manuals to enable consistent replications to be conducted (Puttick and Ludlow, 2013, p. 2).

The case for and against randomized controlled trials

As RCTs have become 'bedded down' in the evidence-based approach to 'what works', so the rigour required of them has increased. 'All well and good', you might say. However, this does not always overcome several issues of validity, reliability and utility, and these present powerful challenges to according RCTs their current place in the sun. Whilst not to conduct an RCT to learn how or whether something 'works' is considered by some to be unethical (Buck and McGee, 2015, p. 7), arguments for and against RCTs in education are many, and these are summarized in Tables 4.1 to 4.9. These are unpacked over the course of the analysis here and in subsequent chapters.

Table 4.1 Ontology

FOR	AGAINST
RCTs override individual behaviour.	RCTs understate agency, motives, intentionality and humanity.
RCTs override differences in human make-up and recognize the essential similarly between people.	RCTs are premised on poor ontology of humans.
RCTs build out contaminating elements of human behaviour and achieve a singularity of focus.	The people factor is underplayed in RCTs.
RCTs override individual behaviour.	Education concerns individuals, not only panels/cohorts.

Table 4.2 Epistemology and methodology

FOR	AGAINST
RCTs simplify what is happening.	RCTs operate as input-output black box models, and rely on supplementary evidence to provide (process) evidence.
RCTs have standardized treatments, protocols and procedures.	There are several ethical concerns and problems in RCTs, which are not easily solved or, sometimes, not solved. People's behaviour is not standardized.
RCTs do not need much prior information: the 'no knowledge required' principle.	The 'no knowledge required' principle in RCTs is suspect. An RCT relies on prior knowledge to make sense of it.
RCTs are more rigorous than teacher-based decisions and evidence.	Whilst RCTs in education might have greater rigour than teacher-based decisions, and return lower effects sizes, account must be taken of teachers, multi-causality and contexts, which are understated in RCTs.
RCTs are objective, neutral and disinterested.	RCTs are unfairly reductionist.
RCTs are 'real world', not only laboratory based.	RCTs understate the role of teachers and professional judgement, expertise and tacit, accumulated knowledge.
RCTs are comparatively straightforward to design and can yield straightforward results.	RCTs understate the role of theory and warrants, and they exclude important factors and variables. They require prior research and warrants before they can be usefully conducted.
RCTs show clearly the effects of one intervention on an outcome.	RCTs overlook the significance of complexity theories and chaos theories, interconnections and interactions of factors and variables.

(Continued)

Table 4.2 (Cont.)

FOR	AGAINST
RCTs compare groups in judging 'what works' in comparative terms.	RCTs have a limited view of criteria, standards and comparison groups for judging 'what works'; standards are relative, not absolute.
RCTs are a clear way of conducting research and finding out 'what works'.	RCTs are based on a limited epistemology to understand and to know if something 'works'.
RCTs are the apex of evidence.	RCTs are unfairly privileged in the arsenal of research.
Education can learn from clinical RCTs.	Clinical RCTs are unlike educational RCTs in key elements, and currently understate educational equivalents of dose-response, side effects, long-term effects, risk analysis, co-medications and contra-indications.
RCTs identify key interventions.	RCTs are atomized and reductionist.
RCTs have standard protocols and procedures for what to do in an RCT.	There is poor and variable implementation of RCT procedures in practice.
RCTs are supreme in the 'what works' agenda.	Other methods are needed to make meaning, significance and application of RCTs to people.
RCTs are easy to operate.	RCTs are expensive, the costs are not worth the benefits, and adverse effects are neglected.
RCTs indicate clearly the outcomes of interventions.	RCTs adopt a narrow view of outcomes.
RCTs are clear and clean in educational research.	Unlike clinical models, there is a lack of pre-trial testing in RCTs in education.
RCTs report clear effects.	RCTs neglect unintended effects and make unfair assumptions about effect size.
RCTs have clear measures.	The validity and reliability of indicators and proxies in measures are questionable.
RCTs show limitations, weaknesses and over-estimations in teachers' judgements.	Procedures are not always followed in RCTs; teachers in the control group do different things and teachers in the treatment group do different things, and randomization does not overcome this problem.
RCTs overcome bias in research.	There is a risk of biased measures (in favour of the treatment). Bias is not removed simply by using an RCT.
RCTs adopt a usefully narrow focus, pinpointing 'what works'.	RCTs have too narrow a focus, to the neglect of other relevant matters that impinge on a situation.
RCTs report 'what works'.	'What works' is ambiguous and a value-laden judgement that varies in different parties.

(Continued)

Table 4.2 (Cont.)

FOR	AGAINST
RCTs are scientific.	RCTs overlook over-determination and under-represent the varied nature of science and experimentation. Science is multiply epistemological.
RCTs yield net effects, regardless of other factors.	RCTs operate a limited, impoverished view of 'science' and 'what works' in specific contexts. Averages are often unhelpful.

Table 4.3 Causality

FOR	AGAINST
RCTs demonstrate simple causality.	RCTs operate with an over-simplified view of causality. RCTs do not address the mechanisms and sub-causal elements of causality, which are essential to understand 'what works' and to generalize.
RCTs demonstrate causality beyond random error.	RCTs require large sample sizes in order to balance the effects of differences; hence, they can be expensive and impractical.
RCTs override the details of causality in determining 'what works'.	RCTs are a dangerous basis for meta-analysis and meta-meta-analysis, with problems in the studies included and how they are included in meta-analysis and meta-meta-analysis.
RCTs override concerns of the mechanisms of causality.	Causes are assumed inductively, not proven.
RCTs show overall causality, i.e. that an intervention probabilistically causes an outcome.	RCTs occupy no privileged position in determining causality: other ways are possible and may be cheaper and better.
RCTs meet counterfactual requirements by having a control group.	It is unclear what the control group is doing in an RCT. True counterfactuals are impossible in education.
RCTs address INUS conditions.	RCTs disregard the complexity of causality and of the requirements for generalizability.
RCTs are useful for trivial, low-level or easily measurable, technical matters and knowledge	RCTs neglect the huge significance of 'causal cakes' and webs, and interaction of many causes: multi-causality.
Despite claims to showing causality, RCTs are not over-concerned with causality, only whether and intervention does or does not 'work'.	RCTs overlook important questions of 'why', 'where', 'how' and 'under what conditions'.

Table 4.4 Randomization

FOR	AGAINST
Randomization improves the balance of differences between the control and treatment groups.	Whilst randomization intends to balance differences between control and treatment groups, this may be unrealistic. Randomization overlooks important small differences; there are limits to the usefulness of randomization.
Randomization overcomes or reduces bias.	Randomization and blinding may not be possible or do not occur; randomization does not remove bias completely, as bias occurs elsewhere in RCTs.
Matched groups may replace randomized groups	Matching the control and experimental groups on some things is not good enough – there may not be a match on many important items, and this is not solved by randomization

Table 4.5 Generalizability, averages and meta-analysis

FOR	AGAINST
RCTs enable generalizability and transfer through meta-analysis.	There are problems of generalizability of RCTs, with insufficient account of what is needed for generalizability, e.g. causal mechanisms and factors.
RCTs contribute to the cumulative building up of effective practice, in meta-analysis.	Important issues are overlooked in meta-analysis, e.g. timing and duration of intervention and measures, the quality, foci and operations of the contributing studies. Meta-analysis is problematic, despite claims made for them.
RCTs are generalizable through meta-analysis.	RCTs have much less transferability/generalizability than is claimed for them, even though overall average effects can be calculated.
RCTs operate beyond the levels of individual teachers, i.e. are generalizable.	RCTs can undermine teacher professionalism, even though many teachers take part in RCTs.
Generalizability comes through meta-analysis.	There are severe limits on generalizability of RCTs, even though meta-analysis is undertaken. RCTs may not be scalable.
RCTs yield average, overall and aggregate effects.	RCTs understate the significance of teachers in teaching and in undertaking RCTs. Using average results commits the ecological fallacy. Distributions trump averages.

(Continued)

Table 4.5 (Cont.)

FOR	AGAINST
Average treatment effects are useful for identifying overall outcomes and their application to the majority of people, i.e. generalizability.	Averages conceal heterogeneity and important sub-group and individual differences (which should concern educators).
RCTs identify net effects and average treatment effects.	There are problems in calculating net effects of RCTs, with error factors being different between control and experimental groups, and outliers being important. Averages misrepresent people and individual differences.

Table 4.6 Controls

FOR	AGAINST
RCTs control in and control out factors and variables.	It is mistaken to control out factors and variables, as these are interconnected in bringing about an effect.
RCTs hold variables constant and compute correlations and differences in order to see the effects of an intervention.	RCTs are premised on linear thinking in a nonlinear world. It is mistaken to identify and control variables and/or to hold them constant and unfair to hold time as if it is constant and nothing else is happening whilst the RCT is taking place.
RCTs have standard protocols and procedures for treatment, and controls to assure fairness and comparability.	It is unlikely, even dangerous, to have entirely the same procedures, as people and classes differ – there is a need for sensitivity and responsiveness, but changing the procedure changes the RCT and its appeal to standardization.
RCTs hold variables constant in order to identify 'what works'.	RCTs neglect emergence and ongoing, dynamic change.
RCTs control several variables in and out.	Holding variables constant misrepresents what is happening in classrooms.
RCTs isolate and control variables, and thereby identify treatment effects.	It is impossible to control out other factors in classrooms and non-laboratory contexts.
RCTs reduce complexity to enable treatments to be controlled and outcomes to be measured.	RCTs are significantly over-reductionist, misrepresenting the 'real' situation of classrooms and people.
RCTs isolate and control variables in and out.	Connectedness, not isolation, is key; worlds are open and dynamical systems, not closed systems. RCTs significantly understate the important of the interconnections of factors, not their separation.

Table 4.7 Sampling and blinding

FOR	AGAINST
Large samples in RCTs address heterogeneity.	There are several problems with studies included in meta-analysis and meta-meta-analysis.
Large samples yield greater reliability.	Many RCTs are underpowered because of small samples, but large samples find weaker effect sizes.
Cluster sampling overcomes contamination problems.	Contamination is still possible. Cluster samples require large numbers of participants and participating units (e.g. schools). A cluster is $n = 1$.
RCTs have clear protocols for sampling.	In practice, RCTs have sampling and retention problems.
RCTs reduce selection bias.	There are many problems in working with, and understanding sampling, effect size and statistical significance.
RCTs reduce bias by blinding.	Blinding and double blinding may be impossible. Randomization and the *ceteris paribus* condition are problematic.
Sufficient replicability may not be possible, but large samples overcome small differences.	In sampling, neither big nor small is useful as these overlook key elements of human behaviour and groupings.

Table 4.8 Context and individuality

FOR	AGAINST
RCTs are clean and untrammelled by a myriad of variables.	RCTs need process evaluations, but process evaluations are unclear on the criteria being used to judge reliability, validity, credibility and utility.
RCTs override contextual factors.	RCTs mistake the importance of including the buzz of the everyday classroom.
RCTs show 'what works' across specific contexts.	RCTs neglect over-determination. Context is essential.
RCTs fit many conditions and contexts.	RCTs operate on a questionable 'one-size fits all' approach.
RCTs demonstrate whether something 'works'.	RCTs take insufficient account of contexts and conditions and the effects of these on outcomes.
RCTs have a rigorous standard of evidence.	Situational specificity is under-represented.
RCTs are useful in specified contexts.	RCTs suffer from the file drawer problem, publication bias, and problems of meeting operational fidelity.
RCTs indicate 'what works'.	RCTs may not help teachers concerned with what to do, as teachers need 'why', 'how', 'where', 'for whom' and 'under what conditions', which are context-specific.

Table 4.9 Usefulness

FOR	AGAINST
RCTs identify outcomes of treatments.	RCTs overlooks the educational equivalents of comorbidities and conditions present in a specific context or individuals.
RCTs promote evidence-based decisions and policy and practice.	Sampling problems, issues of causality and limited utility making and uptake undermine the claims made for RCTs and their utility in policy making. Policy makers rarely use RCTs.
RCTs show whether a policy is working.	There are many badly conducted RCTs.
RCTs enable fair comparisons to be made of methods of teaching.	There are no hierarchies of evidence, but fitness for purpose. RCTs may not compare like with like.
RCTs test 'what works' before putting into widespread use.	RCTs ask and answer wrong or unhelpful questions; efficacy trials and replication RCTs are rare.
RCTs are well proven in clinical practice.	RCTs neglect how they are used as part of many approaches in practice.
RCTs are fit for a range of purpose in the 'what works' agenda.	RCTs neglect fitness for purpose in many areas and overstate the role of RCTs in education.
RCTs are useful for informing practice.	RCTs have limited utilization potential.
RCTs yield results that aid predictability of outcomes.	RCTs understate the significance of unexpected effects, side effects and risks, and are at best probabilistically predictable under specified conditions.
RCTs are useful for many parties.	Different parties want different things from RCTs and they may not want or use RCTs at all.
RCTs are attractive to teachers.	Effective classroom practice is highly teacher dependent, and teachers may not address the full requirements of RCTs, which raises problems of reliability and validity.
RCTs serves educational improvement	RCTs risk making category errors in considering what makes educational research 'educational'.

The case for RCTs in education does not need to be made again; it has already been made strongly for many years. RCTs have their place in evidence-based education. Their claim to provide empirical evidence of the effects of a particular intervention is clear (Hammersley, 2013, p. 48). But what is that place and what does it deserve to be? The answer to both of these is 'it all depends': if we want a limited, linear input/output mode of intervention that purports to be probabilistically causal because of the control and treatment groups being probabilistically the same at the start, accompanied by qualitative data on process evaluation and maybe sub-group analysis, and to comment on a given intervention in a given locale at a given time, then an RCT might be fit for purpose, depending on how well it is conducted.

If we want something more sophisticated, deep, to answer questions of 'how?', 'why?', 'will it apply to my situation and context?', and 'how can I apply this to my situation and context, and with my students in my classroom?', then the RCT may let us down, even if accompanied by qualitative data and other process data.

Joyce (2019) remarks that it is dangerous to *draw* causal inferences from RCTs; rather they *assume* certain causal inferences. RCTs, she avers, are ill-equipped to study causal mechanisms, and yet we need an understanding of these if we are to suggest generalizability. Whilst it is unfair to judge an RCT by criteria that it was not intended to address, e.g. going into *mechanisms* of causality, nevertheless it is fair to state that the claims for causality made by RCTs are only one interpretation of causality, and, indeed, are simplistic and questionable.

If we want to see how RCTs fit into the broader evidential base, then we need much more than RCTs, on their own (as applies to other types of research). Connolly et al. (2017, 2018) make a case for RCTs in education, indicating that, not only is there substantial evidence of their increase, but that important issues of, for example, large sample size, teacher involvement, longer duration of interventions, and inclusion of qualitative and contextual data, contribute to increasing the trust that can be put in their findings and the usefulness of their results for the 'what works' agenda. Similarly, the National Research Council of the National Academy of Sciences (Gersten and Hitchcock, 2009, p. 81) comments that, because of their ability to enable fair comparisons to be made between control and experimental groups, RCTs are the ideal kind of research for establishing whether one or more factors cause a change in outcomes (p. 110). However, it also notes that RCTs cannot test complex causal hypotheses, may have limited generalizability, and cost a lot of money to mount (see also Thomas, 2016).

RCTs in education have their protagonists and antagonists. On the one hand, RCTs claim to provide evidence of 'what works', which is preferable to introducing or using untested interventions in education; they can meet a rigorous standard of evidence and can upset long-held, false myths about education, and they suggest probabilistic causation. Small-scale RCTs acting as pilots can also reduce risk.

On the other hand, Thomas (2004) notes that RCTs, in principle, play largely a 'mundane' and 'dull', minimally useful, 'confirmatory role' rather than making advances in knowledge (p. 11), a concern that can apply to the logic of reliance only on experimentation in education more widely. Boylan and Demack (2018) note that, whilst RCTs may be useful for an evaluation of programs of technical professional development, they may be less suited to evaluation of programs that are more open-ended in their scope, where diversity, adaptation and variation are celebrated in professional development, rather than uniformity, adoption and fidelity respectively. Similarly, Styles and Torgerson (2018) note that some kinds of intervention, e.g. those which require systemic and systematic changes at several levels, are not amenable to evaluation using RCTs because of difficulties in randomizing and measuring outcomes at all the levels concerned (p. 261).

Added to these concerns in RCTs are those reported by Ginsburg and Smith (2016, p. 21) who examined RCTs in the What Works Clearinghouse and identified very many problems encountered in them:

- 'Developer associated': in 44 per cent of the RCTs, an association existed between authors and the curriculum developer.
- 'Curriculum intervention not well implemented', with infidelity to the treatments and an absence of fidelity measures in many of the studies investigated: in 85 per cent of the RCTs the treatment occurred in the first year only, whereas it was planned to take 3 years for change to happen.
- 'Unknown comparison curriculum' and unclear comparison curricula: in 56 per cent of RCTs, the comparison curricula and its characteristics were not identified and reported.
- Differences in 'dosages': the time devoted to instruction was greater for the treatment group than for the control group in 8 out of 9 RCTs studied.
- 'Limited grade coverage' and no longitudinal cohorts: in 19 of 20 studies, a curriculum covering two or more grades did not include a longitudinal cohort, so cumulative effects across grades could not be measured; and 13 out of 27 studies did not cover a sufficient range of grades to enable a clear picture to be provided of the effectiveness of the curriculum.
- 'Assessment favors content of the treatment': in 19 per cent of the studies, the assessment was designed by the curricula developer and was likely to be more closely aligned in favour of the treatment.
- 'Outdated curricula': in 19 out of 27 students, the RCTs were conducted on outdated curricula.
- Outcomes were not fully reported by grade.
- There was a failure to report significant interactions of the RCTs with student characteristics.
- There was a failure to report significant interactions of the RCTs with teacher/teaching characteristics.

The authors commented that 'the magnitude of the error generated by even a single threat is frequently greater than the average effect size of an RCT treatment' (p. ii), and that 26 out of 27 RCTs evaluated by the What Works Clearinghouse in the field of mathematics had multiple problems.

Whilst RCTs have their place in educational research, this does not obviate the importance of other research approaches, e.g. observational studies, quasi-experiments, case-cohort studies, analysis of multiple data sources, longitudinal studies, retrospective studies and research that addresses the whole person and the person-as-individual. Indeed, one can question the vehemence with which observational studies are consigned to a status below experimental studies (as happens, for example, in Buck and McGee, 2015).

Morrison and van der Werf comment that:

> RCTs, meta-analysis of RCTs, and large scale research certainly have their place in educational research, but what is their place? Discourses of RCTs, meta-analysis of RCTs and large scale research from policy hegemons, if they become the sole order of the day or the dominating discourse of educational research, risk becoming a race to the bottom in terms of the benefits from adopting a wealth of approaches to researching 'what works' and what counts as robust research evidence in education. Fitness for, and of, purpose suggests keeping an open mind on what kind of educational research to conduct, how to plan, implement and evaluate it, whilst still staunchly defending the need for rigour and high standards of planning, design, operationalization, conduct, ethics, data, data analysis and interpretation… . RCTs, meta-analysis of RCTs and large scale research should not be totalizing; alternative types of research clearly have, and have to have, their places in education, e.g. tests, surveys, a whole panoply of qualitative research, case studies, small scale research, action research, historical and documentary research, big data research, virtual worlds research, critical theoretical approaches and so on; the list is immense.
>
> (Morrison and van der Werf, 2017, pp. 75–76)

Thomas (2016) argues that multiple forms of inquiry (e.g. descriptive, experimental, interpretative, correlational) are required, using a variety of research designs, in order to address the multi-factorial and multi-directional nature of causality (p. 395). Whether the complexity of education lends itself to RCTs is discussed below, even if pragmatic, 'real world' RCTs hold prominence over laboratory-like trials. The push for RCTs in educational research, if they marginalize other kinds of research, is counterproductive.

Scriven (2009) notes that much scientific research (e.g. in the natural sciences) is conducted without an RCT in sight. Schwandt (2009, p. 198) questions the positioning of RCTs as the 'gold standard', and St Pierre (2002) notes that it is very dangerous to claim that a 'single epistemology alone governs the whole of all science' (p. 26). Greene (2009) comments that adopting the principles of hard science to the human sciences is a form of scientism (p. 158), and Rallis (2009), echoing Kuhn, notes that 'scientific knowledge is a social construct' and that what counts as 'credible evidence' is that which the 'relevant communities of discourse and practice' hold to be reliable, valid or 'trustworthy' (p. 171).

Causality and controls in a randomized controlled trial

RCTs claim to enable probabilistic causal inferences to be made. RCTs, by including comparison groups (control groups), claim to address the counterfactual requirement of research. However, as Scriven (2009) remarks, this is not always the case in education, as: (a) it is rare for them to be blind or double-blind or triple-blind, as in clinical trials, i.e. the Hawthorne effect may be present; (b) whereas in clinical trials the only difference between the control and experimental groups is the treatment, in human studies this is not the case, as the beliefs, values, agency, behaviours, intentionality, and contextual, situational and interpersonal factors within and between the participants, experimenters and others involved are also present and may differ, and that such differences may cause different effects (p. 142). The researcher in education has to ask how possible it is really to obtain a counterfactual in an RCT, e.g. those who haven't been exposed to features which appear in the intervention and who are sufficiently matched on other characteristics.

Causation still operates in the absence of a counterfactual; causation is not the property solely of an RCT and anyway, even if counterfactuals are present in an RCT, other factors present may be contributing to the overdetermination of an effect. For example, an RCT might show that increased homework improves Mathematics achievement, whereas other factors might be exerting equal or more powerful causal influences, e.g. parent pressure, high stakes examinations, cultural factors, risk of being shamed for poor performance, such that, even if increased homework were removed, other factors would still lead to the increased achievement of the intervention group, and these cannot be controlled out by randomization or exerting controls in the data analysis. The familiar example here is that, if two shots are fired at a person, if bullet A does not kill him then bullet B will.

RCTs have no privileged position in inferring causality (Bickman and Reich, 2009; Scriven, 2009) simply because they strive to hold constant all factors between the control and experimental groups and provide the intervention only in the experimental group, thereby attributing any change to the intervention only. If only it were that easy in the rough-and-tumble of the everyday, multi-dimensional, multivalent world of classrooms, even though teachers in the 'real' world might welcome RCTs and be involved in them (Connolly et al., 2017, 2018). Indeed, as Petersen (2014) remarks, if we really wish to understand the relationship between inputs and outcomes then we have to control for all factors, which is impossible (p. 130). Other kinds of high-granularity research might yield much greater insight into causality, e.g. observational methods and case studies (Cook and Payne, 2002), even though case studies lack the counterfactuals that RCTs claim to address.

Deaton and Cartwright (2018) comment that, in fact, for much of what we wish to discover and know in education, there may be superior ways of finding out than by using RCTs, or by using RCTs in combination with a range of other data (p. 2). They note that the method which researchers select in order to investigate causal inference depends on what they are seeking to discover (p. 2), and that RCTs have no privileged position here.

Users of RCTs are likely to want to know 'why' something 'works', not simply that it does or does not, and RCTs have problems here. This raises the challenging issue of demonstrating causality. The idea in an RCT is that: (a) if randomization in sample selection and allocation is conducted to distribute and balance out the effects of many small differences between individuals (e.g. Slavin and Smith, 2009), and then (b) the control and experimental groups are matched on the pre-test object of interest, and then (c) all the other factors are controlled apart from the intervention with the experimental group, therefore (d) causality can be attributed to the intervention, the other factors having been controlled out. This is very appealing, but how does the researcher know that the controls being exercised are sufficient and that all the relevant controls have been applied (Alt, 2009, p. 150)?

Attributing causality from an RCT is unclear. For example, let us say that an experiment is conducted to increase security and reduce theft in two schools through the installation of closed circuit television (CCTV) (Morrison, 2001). The effect is a reduction in theft in the experimental school. Exactly what causes the reduction here? Maybe potential offenders are deterred from theft; maybe offenders are caught more frequently; maybe the presence of the CCTV renders teachers and students more vigilant, thereby making the teachers and students more security-conscious so that they either do not bring valuables to the school or they store them more securely. The experiment might succeed in reducing theft, but what exactly is happening causally in the experimental school (even though the transitivity argument is often advanced, i.e. if A causes B and B causes C then A causes C)? Are the changes occurring in the teachers, the students, the thieves, or a combination of these?

Consider this example: two groups of children were formed by random allocation, a control/comparison group and a treatment group. The RCT was designed to see the effects of using a new text book on students' mathematics achievement. At the pre-test stage the mathematics scores of the two groups were very similar. What were thought to be all the key variables were isolated and controlled, so that the only difference in the RCT was the application of the intervention to the treatment group. The experiment ran for an entire year. At the end of the year the mathematics scores of the treatment group were much higher than those of the control group. Given that all other variables were held constant, the researcher concluded that it must have been the new text book that was making the difference. True? Not necessarily.

In fact, the parents of the students in the intervention group were concerned about the new text book, and the end-of-year test (being a relatively high-stakes test, since the placement of students in the following year depended in part on it) had not only put pressure on their children to work hard, but had also arranged for them to have additional private tutorial support in mathematics; these had not been factored into the RCT's variables to be controlled. Was it the text book, the parental pressure, the private tutoring, the high-stakes test, or some combination of these, that had brought about the high post-test scores in the treatment group? Alternative, rival, possible disconfirming explanations of causality (Weiss, 2002, p. 220) have to be considered and eliminated in addressing 'inference to the best explanation' (Lipton, 2004).

In a sense the RCT had 'worked' – it had brought about a noticeable rise in students' mathematics achievement (using the transitivity claim of causality). But the causal chain involved is unknown. It might have been that the experimental text book (A) had caused parental concern (B); parental concern (B) had caused the student to work harder for the high-stakes examination (C); the parental concern (B) and the high-stakes examination (C) had led to the employment of a private tutor (D), and the combination of these (A + B + C + D) or the transitivity argument (if A causes B and B causes C and C causes D then A causes D), or any one of A to D on its own or in combination, had led to the high scores in the post-test, high stakes examination. Or indeed other unnamed factors were operating, with many degrees of freedom between the pre-test and the post-test. Such causal chains are important for teachers to know, but they are often unexamined in the black box of the RCT, though recent moves towards including process evaluation with qualitative data might attenuate this (Siddiqui et al. (2018) and Joyce (2019) make a strong case for process evaluations in order to obtain the rich data needed for understanding how outcomes have been achieved). That said, a salutary warning is given by Feinstein (1995), arguing that observational data can be prone to bias (p. 76) and the quality of protocols for qualitative data does not currently match the careful protocols that are emerging in RCTs in education. Indeed, thinking causally is best undertaken not by thinking in terms of linear causal chains but in terms of 'causal cakes' (Chapter 3).

Advocates of RCTs might respond by saying that the experiment has generated further hypotheses to be tested experimentally (Coe et al., 2000, p. 4), the results of which can be combined in meta-analysis, but this is very far from claiming knowledge of 'what works' or attributing actual causality. As Chomsky's withering critique of Skinner's behaviourism (Chomsky, 1959) argued, it is dangerous to believe that we can isolate, control and predict social behaviour from, and in, naturalistic settings. Indeed, understanding *how* an intervention or experiment actually operates in practice is important, and yet it is precisely this *explanatory* understanding that is missing in RCTs, i.e. exactly what is needed to inform practice.

The RCT (as in other types of research) is still a comparatively opaque black box, disabling the identification of detailed causal mechanisms that produce treatment effects (Morrison, 2001, p. 73; see also Clarke and Dawson, 1999, p. 52; Bickman and Reich, 2009; Julnes and Rog, 2009; Joyce, 2019), and it is precisely these detailed mechanisms that are needed in order to understand complex situations if we wish to improve education; other kinds of data and research are necessary to fill the gaps left by RCTs in determining causality (Morrison, 2001). As Goldstein (2002) noted, RCTs do not enable causal connections to be made. Between an input and an outcome lie a potentially infinite number of degrees of freedom and how they operate.

Proponents of RCTs might argue that, in fact, this does not matter, for the experiment appears to have identified 'what works' (Coe et al., 2000, p. 5), particularly in large-scale RCTs, thereby overriding other variables that might be operating in the situation, i.e. the similarities between situations and interventions might outweigh the differences between them. However, this is to neglect the central part that *people* play in the RCT – their perceptions, motivations, intentions, agency, imagination, creativity, attitudes, wishes, responses – and all these have an effect on the RCT. An RCT, as Pawson and Tilley (1993, p. 8) observe, might be 'splendid epistemology' but it is 'lousy ontology', as programs are mediated by their participants and have to build in the 'human factor'. People matter. Participants in an RCT might choose, agentically, to make an intervention work or not work, and teachers' and students' motivations in, commitments to, and involvement in an intervention might be the critical factors rather than the intervention itself, or to be considered as 'noise' to be controlled out of the RCT.

The need for protocols and procedures in establishing causality

RCTs require protocols (the design of the RCT) and procedures (the same treatments to all participants in the control group and all participants in the treatment group) to be observed, with faithfulness to the procedures for each group (Joyce, 2019, p. 46). This is the issue of fidelity and standardizing the intervention amongst the treatment group(s) (Hammersley, 2013, p. 48) and ensuring the same practices occur amongst the control group(s), i.e. ensuring that the same implementation takes place across the entire RCT, without which the RCT is invalidated and certainty is called into question as to whether the RCT has 'worked'. It raises the question of what level of detail is required in the procedures for the implementation and conduct of the 'treatment' in the RCT, what happens in the control group (Simpson,

2020), and what constitutes fidelity and infidelity to those procedures in practice. It is unlikely, even undesirable, that standardization of treatments is possible or operates in social contexts (Hammersley, 2013, p. 48), and 'control' over this is a fiction in many cases.

It is essential that procedures are followed scrupulously in the RCT, but this is often impossible, even undesirable, in education. Because sentient people tailor their behaviour to each other and to the situation, their behaviour differs, and, therefore, the planned intervention changes (Thomas, 2016). Changing one element of the implementation changes other conditions and factors in the RCT: changing one element has a knock-on effect on other elements and conditions (Kvernbekk, 2018): their influence, interactions and outcomes.

In question here is how far exactly the same will be occurring in the relevant parts of the RCT, be they control group or treatment group or, indeed in the way in which the intervention or program was intended to run. Indeed, Simpson (2020) notes that insufficient attention is given to what the control group is doing, and that variances here affect effect sizes.

For example, a teacher may modify, intentionally or unintentionally, a part of a program or its 'delivery' to suit the students, perhaps because she does not agree with one part of it, or she is particularly enthusiastic about another part, or because she is certain that a particular part of the program, based on her experience of the participants, will not work or will cause other problems in the class. The task for researchers, then, is to retain consistency, yet this could cause the researcher and the practitioner to come into conflict with each other if they give rise to ethical, interpersonal, administrative or management problems coming from the practitioners. What if the practitioners object to the conditions of the research? Do they withdraw (and attrition can cause bias in an RCT)?

Further, if all practitioners must obey without question given procedures, given scripts, a rehearsed narrative and rules, then their professionalism is undermined; their judgement – an essential part of teaching – is rendered redundant (Biesta, 2007; Phillips, 2019, p. 20). As Kvernbekk (2018) avers, evidence should serve professional judgement, not replace it. Teachers have professional knowledge, experience and wisdom that might not score highly on the canons of evidence-based research, but, nevertheless, they are essential and powerful ingredients of teaching and learning (Albrechtsen and Qvortrup, 2014, p. 73). What arrogance it is for RCTs to demote such wisdom and judgement.

Social processes at work in the experiment may be the determining factor, and RCTs may be unable to control for these. We delude ourselves if we believe that we can control everything of importance. This is the well-rehearsed problem of causality – behind or alongside an apparent cause (A causes B) lurk other causes (e.g. C causes A which causes B, and D causes A and B). The search for simple mono-causality is naïve; it may be the interplay and differential weighting of causes and factors that are producing the effects observed (Chapter 5). It is unclear how an RCT can disentangle this or even take account of multiple mechanisms interacting with each other in a single RCT other than ignoring or over-riding them. It is akin to taking ten medicines for a stomach pain: I take the medicines and the pain goes – which medicine(s) was/were effective, or was it the synergy of them all that caused the relief, and *how* did these combine to relieve the pain? This is important if efficacy, effectiveness and efficiency – even value for money – are to be ensured. Webs of causality and 'causal cakes' operate here (Chapter 3), and RCTs, in purporting to over-ride these, are simplistic, ignorant and neglectful.

The researcher, then, must determine under what combination of conditions, causes and conditions, something does or does not 'work'. As mentioned in Chapter 3, I may have a dry match, a rough surface on which to strike it, flammable material and a strong striking action, but still it does not light up, as there is insufficient oxygen. We need to know the circumstances – the conditions – operating in the intervention in order to attribute causality.

'Causal cakes' and 'causal webs' in RCTs

To replace linear, singular causality, Chapter 3 noted the importance of Cartwright's and Hardie's (2012) 'causal cakes' and Morrison's (2012) 'causal webs'. 'Causal cakes' are the necessary and sufficient ingredients that, together, contribute to the effects required (with 'support factors' such as heat). 'Webs of causality' are the webs of multi-directionally interacting causes that produce the outcome. In both of these, there is not one simple or sole cause, but the interaction of many causes, conditions, triggers and contexts in a situation (Chapter 3's reference to Mackie's 'INUS' conditions).

RCTs operate from an impoverished, over-simplified view of causality, thereby undermining generalizability. To answer this, Makel and Plucker (2014) note that, whilst having limitations in terms of causal validity, RCTs have the advantage of simplicity here. Cook and Payne (2002) note that RCTs have a less ambitious project than working with multiple causes (pp. 151–154); rather, their purposes are narrower and more practical, simply to see if one or more possible causal agents lead to changes in an outcome (p. 153). Further, RCTs can embrace complex schooling situations as they can take account of both similarities and heterogeneity in schools in using large samples and stratified samples (pp. 158–160). Cook and Payne contend that generalizability is less important than the results within a bounded sample (i.e. efficacy – internal validity in a single, perhaps ideal, RCT – rather than effectiveness – external validity in the general public). Indeed, they argue that, simply because RCTs operate on a simplified view of causation is not a sufficient reason for dispensing with them, and that the purposes of an RCT are not to explain all possible sources of variation, but, rather, to determine whether an intervention makes an overall, net improvement regardless of background factors (p. 159): a powerful but questionable argument. Why are factors rendered 'background' and why disregard them?

RCTs are inherently reductionist and atomizing in their focus and methodology; they are incapable of taking in the whole picture and they fail to catch the unavoidable complexity of phenomena and their multi-causal nature (Wrigley, 2019; Wrigley and McCusker, 2019). Wrigley contends that 'the purpose of experiments is to artificially simplify and close situations in order to make a particular relationship more visible' (Wrigley, 2019, p. 150) by stabilizing mechanisms, variables and forces, so that the impact of an independent variable on a dependent variable can be exposed clearly. Whilst this might be an interesting enterprise, it comes at the cost of over-simplifying, and therefore the risk of falsifying the nature of, the noise and bluster of, and the interacting diversity and confusion of everyday life, in which it is rare for things to happen only one at a time (Wrigley and McCusker, 2019, p. 112), i.e. the reality in which people actually operate and in which outside factors and forces impinge on the inside world of the RCT, and *vice versa* (Morrison, 2008), as embraced by complexity theory (Chapter 5).

Wrigley (2019) notes the current hegemonic embrace of reductionist approaches in many areas of schooling (p. 145), e.g. in defining achievement, high quality, social justice and evidence from research (pp. 145–146). He suggests that these distort the nature of education and serve 'ideological misrepresentation, which disempowers practitioners' (p. 146) and the zeitgeist of 'greedy reductionism' in its press for 'fast answers and quick fixes' (*ibid.*). Such reductionism also neglects individuals' agency, purposefulness, consciousness and freedom and which lead to emergence of unpredicted changes in dynamical, nonlinear, non-deterministic, creative, open systems and situations (Chapter 5). This is coupled with a failure to recognize that quantifying everything (as in, for example, effect size) fails to tell a credible, sufficiently rich or valid story of what really is happening in living, agentic humans and groups; causality is complex and multiple, and to reduce it to single causes is not even wrong.

The RCT adopts a linear view of causality, but causality is almost anything but linear, and classrooms, schools and education are anything but linear. RCTs are like fitting a square peg into a round hole; the world is no longer linear, even if it ever was (Chapter 5).

Conclusion

Whilst RCTs have come into prominence, their position in a hierarchy of 'evidence' is questionable, even unacceptable. Different purposes of educational research demand many different kinds of research and many canons for demonstrating fitness for purpose, and RCTs cannot meet many of these. Even though RCTs are conducted in 'real world' settings and include process evaluations and supplementary qualitative evidence, this does not guarantee reliability, validity or usefulness for a range of parties, as they neglect key questions of causality and the 'why' and 'how' of education. RCT's view of causality is limited and simplistic, overlooking mechanisms of causality; that is both their positive claim and a source of criticisms against them. Whilst RCTs may be useful in some areas of educational research, these are far fewer than is claimed for them, and it is little surprise, there-fore, that they are seldom fully used in policy making, and indeed, it is right, even ethical, that their limitations for policy making are exposed and made transparent (Chapter 13). The appeal to RCTs too easily dismisses other important and necessary ways of conducting research in education, and adopts an impoverished and too-limited a view of 'science', neglecting important paradigms of science and being over-reductionist.

The chapter set out the claims made for and against RCTs, and suggested limiting claims made for RCTs in education. RCTs have limited utility in edu-cation; they don't actually offer much, they occupy only one position in the realm of fitness for purpose, and they are only one of many kinds of important and necessary forms of research in education in serving a range of purposes in education. They do not warrant their emergent ascribed hegemonic position. As Norman remarked:

> What effects can be identified from such randomised designs are likely to be of such minimal importance as to be of little practical con-sequence. It is not that randomised trials are not possible to do on educational interventions; it is that they are not worth the effort involved in doing them.
>
> (Norman, 2003, p. 582)

Chapter 5

The impact of complexity theory and chaos theory

Introduction and overview

RCTs appeal to the cachet of being 'scientific'. However, developments in paradigms, ontologies and epistemologies of science call into question several of the principles underpinning RCTs in education. Here, those that relate to scientific theories of complexity and chaos are introduced, and are shown to undermine the claims of RCTs to be useful in understanding, interpreting and developing the 'real' world of education. The chapter focuses on:

- Limitations of the linear thinking that underpins RCTs.
- The importance of unpredictability, indeterminism and emergence, of which RCTs take insufficient account.
- The importance of the effects of small differences in initial conditions, which randomization, in its appeal to balancing out the effects of these between control and treatment groups, does not address sufficiently with regard to starting points and effects.
- The understatement of diversity, irregularity, heterogeneity, discontinuity and turbulence, and the inability of standard protocols and procedures in RCTs to address these.
- The importance of recognizing that RCTs operate in dynamical, nonlinear, open and self-organizing systems, with interconnections and interactions within complex networks of causality, agency and ongoing change.
- The contention that RCTs require artificial selections from a complex whole, and that the unit for understanding what is happening is the whole rather than a selected extraction from it. Whilst this might work in clinical trials (but Chapter 6 questions this), this is not so in education, and to argue that RCTs take place in 'real' classrooms, does not solve this matter – selection is selection. To focus on a few elements rather than addressing how these relate to, inform and are informed by, the operation of the units at a whole and multiple-component level, is to misrepresent the nature of the phenomenon under investigation.

- The complexity of the agentic, evolving, human and social world is distinct from the natural world, and the two are insufficiently comparable and commensurate.
- The problem of holding variables constant over time, which misrepresents the significance of the 'arrow of time' in bringing about changes.

In short, the chapter argues that, far from meeting their own claims of being 'scientific', RCTs neglect the significance of chaos and complexity sciences.

Key elements of theories of complexity and chaos

Complexity theory and chaos theory constitute a powerful challenge to arguments for randomization in RCTs. Chaos theory tells us that small *initial* conditions can have major effects (Gleick, 1987), and complexity theory tells us that small, *emergent* conditions and contingencies can cause major, unpredictable changes (Bak, 1996). A small cause may have a large effect and a large cause may have a small effect, i.e. effects are not proportional to their causes (Morrison, 2008). One excludes apparently insignificant variables or tiny variations at one's peril in establishing causality. The butterfly beating its wings in the Caribbean, thereby causing a hurricane in another part of the world, frustrated Lorenz's attempts at long range prediction of weather patterns (Gleick, 1987); so it is in classrooms. Small events cause major upsets and render long term prediction and generalizability futile. How do we know what the effects of small changes will be on an RCT?

The impact of chaos and complexity theories here is important, for they argue against the predictable, linear, deterministic, universalizable, stable, atomized, modernistic, objective, mechanistic, controlled, closed systems of law-like behaviour which may operate in the world of the laboratory but which do not operate in the social world of education. Thomas (2012) remarks that '[e]ducation is no better on prediction than are meteorology or economics; nor should we expect it to be' (p. 34). Biesta (2014) notes that attempts to reduce complexity lead to a 'critical tipping point' whereby education is transformed into indoctrination (p. 22), obstructing interactions with the outside world and limiting the agency of participants in education.

Chaos and complexity theories raise several questions against the value of RCTs in education (e.g. Gleick, 1987; Waldrop, 1992; Lewin, 1993; Morrison, 1998, 2008, 2010; Biesta, 2010, 2014; Jensen and Kjeldsen, 2014; Cohen et al., 2018; Wrigley and McCusker, 2019):

- Small-scale changes in initial conditions can produce massive and unpredictable changes in outcome.
- Very similar conditions can produce very dissimilar outcomes.
- Regularity and conformity break down into irregularity, diversity and entropy.

- Even if differential equations are simple, the behaviour of the system that they are modelling may not be simple.
- Effects are not straightforward, continuous functions of causes.
- The universe is largely unpredictable and nonlinear.
- If something works once there is no guarantee that it will work in the same way a second time.
- Determinism is replaced by indeterminism; deterministic, linear and stable systems are replaced by 'dynamical', changing, evolving systems and nonlinear explanations of phenomena.
- Continuity is replaced by discontinuity, turbulence and irreversible transformation.
- Universal, all-encompassing theories and large-scale explanations provide inadequate accounts of localized and specific phenomena.
- Long-term prediction is impossible: we can know 'what worked' rather than 'what works' (Wiliam, 2019).
- Order is not predetermined and fixed; it emerges, rather than being imposed.
- Social behaviour, education and learning are emergent, and are marked by recursion, feedback, evolution, autocatalysis, openness, connectedness and self-organization.
- Human life is agentic, deliberate, creative, spontaneous, emergent, purposive, volitional, intentional, imaginative, not simply a biological reactive, mechanistic or passive process or a closed, situation in which RCTs hold variables steady and constant – to do so is to misread social complexity and to commit the fallacy of seeking averages in a non-average, often unmeasurable world.
- Social life, education and learning take place through the interactions of participants with their environments (however defined, e.g. interpersonal, social, intrapersonal, physical, material, intellectual, emotional) in ways which cannot be controlled through RCTs, even with appeals to the *ceteris paribus* condition and to randomization.
- Local rules and behaviours generate diversity and heterogeneity of practice, undermining generalizability from RCTs about 'what works'.

These call into question some of the key principles underpinning RCTs, and are addressed below.

Linearity and nonlinearity

Researchers cannot confine themselves to simple linear thinking; they must take account of nonlinearity. However, much of the statistical debate on causality and RCTs assumes linearity and stability of relationships, i.e. the more we have of cause X, the more we have of effect Y. A little homework may improve a student's performance at school, but it does not follow that a large amount of homework will improve it further, as stress, tiredness and demotivation set in. For example, in a curvilinear relationship, a statistic that is premised on linearity (e.g. correlation, difference or regression as used in RCTs) might *find* no relationship, as the negative correlation cancels out the positive correlation, but in fact there may still be a very strong causal relationship. One paracetamol tablet may be curative, e.g. for a headache, but five hundred may be lethal. Jensen and Kjeldsen (2014) comment that evidence-based practice, based on a 'linear view of knowledge production and transfer' (p. 29), not only misrepresents the nature of education as individualized, contextualized and complex practice but threatens the autonomy and integrity of educationists (p. 34).

Unpredictability and emergence

Complexity theory tells us that effects emerge unpredictably when the interplay of factors reaches a bifurcation/tipping point that leads to unpredicted outcomes (Bak, 1996) from the self-organizing, multidirectional, multivariate, nonlinear interplay of variables. We cannot know in advance which variables will be important to include or exclude, and we cannot decide that, because variables happen to exert little, if any, influence at one particular point in time, this means that either they are unimportant in any causal account (Cilliers, 2001, p. 138). In a nonlinear world such prediction is impossible or dangerous. A small variable now may not be a small variable tomorrow.

Some of the purposes of RCTs are clear: to establish causality and predictability. Causality here is premised on control (Cohen et al., 2018) and manipulation, however benevolent. Regardless of the perhaps questionable desirability of predicating human sciences on the natural sciences, with its subject/object split, its appeal to value-neutrality, and its procedures for manipulating variables, there is the *de facto* problem of whether this, in fact, can be done. The impact of complexity theory and chaos theory (Gleick, 1987; Waldrop, 1992; Lewin, 1993; Kaufmann, 1995) suggests that predictability is a chimera. For example, Tymms (1996, pp. 32–33) suggests that different outcomes might be expected even from the same classes taught by the same teacher in the same classroom with the same curriculum; if something works once there is no guarantee that it will work again (Phillips, 2019). Hence, RCTs may have limited utility.

Open, dynamical systems, controls and holism

Complexity theory is premised on a view of education as an open system in which changes constantly occur in a dynamical, ever-evolving world, happening as interaction between the education system and the outside world unfolds. The classroom situation at the end of an RCT is not the same as it was at the start, and unpredictability and emergence feature here. To try to hold constants, as in an RCT, is to misrepresent what classrooms are really like. As Cowen (2019) observes: the world keeps moving, rather than standing still whilst schools consider or enact changes and practices as a consequence of RCTs (p. 94). Indeed, MacIntyre (1985) contends that the social world is characterized by its lack of susceptibility to generalization and unpredictability (p. 103), and in which induction is dangerous. Given this, 'inference to the best explanation' (Lipton, 2004) is more the stuff of educational research rather than generalization in a situation in which under-determination and induction can be fallacious (Lipton, 2004, pp. 5–7; see also Thomas, 2016, p. 399).

Further, Kvernbekk (2019) notes that practice must be regarded as a whole, and the whole is not amendable to an RCT, which is essentially a selective part of an open, complex system of multiple, interacting parts (pp. 26–27). As Cartwright (2019) observes, education, as an open system, requires including, rather than excluding social complexity and reflexivity (p. 66).

Complexity theory replaces an emphasis on simple causality with an emphasis on networks, linkages, feedback, impact, relationships and interactivity in context (Cohen and Stewart, 1995), emergence, dynamical systems, self-organization and distributed control (rather than the controlling mechanism of RCTs), and open systems rather than the closed system of the RCT (Morrison, 2012), which has its parallel in the moves in health care towards going wider than natural science into qualitative/subjective research (Davies, 1999, pp. 112–113).

Even if we could conduct an RCT, and Connolly et al. (2017, 2018) make a case for this, the applicability of that RCT to ongoing, emerging, interactive, relational, changing, open situations, may be limited in practice, even though some general similarities may be *calculated* through meta-analysis (Chapter 12). To hold that policy making must be based on the evidence of 'what works' as derived from comparatively crude equations used in meta-analysis (Glass et al., 1981, pp. 29, 102; Tymms, 1999) is perhaps little more than an article of faith. It is dangerously optimistic and overambitious to base policy making on a few relatively simple equations; perhaps mercifully, this rarely happens.

It is questionable whether one should hold variables constant in a dynamical, evolving, fluid, idiographic, unique situation (a feature which is recognized in health care research (Davies, 1999, p. 115)). It is a commonplace truism to say that natural settings such as schools and classrooms are not the antiseptic, reductionist, analysed-out or analysable-out world of the laboratory or the controlled classroom, and that the degree of control required for experimental conditions to be met renders classrooms unnatural settings, despite the advocacy and evidence of classroom RCTs by Connolly et al. (2017, 2018); the implications of this are perhaps understated in advocating RCTs. Even if one *wanted* to, or did, undertake an RCT in classrooms, to what extent is it *actually* possible to identify, isolate, control and manipulate the key variables in RCTs, and, thence, to attribute putative causality? As Norman (2003) remarks, it may not be the case that the RCT has an 'uncanny ability ... to isolate everything except the overall effect of the intervention' (p. 583).

Further, Joyce (2019) argues that, in isolating variables in order to control them, and in considering some processes in isolation from other processes, misrepresents how processes actually operate in practice, with *causal pathways* and causal mechanisms being established by the context. These, she avers, are necessary to include for generalizability to work (p. 57). Indeed, she argues for the necessity of using non-experimental methods in providing this required causal analysis in supporting generalizability and regularities (pp. 57–58).

There is an important double message from complexity theory. Firstly, we must treat people and situations as wholes, i.e. we cannot fairly separate out single elements from 'causal cakes' (Cartwright and Hardie, 2012) and attribute causality to these, as in RCTs. Causes operate *together, collectively* in tandem with an array of other causes, triggers, intentions, agency, volitions, social contexts, histories, psychologies, social systems, norms of behaviour, emergent and non-static open systems in which predictability is diminished in collective as well as individual behaviours and situations (Phillips, 2019, p. 15).

Secondly, humans are agentic and, rehearsing the mind/brain difference, they act volitionally and consciously. As Simpson (2019a) puts it:

> A stomach ulcer does not have consciousness and agency to decide to respond to an intervention, while different patients do have that freedom.... When we move from treating the body part to treating the patient, evidence from even well-designed RCTs may not be enough. Complex systems in which conscious agents interact and which co-evolve with other systems are not susceptible to randomised controlled trials or their derivatives, and the UK's Medical Research Council is now recognising the difficulties of using methods designed for simple, non-interacting situations for complex social ones ... . In education, there are few obvious analogies of body parts: all the components in education have agency and consciousness and are part of a complex, networked social system.
>
> (Simpson, 2019a, p. 2)

Similarly, Manzi (2012) notes that one cannot proceed from biological models to 'political institutions' without invoking absurd reductionism (p. 205). Wrigley (2019, p. 153) recalls Vygotsky's comment that animals passively adapt to the environment, whilst, by contrast, humans actively adapt the environment to their own needs and situations. This is akin to familiar critiques of behaviourism in striving to understand learning but neglecting human imagination and creativity, overstating prediction and control, understating consciousness and intentionality, and unfairly importing methods from the natural sciences into human sciences (*ibid.*, pp. 153–154).

Put simply, to pull out a single variable from a necessarily and unavoid-ably combined set of variables, and then to attribute causality to that single variable, is to misrepresent the reality of the situation and the players that are playing out over time. And to suggest that randomization overcomes this, is an all-too-easy and all-too-wrong way out, even if, as Connolly et al. (2017, 2018) argue, teachers themselves respond positively to RCTs; the pied piper of RCTs leads them into a world in which over-simplistic, over-reductionist, under-warranted, over-generalized assertions and conclusions have dominion.

Further, there is an 'arrow of time'; Prigogine and Stengers (1985) argue that situations evolve irreversibly and that to overlook this by holding time and situations as constant as possible in RCTs is to misrepresent reality. Though Campbell and Stanley's (1963) influential work on RCTs discusses threats to internal validity caused by history and maturation (p. 5), and they suggest that randomization can overcome these (pp. 13–14), there is a nag-ging worry that the importance of these factors – of the people involved in the RCT – might be underestimated. How these can be addressed in RCTs is an open question.

Holding variables constant over time misrepresents the significance of the 'arrow of time' in bringing about irreversible changes which, even though RCTs claim to be able to address them (e.g. as the same time period holds true for both the control and treatment groups), they do not sufficiently address. Emergence leads to divergence, i.e. the situation which might have been the same for both groups at the start is not the same both groups at the end of the RCT, and contexts influence practices. Campbell and Stanley's (1963) seminal volume on RCTs include 'history' and 'maturation' as pro-blems, and the impact of complexity theory potentates them.

Conclusion

The sciences of complexity and chaos call into question the claims of RCTs to 'work' and to yield reliable and valid evidence of 'what works' in the 'real' world of education. Linear thinking that underpins RCTs misrepresents the actual nonlinearity of causality and of the world in which RCTs are set; RCTs understate the significance of unpredictability, indeterminism and emergence; they neglect the importance of the effects of small differences in initial conditions; even though randomization is an attempt to balance out the effects of these between the control and treatment groups, this is insuffi-cient, as small differences in initial conditions can lead to significant differ-ences later, e.g. at the outcome stage of an RCT.

RCTs lack attention to diversity, irregularity, heterogeneity, discontinuity and turbulence, and, even though their appeal to randomization attempts to address and overcome these, it is inherently unsuccessful as it strives to build them out rather than to build them into the RCTs, and standard protocols and procedures for the operation of RCTs are a pious aspiration rather than a practical reality, as humans are not standard and they do not behave in a singular, standard way; to think otherwise is a fiction, a wish.

It is fundamentally misconceived to isolate practice in an RCT from the world in which it takes place, and the suggestion that, in fact, RCTs do not isolate practices from the 'real' world, and that they operate in 'real' class-rooms, is unsatisfactory, as RCTs are required – in their procedures – to isolate and control variables (which many classroom RCTs actually do not). RCTs are extractions from a complexly interconnected world in which it is simply wrong-headed to remove or overlook these factors in the search for identifying whether an intervention 'works', as they are key to what is hap-pening; it is wrong to relegate them to 'noise'. It is fanciful to think that, by conducting an RCT in the real world, this is sufficient for it to over-ride the *significance* of the interplay and multiply causal and multiple directionality of causes of a myriad of factors which are not the same in control and treat-ment groups. How RCTs take account of human agency, interaction, and the consequent changes in phenomena over time is neglected, despite their claims to be able to control for history and maturity; these are simply inadequate. Classes of children in a control group or a treatment group at the start of an RCT are not the same as at the end of an RCT; they have diverged and changed; thank heaven.

Chapter 6

'Medical models' and randomized controlled trials in education

Introduction and overview

Much reference is made to RCTs in clinical practices and 'medical models'. Medical models have often been cited as examples from which educational research might learn (e.g. Torgerson and Torgerson, 2003; Connolly et al., 2017; Cohen et al., 2018). This chapter argues that, whilst much can be learnt from 'medical models' and RCTs in clinical practice, the worlds of education and medicine differ. The chapter sets out a range of similarities and differences between the two, and argues that, whilst such similarities are informative, differences between the two are important, as they call into question the appeal to applying RCTs from one to the other. What is happening in control groups is not the same as a placebo in clinical trials. There is a clear distinction between clinical and educational RCTs, as the scope of the former is narrower than the latter, and it is impossible to rule out the wide scope of the latter; the former has clear input and outcome measures which operate with questionable validity, reliability and utility in the multifactorial and multiple-outcome world of education.

The chapter notes that the rigour which applies to clinical trials has much to teach RCTs in education, for example in terms of:

- pre-trial development and testing (e.g. and efficacy testing);
- approvals for RCTs;
- risk analyses and cautions;
- protocols and procedures for operating the RCT;
- recognizing that attention to personal factors must be included (people are at different stages of an illness and with different auxometry (rates of clinical progress or decline), the educational equivalent of which is an argument for differentiation, a feature recognized for decades (e.g. Department of Education and Science, 1985));
- attention to what counts as 'effective', and for whom;
- decisions on what counts as 'successful';
- patient/client screening: people differ;

- the attention to the educational equivalents of: dose–response (variations in strength, frequency and intensity for different people and in different time periods, e.g. at the start of the treatment and later in the treatment); personalized treatments; contextual factors and 'noise'; co-morbidities; co-medications; side effects and risks; long-term effects; sub-group outcomes and outliers as well as averages; unanticipated outcomes; fidelity to protocols and procedures for treatment; careful initial diagnosis; blinding (double and triple); caution in claiming generalizability; attention to causality; ongoing monitoring; the complementarity of other sources of evidence in evaluating and contributing to RCTs;
- statistical power analysis;
- recognizing that RCTs are fallible.

Whilst RCTs in education can learn from clinical trials, the two differ in scope and operation. One cannot and should not model itself on the other, and discourses of RCTs in education have noted this.

Similarities and differences between RCTs in medicine and education

RCTs in clinical and educational research are both similar and different. Sullivan (2011, p. 287) identifies six differences:

i in clinical trials the 'mechanism of the action is well understood' (e.g. the positive effects of aspirin) whereas in education the mechanism of learning is less clearly understood;
ii in clinical trials the 'endpoint is easily measured' whereas outcomes in education are diverse;
iii in clinical trials the 'targets likely to benefit from intervention' are 'easily understood', whereas, in education, the responses from individuals may differ and identification of target individuals may not be feasible;
iv in clinical trials the effect size is 'expected to be small' (e.g. 0.07 for aspirin) whereas in education it might be 0.5;
v in clinical trials the effect of the intervention is independent of who happens to be administering it, whereas in education the characteristics of teachers and their interactions with students may exert a significant effect on the success of the intervention; and
vi in clinical trials there is a 'major impact' if the trial is successful, whereas this is much less likely in education.

To this can be added the important difference set out by Manzi (2012), which is that, whilst clinical trials operate in an environment of relatively high 'causal density' (p. 81), RCTs in the social sciences operate in an environment of much greater 'causal density' and in the presence of many hidden or known conditionals, thereby confounding attempts at reliable, easy prediction or certainty. 'Very high causal densities' replace compact, powerful and generalized laws with 'extremely conditional, statistical statements' (p. 204). Indeed, he suggests that 'core questions' in social science, being strongly 'holistically integrated', render experiments impossible (p. 204). To use simple measures of outcomes is to take insufficient account of the reality of multiple outcomes of RCTs in social research, and the more one tries to take account of these, the more difficult or imprudent it is to generalize (Hammersley, 2013, p. 49), even with large samples.

Control groups

Wrigley (2018) notes that, in educational trials, there is no parallel to the placebo that one finds in clinical research, as not only are children and teachers already allocated to classes, but also it is almost impossible to change what is happening without the participants – students and teachers – noticing that such changes are happening (p. 363). Further, he asks whether the control group should experience the deliberate *absence* of the practice that is being trialled in the RCT, or simply go about 'business as usual' (p. 363). He notes that lack of clarity here can mean that the RCT groups are unfairly matched in practice. He gives the example of an RCT concerning the use of open questions, and he asks whether the control group should have only closed questions or whether the teacher should continue as normal and without thinking particularly about question types that he/she is using (p. 363). What the control group is actually doing has a significant effect on the findings e.g. in effect size (see also Wrigley and McCusker, 2019, p. 115; Simpson, 2020). Sufficient controls are often missing on what the control group should be doing.

Further, control groups may not be reliable counterfactuals as they differ on unmeasured and non-controlled factors, and, as Oakley (2000) notes, they often they provide data to the research team, e.g. interview data, and that this constitutes an intervention, such that the control group is no longer 'outside the dynamics of the research process' (p. 238), i.e. a form of the Hawthorne effect.

The scope of RCTs in medicine and education

RCTs in education raise issues concerning the irreducible complexity and multiplicity of purposes, intended outcomes and contents of education, which stand in contrast to the 'medical model' which seeks to cure a single or limited number of illnesses at a time (Wrigley and McCusker, 2019, p. 124). Further, caricaturing for heuristic clarity, there is incongruence between the 'medical model' which is pathological, seeking to cure a disease, and the educational model which has more positive aims, unless, perchance, one believes in original sin.

Whilst some of the responses to potential criticisms of RCTs suggest having yet more, and more rigorous, RCTs, other criticisms are at the level of principle. Here, unlike the explicit, relatively narrow focus of clinical trials, RCTs in education betray the complex world of education and, thereby, are simply not a 'good thing'. Similarly, quasi-experiments, even though field experiments are often advocated (e.g. Shadish, Cook and Campbell, 2002), are risky, as they do not take sufficient account of the many unmeasured and uncontrolled factors obtaining in a situation (for both the control and treatment groups), thereby compromising what can legitimately be inferred from the results.

Whilst RCTs might be useful in medicine, it is infinitely more difficult to operate them validly in education because, in medicine, outcomes and boundaries are easier to predefine. Even if we could define and identify such outcomes in education, measuring them is much more challenging than in medicine, and surrogates and proxies in medicine may not have their equivalents in education (Smith, 2013, p. 2).

The human factor

RCTs have a prominent place in drug testing, clinical and other therapies. Clinical RCTs are conducted in less controlled, 'real world' settings, replacing *experimental* RCTs (e.g. efficacy testing) with *pragmatic* RCTs (e.g. effectiveness testing) (de Leon, 2012; Liu et al., 2011; Sullivan 2011; Torgerson and Torgerson, 2013). Indeed, Campbell, a towering figure in experimental research in education, was an advocate of quasi-experiments and field-experiments (Pearce and Raman, 2014; Shadish et al., 2002). Pragmatic trials fit clinical settings well, addressing, for example: patients who forget to, or refuse to, take medicine or take it irregularly; comorbidities; patients taking multiple medications; doctor-patient relations etc. RCTs also address the rise of personalized medicine. What are the equivalences in, and implications for, educational research?

On another level, regarding the 'human factor' in clinical practice, Peile (2004) notes that clinical trials rarely provide all the evidence that is needed to answer clinical practice questions, e.g. concerning harms, and this supports the significance and essential contribution of observational studies (p. 107). The contribution of RCTs is tempered by the importance of recognizing that people, not evidence, make decisions on clinical practices (p. 108). So it is in education, with teachers making hundreds of decisions each day (Clark and Peterson, 1986). Peile (2004) comments that, in clinical practice, research evidence has to take its place alongside, rather than being superordinate to, patients' preferences and actions, clinical states and circumstances (p. 109). He argues for the importance of informed experience, tacit knowledge and informed intuition within an evidence-based culture (pp. 113–114).

Greenhalgh et al. (2014) note that the evidence-based movement in medicine risks being 'in crisis', as technology-driven prompts and inflexible rules can lead to patient-centredness being superseded by management-centredness, with guidelines taking insufficient account of comorbidities (p. 2). Education can do better than being bound by 'algorithmic rules' (p. 2). Greenhalgh and her colleagues advocate the greater concern for the individual patient, for placing the exercise of judgement over naïve obedience to rules, for the importance of the interactional relationship between physician and patient, i.e. human-centred clinical practice, and for more imaginative research, including qualitative research, than simply RCTs. Educationists, take heed.

Personalized medicine, with targeted therapies, is a massively growing field. It involves the whole person, the severity or stage of their disease (Feinstein, 1995), environmental and sociodemographic characteristics, socioeconomic, cultural, personal factors, health-related behaviours, the presence of other risk factors and comorbidities, in short the elements affecting the whole person (Goodman, 2009) which require careful screening and diagnosis:

> 'Personalized medicine' refers to the tailoring of medical treatment to the individual characteristics of each patient. It does not literally mean the creation of drugs or medical devices that are unique to a patient but rather the ability to classify individuals into subpopulations that differ in their susceptibility to a particular disease or their response to a specific treatment. Preventive or therapeutic interventions can then be concentrated on those who will benefit, sparing expense and side effects for those who will not.
>
> (President's Council of Advisers on Science and Technology, 2008, p. 1)

Frueh (2009) notes that a range of factors, e.g. environment, co-medication, 'play a critical role' (p. 1080) in treatment. Do RCTs in education currently take account of this?

Dose–response

In clinical trials for new drugs, attention is given to the dose–response factor: what level of dosage brings about what kind of response in the patient? Too little, and the medication is seen to be ineffective; too much, and it can be lethal. In considering the dose–response factor, attention is paid to: the amount, quality, strength, frequency, intensity, duration, and recognition that a person is a complex system which combines and connects very many elements whose interactions and outcomes change over time (with concomitant changes to interventions over time). The same applies to RCTs in education. How many RCTs in education take into account the varying amounts, quality, strength, frequency, duration and intensity of 'treatments' in the treatment group, e.g. in factorial experiments or other types of experiment?

In clinical practice, some treatments require initial intensive medication, kick-starting treatment, then tailing off to a maintenance level (e.g. many people start a course of antibiotics with a double dose and then maintain a single dose for several days); some medication requires a gentle start, with an increasing, cumulative dosage as the body responds to treatment. Some drugs (e.g. lithium, insulin) require ongoing, regular, close monitoring, whilst others need a less watchful eye. The point here is that medication is not a single event but, as the career of a disease and a patient change over time, so does the treatment. How much does this operate in the simple input-output model of current RCTs in education? Some patients need intensive treatment, others do not; how is this addressed in RCTs in education, and how is this both monitored and factored into the assessment of 'what works'? The importance of these from the protocols and procedures for clinical trials is clear.

In addition to needing to know 'how much' effect a treatment has, and on whom, Hogarth (2012), referring to the medical model, comments that RCTs generally do not indicate why: (a) some patients do or do not respond to treatment; (b) others have an excessive response; and (c) others experience side effects or adverse effects. It is difficult to find an RCT in education that states in advance the level of success that it requires in order to be judged efficacious or effective, and how it will address contingencies and responses to interventions. Many have no specified targets, though some may pre-specify an *overall* effect size sought, e.g. to ensure statistical power (Ellis, 2010). Indeed, it is difficult to find RCTs in education which, unlike personalized medicine, state their prognoses, targeted improved benefit (for whom, how much and about what) (though efforts to address this are appearing in the work of the Education Endowment Foundation), predicted benefit or its lack (and for whom), predicted risk and its acceptance/mitigation/avoidance/transference/exploitation (though ethics committees/boards are supposed to act here), and estimated dose.

Whether or not average effects are found, the point is that, given the variability of dosage and responses in clinical trials and personalized medicine, targeted therapies are required rather than a 'one size fits all' approach. Moving from RCT to treatment is an art as much as a science (de Leon, 2012). Indeed, as Osler, a key early figure in medicine remarked, 'if it were not for the great *variability* among individuals, medicine might have well been a science and not an art' (quoted by Roses, 2000, p. 857). So, too in education; how one conducts and subsequently uses an RCT is open to question.

The importance of analyzing the dose–response equivalent in education is not lost. Glass (2000) commented that 'we are not testing grand theories, rather we are charting dosage-response curves for technological interventions under a variety of circumstances' (p. 12). Thomas (2016, p. 400) harks back to the work of Cronbach (1975) who drew attention to the high variance within and between groups, i.e. there was inconsistency of effects across sites. In medical practice, Thomas (2016) reports that the same kind of psychotherapy was practised differently by different psychotherapists, and that these differences exceeded differences in the kinds of psychotherapies being practised (p. 400). He applies this to the field of teaching, noting that differences in teachers – their personalities, values, likes, dislikes, expectations, practices, contexts and experiences – turn out to be more significant than the pedagogies they adopt, i.e. people feature very strongly in an RCT, and are far less susceptible to control than might be desired in the standard protocols and procedures set out in an RCT (p. 401).

Teacher effects are vast. Behaviour is situationally specific, and teachers call on a vast store of experiences and knowledge to handle and adapt to situations in specific classrooms ('arenas') with specific students in specific conditions, and with specific needs, interests, capabilities, motivations, etc. (Thomas, 2016, p. 402). These are far removed from the controlled-out/controlled-in world of the RCT, indeed of experimentation itself. Thomas strongly defends the essential '"person-ness" of the teaching situation' (p. 403) which, he notes, is sorely neglected in RCTs.

Variable responses ('heterogeneity of treatment effects') are almost inevitable in heterogeneous patients and their sub-groups. RCTs often overlook such heterogeneities, leading to claims for results being more broadly applicable than they are in reality. Goodman (2009) cites plentiful evidence to show that clinical trials often overlook or exclude sub-groups, comorbidities, co-medication and other patient characteristics. Patients with comorbidities (more than one illness for which they are taking more than one treatment or medication), are often excluded from RCTs in order to try to establish the causality of X alone with greater certainty than would be possible if other illnesses or medications were present. This risks distorting, even invalidating findings (Wrigley, 2018, p. 362; Wrigley and McCusker, 2019, p. 115) and misrepresents the 'real' world in which patients really do present with comorbidities for which they are taking different combinations of medication (Fortin et al., 2006; Greenhalgh, 2016). So too in education.

This is a warning for educational research which too easily assumes that it is acceptable to exclude certain samples if they have additional features (which, in reality, is very likely to happen), and which is too accepting of the naïve view that a single intervention will have a single effect or that a single intervention operates in isolation from other events, situations, activities etc. which obtain simultaneously in the situation. It is impossible to rule out contextual factors, such that many RCTs are a blunt instrument with a blunt measure, i.e. not knowing exactly what it was that caused such-and-such. Conversely, it is unacceptable to inure, shield or exclude RCTs from the effects of other causal factors and 'noise' operating, for example in classrooms. Indeed, Thomas (2016) comments that, in contrasting the 'signal' and the 'noise', 'noise' might contain several 'signals' of other dimensions of contexts and individuals that should be included in understanding a situation (p. 400). 'Noise' may actually be the 'signal' rather than the 'noise'.

Clinical and educational RCTs typically use averages in their measures (Woodcock, 2007); this may be their strongest point or their Achilles heel, depending on the purpose of the research. De Leon (2012) observes that whereas clinical trials seek to identify the most suitable treatment for the 'average' patient, and, thereby, ignore outliers, personalized medicine focuses on outliers (p. 153). Patients, average or outliers, may or may not benefit equally from the treatment. Personalized medicine, de Leon (2012) notes, does not assume population or response homogeneity; a 'drug response is a statistically heterogeneous phenomenon' (p. 153). It is all too easy to dismiss outliers, regardless of the levels at which they are defined: 1 per cent, 5 per cent, 10 per cent, or whatever (p. 156). The same could be said of education: the more difficult, extreme and small in number is the sub-group, the more it risks being overlooked or excluded. So much for inclusive classrooms and students with special needs. Medicine seeks to identify the 'right treatment' for the 'right patient' at the 'right time' (Goodman, 2009, p. 3); does this happen in education which is informed by RCTs? Where is the evidence?

Personalized medicine places store on detailed diagnosis. This stands in contrast to many RCTs in education which seem to take a largely undifferentiated approach to diagnosis of who might and might not benefit from an intervention, and then proceed to a relatively crude RCT that is targeted at an undifferentiated group (maybe in the interests of randomization and large samples).

One lesson here is that RCTs in education may benefit from being differentiated to targeted groups, based on careful diagnosis; the other lesson is that treatments will need to take account of the whole person, not just a few variables: focus on the person as a whole, not solely on particular elements in isolation. A person is not just a bundle of variables. Be prepared to change treatments over time for the individual. In other words, take people seriously. Jadad and Enkin (2007, p. 13) note that there are many types of RCT in medicine, and that they vary by attention to differences in: aspects of the intervention; how participants are exposed to the intervention; the units used for analysis (e.g. parts, wholes, groups); the number of participants; blinded or open trials; participants' preferences (e.g. Zelen's design, in which eligible participants are randomized *before* they give consent to participate in the RCT) (p. 22).

Clinical trials stress the importance of researchers taking account of many other factors, contexts and systems in which RCTs exist; rather than trying to control out such factors, contexts and systems, they occupy a central position. Clinical practice does not rely on RCTs alone but takes account of the personal characteristics of the patient, the patient's history, and other sources of evidence. In education, minimally speaking, this echoes calls for process evaluations in RCTs (Siddiqui et al., 2018). As a former Vice-President of the British Educational Research Association, Ian Menter (2013) observed: RCTs '*must* be complemented by other approaches including evaluation research, qualitative research, action research and theoretical research' (p. 39) (italics added). Connolly et al. (2017, 2018) argue for mixed methods RCTs.

Patients differ from each other and respond variably to the same drug. Average effects, as measured in an RCT, may differ markedly from effects on a given individual. Whilst randomization, harking back to Fisher, is designed to balance out the effects of a myriad of within-group and between-group differences, this might be all well and good for the agricultural model in his *The Design of Experiments* (Fisher, 1966), but humans are infinitely more complex and less passive than seeds which are affected by soil, heat, light, weather, location and water. Medicines are not fertilizers; a fertilizer may have only one effect, whereas a medicine may have many (Healy et al., 2014, p. 81), and, whereas fertilizers look for average effects, medicine is 'critically concerned with the benefit to an individual patient' (p. 81) (see also de Leon, 2012).

The 'science' in scientific experiments

Medical research, like science itself, is far from being confined to RCTs (Thomas, 2016). Close, careful, detailed, systematic observation is a characteristic feature of much medical research, without an RCT in sight, and, indeed, medics, ideally, are concerned to treat each individual as an individual case/person, not an average or by following a rule mechanically (Wrigley, 2018, p. 360); they draw on their nuanced, expert judgement and experience, communicated sensitively in a patient–doctor relationship.

Thomas (2016) and Wrigley (2018) argue that many scientific discoveries have not come from experiments, that causality in sciences often relies on close observation rather than experiments, and, anyway, the social world is very different from the natural world (p. 361). Thomas (2016) notes that RCTs are only one form of experiment in science, and that other forms of experiments are common in science, with conjectures, hypotheses and refutations, testing ideas and theories in controlled situations, with systematic testing, meticulous observations and consideration of explanations of findings, and not necessarily in RCTs (p. 395).

Wrigley and McCusker (2019) note that to appeal to RCTs as the only true scientific method is to adopt an impoverished view of sciences, and that, in reality, a huge amount of non-RCT-based scientific work takes place *before* any RCT is conducted, including observations, 'intelligent noticing', trial and error, intuition, creative thinking; indeed, they comment that experiments tend to be used to verify rather than to advance knowledge (p. 111). In clinical research, before any RCTs are undertaken, years of theory-based and carefully tested research are undertaken; indeed, the case has to be made persuasively and approved by regulatory bodies, for the research to be ready to go to trial in RCTs; not so much in education, at present, though the What Works Clearinghouse sets rigorous requirements for registering RCTs.

Frieden (2017) remarks that observational studies in clinical practice remain 'the foremost source' of research evidence (pp. 465–466), even though they may over-estimate some effects, and that it is counterproductive to elevate RCTs 'at the expense of other potentially highly valuable sources of data' (pp. 569–570). He comments that even if we know what the established risk factors are, 'RCTs can yield answers that are simply wrong' (p. 468). He cites a range of alternative, suitable ways of conducting clinical research, e.g. meta-analysis, systematic reviews, prospective cohort studies, retrospective cohort studies, case control studies, cross-sectional studies, ecological studies, pragmatic and large observational studies, program-based evidence, case reports and registries (see also Phillips (2019), who argues for RCTs taking their place alongside interviews, observations, simulations, case studies, and logical analyses (p. 21)). As McKnight and Morgan (2019) note, medicine recognizes that there is a much wider evidence base than RCTs (p. 2).

Advances in medicine are being made in 'real world evidence' (Faulkner, 2013), i.e. data which do not come solely from RCTs but from a range of sources, e.g. registries of patients, databases of claims, electronic health records, outcomes reported by patients, and reviews of literature (p. 12). Faulkner comments that RCTs on their own are part of 'yesterday's toolkit', whereas the 'New Health Toolkit' includes RCTs but also, *inter alia*, stakeholder research, observational studies, registries, budget impact models, cost-effectiveness models, data on values, surveys conducted through social media etc. (p. 43). Data, he avers (p. 51) should include patients' biomarkers, comorbidities, confounders, comparative effectiveness, and should consider multiple, alternative and mixed approaches in generating evidence (p. 91). So too, in equivalent form, in education.

Whether, or how far, RCTs in education are sufficiently whole-person centred and systems-centred, rather than focusing on a limited range of elements, is an important area for investigation. Noble (2006) comments that systems approaches (e.g. to biology) seek integration and combination of elements rather than reduction (p. 176), and this applies equally well to educational research, but often runs counter to RCTs.

Risks

Risk analysis addresses risks and benefits, and whilst risk frameworks and registers abound in some parts of the world, it is unclear how far RCTs in education address these. Costs should also be provided alongside benefits in reporting evidence of 'what works', and these should be mandatory in published research, teachers' textbooks and program details from publishers.

Risk analysis and risk management are important, and it is essential to identify and evaluate potential risks that could be encountered in the RCT (the risk events), what they are, for whom and to whom or what, where they come from (the sources), the causes and drivers of the risks, the likelihood of the risks actually occurring (e.g. 'almost certain' to 'very highly unlikely'), and their severity level in terms of potential consequences and for whom, e.g. from 'catastrophic' (e.g. loss of life) to 'extreme', to 'major', to 'moderate', to 'low' (International Organization for Standardization, 2018; International Electrotechnical Commission, 2019).

For example, in education, it is very highly likely that a snowstorm in winter in the UK will occur, but the consequences could be low, e.g. the school is closed for two days, and, thereby the standard RCT procedures, e.g. two class lessons with the 'treatment' for the intervention group, are disrupted but have minimal effect on a one-year-long RCT. By contrast, the likelihood of a salmonella outbreak in a school might be very low but its consequences could be major, as large numbers of participants could be absent from school for up to two weeks, absences will vary, and the school may have to close for disinfecting, and such attrition and closure respectively could have a significant effect on the operations and results of an RCT that was only designed to run for 8 weeks.

Once the risks have been identified and their probability and severity have been assessed, the task is to decide how to address them (risk management). For example, this could be:

- whether to accept the risk (e.g. if it is a low-severity risk or unlikely (or even likely) to occur) and proceed with the RCT; in the example of the snowstorm above, to go ahead with the RCT in the winter months, even though a snowstorm is almost certain;
- whether to take steps to avoid the risk; in the snowstorm example above, it might be to plan for the RCT to take place in the summer;
- whether to exploit the risk (prepare to take on the risk, as it could bring advantages); in the snowstorm example above, it could be to persuade all parents to purchase the school's home-produced software and textbooks for mathematics and English learning, so that children can work at home;
- whether to take steps to mitigate (reduce) the risk; in the example of salmonella above, to increase the number of times each month for disinfecting eating places in the school;
- whether to transfer the risk; in the salmonella example above, it might be to outsource the hygiene and cleaning of the school to a private company.

Whilst risk assessments are commonplace in many schools (e.g. in terms of accident prevention, security and visitor check-ins, students going out of the school), the questions posed by risk assessment and risk management in RCTs are under-addressed in proposals for RCTs in education, whereas in clinical trials they are requisites.

Side effects

Side effects in RCTs are important, be they positive or negative. Zhao (2017) comments that, whilst these are taken seriously in clinical trials, looking at unintended or unexpected side effects, they are frequently overlooked in RCTs in education (and, indeed, in other kinds of intervention in education). A treatment for cancer in multiple RCTs might show it to be effective in reducing cancer, and hence might justify its use; however, it might bring a host of other effects which, on balance, and in the eyes of the sufferers, are worse than the cancer. Whilst clinical research may seek to minimize side effects, how far this is true in education is unclear.

Zhao (2017) comments that very little research in education comments on adverse effects, and research is more concerned with proving how effective an intervention has been (p. 1). When one purchases medicine, it typically comes with warnings on the box, packet, bottle, or from the doctor who has consulted a pharmacopeia. Not so in education, or not yet.

Zhao cites the example of East Asian students who perform well on international tests of achievement (e.g. PISA) but such international tests have adverse effects in terms of cramming, practice tests and test preparation, rote learning, dislike of, and low interest in, the subjects, and the lowest student self-confidence in the world (see also Zhao, 2014). He indicates the policy implications of such high-stakes testing in that some teachers cheat on results, schools exclude low-performing students from education, curricula become narrow, teaching becomes test preparation, and hot-housing takes place for students who will be entered for such tests (see also Muller, 2018).

Zhao (2017) contends that having too narrow a focus on pre-specified outcomes renders it difficult to ascertain side effects, particularly those of a non-observable nature such as motivation and personal qualities (p. 4). This is compounded by the fact that some effects of an intervention might take a long time to manifest themselves, and in an age of short-termism, this may go unassessed. For a full countenance of the outcomes of an intervention, as an ethical requirement the side effects (positive and negative), risk analysis and management, and adverse effects should be included.

Zhao provides the example of direct instruction, in which two very different, even irreconcilable literatures exist (p. 5): one stating its benefits and one stating it downside. Rather than opting for one or the other, it is important in reporting outcomes to report both: such-and-such an intervention can be effective in terms of such-and-such a set of outcomes but it can also have such-and-such negative effects. Zhao indicates that direct instruction can be effective in knowledge transmission but that it can also suppress curiosity and creativity (p. 7). Such information, he avers, enables stakeholders to make informed choices.

He also suggests that it is important to state the long-term effects of an intervention. For example, with regard to direct instruction, one-off exposure to it is unlikely to have long-term negative effects whereas longer-term exposure might damage students' curiosity and creativity (p. 7). This alludes to the issue of dose–response, introduced above, and to the importance of the timing of outcome evaluations, discussed below.

RCTs in education could benefit from the rigour attached to RCTs in medicine, as pharmacopoeias (e.g. the British National Formulary) indicate:

whether a medicine is freely available or a controlled drug; dosage strengths, frequency and quantities; patient screening and diagnosis; security, safety and misuse; indications; contraindications, side effects and adverse effects; delayed effects; register of providers and users; treatment regimens; cautions; patients at risk (e.g. by age, abnormality, special features); presence of other illnesses and other medicines (co-medications); and methods of treatment. The equivalents of these in RCTs in education is often difficult to find in their planning, design, conduct, analysis and reporting.

Sampling and generalizability from RCTs in medicine and education

Medical trials emphasize the need to ensure that differentiated groups are included in the sample, otherwise important groups and sub-samples might be excluded or neglected, risking Type II errors: false negatives. For example, Liu et al. (2011) note that a false negative was found for a cancer drug because none of the trial patients included participants with evidence of epidermal growth factor rejector activity (p. S100), and yet this specific subgroup actually benefited from the drug, i.e. a sampling problem. The subsample should be planned in advance rather than conducting *post hoc* data analysis in the hope of finding something with statistical significance ('dredging'), and have statistical power to avoid a Type II error (Ellis, 2010), particularly if small samples and sub-samples are involved (Torgerson and Torgerson, 2008).

In clinical trials, the issue of generalizability has long been recognized as problematical (Clarke and Dawson, 1999, p. 131), as, in order to ensure that causality is clear, patients suffering from more than one illness (co-morbidity) might be deliberately excluded from the RCT. This results, characteristically, in small or very small samples, generating limits to generalizability, typicality and representativeness. The problem here for RCTs is that, in terms of sampling, big is not necessarily beautiful, as it overlooks differences between individuals and between groups, but neither is small, as it limits generalizability (Morrison, 2001).

Sampling problems encountered in clinical trials can also apply to education: in order to establish clear causality, the reduction of the sample to a subset might lead to very small samples. Often patients have more than one related illness, so to isolate one illness from the others for the sake of an RCT is to overlook the possible connectedness of one illness with another. For example, depression may be linked to cancer, or hypertension may be linked to diabetes, kidney problems and circulation problems. To isolate one from the other may overlook their interconnection. The educational equivalent is the recognition that several relevant factors may be present in any one RCT and that to isolate one from the other(s) is to misrepresent their interconnections and influences.

Clarke and Dawson (1999. p. 130) draw attention to the fact that, in health care, treatments may produce adverse reactions, in which case patients are withdrawn from the experiment. Others might simply leave the experiment. Such 'experimental mortality' or attrition has been long recognized (Campbell and Stanley, 1963). Less clear in education, however, is how the problem has been, or might be, addressed (Rossi and Freeman, 1993). Attrition might undermine putative parity between the control and experimental groups (See, 2018), a parity which, from earlier arguments about the range of participants and characteristics within and between groups, is already suspect. As the constitution of the groups changes, however slightly (and chaos theory reminds us that small differences and changes can result in massive effects), so the dynamics of the situation change (how many teachers have heaved a sigh of relief when a challenging child is absent for a day!), and the consistency and comparability of the research protocol, conditions, contexts and contents are undermined. To address this involves identifying the exact factors on which assignation of the sample to control and experimental groups will take place, and recognizing significant ways in which the two groups differ, and the effects of these. The judgement then becomes about the extent to which the dissimilarities between the two groups outweigh their similarities, which randomization over-rides.

Ethics

In addition to the ethics involved in RCTs in drug research, the USA's Food and Drug Administration has regulatory oversight of the drug and its trials; there is currently no clear compulsory educational equivalent of this apart from ethics committees and their equivalents in educational institutions, and peer review (though organizations, e.g. the Education Endowment Foundation, set their own non-statutory requirements). Would that education had the same stages of trialling as apply to drug testing (Lyman and Hirsch, 2010; Vaidyanathan, 2012). Moving to clinical trials has several stages, for example:

Stage One: the dose–response stage of laboratory testing to identify safe dosages and to derive the medicines and to remove problems in implementing the drug (derivation).
Stage Two: trials (randomized and non-randomized) in ideal conditions to determine levels of efficacy of the drug (validation; efficacy trials).
Stage Three: large sample testing on the general public, to compare the drug with the standard regimen (comparative effectiveness studies).
Stage Four: the post-marketing stage to study longer-term effects (including negative effects).

An efficacy trial is designed to see if an intervention *can* work (i.e. in restricted, ideal conditions). It is conducted under optimal conditions with a particular group or population, and the sampling tightly controls eligibility to participate and whom to include. An effectiveness trial is designed to see if an intervention which has been successful in an efficacy trial, *does* work for a wider, heterogeneous population in normal, 'real world' clinical situations and practices (Jadad and Enkin, 2007, pp. 13–15). It is difficult to discern such safeguards in RCTs in education, though, at the time of writing, regulation and staged interventions in RCTs are appearing in the Education Endowment Foundation's four kinds of trial: 'effectiveness'; 'efficacy'; 'pilot'; and 'scale-up' (https://educationendowmentfoundation.org.uk/tools/promising/).

Ethical requirements for clinical trials are legion, involving: informed consent (as a continuing process rather than a single event); rights to withdraw; do no harm; correct and full randomization; blinding (single, double, triple); risk analysis and risk management; protections for vulnerable participants; protections and liabilities; avoidance of bias; Zelen's design; ensuring that the RCT is essential and important; ensuring that the RCT answers a significant question to which a current answer is not available or which cannot be gained by an alternative method; and ensuring that the intervention is designed to bring about improvements in participants and society in comparison to the existing situation – the issue of beneficence.

Such ethical matters apply to RCTs in education. Additionally, Cohen et al. (2018) identify ethical issues, many of which resonate with those in clinical trials, including:

- informed consent;
- confidentiality and anonymity;
- identification and non-traceability;
- privacy;
- dignity and respect;
- non-maleficence;
- beneficence and duty of care;
- responsibilities (for what and to whom);
- gaining access;
- avoidance of coercion;
- disclosure and public versus private knowledge;
- relationships and differential power relations in research;
- interests at stake in the research (in whose interests the research is operating);
- rights, permissions and protections;
- ownership and control of data;
- access to data (and its archiving);
- the roles and power of research sponsors and commissioners;
- sensitive research;
- gender, age, colour, (dis)ability and ethnicity issues;
- researching with children;
- researching with vulnerable parties;

- avoidance of selective, partisan and skewed data analysis;
- value positions in data interpretation;
- responsibilities to different parties;
- being judgemental.

To this can be added, from clinical research, the issue of equipoise (individually or collectively): the researcher or research community is genuinely uncertain as to whether the intervention will 'work' in terms of making a positive difference both in efficacy trials and effectiveness trials, i.e. to rule out researcher bias (Jadad and Enkin, 2007).

Many RCTs in the social sciences are expensive (e.g. the Education Endowment Foundation was reported to be spending half a million pounds sterling per RCT; Lortie-Forgues and Inglis, 2019a) and collective (located within specific research communities; Upshur, 2000).

Finally, medical evidence is not a 'once and for all' matter; it is provisional (never absolutely certain), defeasible (revisable in light of further findings and research), emergent (changes over time), incomplete (for many reasons, including ethics and politics), constrained (by resources at the time). In short, medical evidence is fallible. So are RCTs in education.

Conclusion

RCTs in medicine and education, whilst sharing some common features, are inherently different. Some of the care and cautions observed in clinical trials can and should apply to education, e.g. pre-trial development and testing; oversight of ethics and approvals for RCTs; risk analyses and cautions; ensuring that standardized protocols and procedures are in place and operating in the RCT; attention to personal factors; ensuring that measures of efficacy and success are differentiated for different groups and individuals; ensuring validity, safeguards, reliability and utility; patient/client screening; attention to the educational equivalents of a range of factors: dose–response (strength, quality, intensity, duration and variance); personalized treatments; risk analyses and management; contextual factors and 'noise'; co-morbidities; co-medications; side-effects; long-term effects; sub-group outcomes and outliers as well as overall averages; unanticipated outcomes; initial diagnosis; blinding; claims for generalizability; attention to causality; ongoing monitoring; the complementarity of other sources of evidence in evaluating and contributing to RCTs; and statistical power analysis.

RCTs in education can learn many lessons from the care that attends their counterparts in clinical trials, addressing, where appropriate, the educational equivalents of the clinical practices set out in this chapter, i.e. to be more demanding. Clinical trials bound carefully their scope and admit that they might be fallible; that is a salutary lesson for RCTs in education, which should be more rigorous, claiming less for their generalizability, and being massively more modest in their claims.

Chapter 7

Contexts and outcomes in randomized controlled trials

Introduction and overview

RCTs in education require strict, rigorous, targeted and differentiated RCTs, with attention to sub-sampling. RCTs must also target and take account of the whole person, contexts, of the dynamical systems nature of the 'careers' of participants, and of the social situation and contingencies operating at the time, but Pawson (2006) remarks that 'human volition', agency and voluntarism, an essential part of being human, are regarded, regrettably, as contaminators in RCTs (p. 27).

This chapter has several points:

- The importance of including context in RCTs (which often over-ride or neglect context). Whilst process data can make a contribution here, the issue concerns the importance attached to context. RCTs are not good at addressing the significance of context.
- Whilst real-world and field RCTs might claim to include context, the *role* of context is understated, and this bears on reliability, validity, generalizability, credibility and utility of the RCT.
- An RCT does not happen in a vacuum, yet the mire of everyday worlds is often put down as 'noise', whereas it is an essential driver of what happens and 'what works'. It is not simply 'noise'; it is the 'signal' rather than the 'noise'. Building out context and what happens in the everyday world surrounding the RCT, impinges directly on the RCT.
- Contextual factors are central to understanding 'what works', why and how, as they enable an intervention to work or obstruct it from working, moderating and/or mediating its operations and outcomes.
- If one builds context and contextual variables and factors into the RCT, how one controls for these is problematic, as controlling them out overlooks their influences and real effects on the outcomes. RCTs' claims to over-riding such factors limit their usefulness.
- Conducting an RCT in classrooms does not necessarily *build in* context.

- To say that an RCT finds outcomes once variables and factors are controlled, singling out an independent variable as being the cause of an effect, is to miss the point: outcomes are what they are *because of* the context.
- In order to be fair, an RCT must adhere to standard procedures and protocols, but these rarely, if ever happen or can happen, as participants (e.g. teachers and students) tailor what happens and what they do to their own situation.
- How acceptable or possible is it to 'control' – to hold variables constant – in real life?
- What outcomes really indicate, and whether they really show that something 'works', is questionable, raising issues of validity and reliability.

The chapter makes the case for a nuanced analysis of 'what works', something that is difficult, if not impossible, for an RCT to address sufficiently.

The importance of context and controls

'Context matters' (Cartwright, 2019, p. 72). That the interaction between the intervention and the setting or the context can exert an effect on the outcome is neither novel nor unnoticed (e.g. Campbell and Stanley, 1963). During the course of the program, a range of factors might come into play which were unanticipated, which cannot be 'controlled out' and which might exert a sometimes massive influence on the program. Unlike the world of the laboratory, this is the reality of social and human settings (Slavin (1986) suggests that RCTs undertaken under laboratory conditions might not translate into actual classrooms). It is difficult to see how RCTs handle matters of context, despite Connolly's et al.'s (2017; 2018) assertions to the contrary and their reference to the increasing use of classroom-based RCTs. Connolly et al. (2018) comment that it is incorrect to say that RCTs ignore context, as 38 per cent of studies that they found included process evaluations (though, as they say, this is not a reliable indicator that they have taken account of context) (p. 288).

Controlling factors and variables in the classroom to the extent required for an RCT to be reliable and valid may be impossible, and asserting that randomization overcomes this is a chimera, even though large scale RCTs might move towards greater balance of the effects of many small differences in participants. How can, or should, a teacher/researcher really control out variables? It is a nonsense. The issue concerns the reliability and validity of the RCT and what can be taken from it, including matters of attrition.

There is a need to identify exactly what is happening in the program or intervention, i.e. the processes that are taking place in them. RCTs need more process data in order to avoid their black box nature (Sheffield Hallam University, 2015, p. 1), yet they may be unable to take sufficient account of, or may not be concerned with, processes (and having process data does not guarantee that they are used to identify exactly what is happening during the RCT), yet it is precisely this sort of evidence that is important. Non-cognitive outcomes may be neglected in RCTs, and RCTs focus on whether a particular intervention brings its desired and/or intended outcome, regardless of the cost (widely defined).

Other things are happening in classrooms at the same time as the RCT takes place, and to imagine that these do not affect the RCT is fanciful, even though randomization attempts to balance out the effects of these in the control and treatment groups. RCTs, operating in arenas where other events and activities are taking place at the same time and producing outcomes of their own, cannot simply rule these out or hold them static and/or fixed, as: (a) classrooms are dynamical, displaying the emergence of open systems in complexity theory and dynamical systems theory (Morrison, 2002, 2008); (b) the connectivity of variables and factors in classrooms means that changing or manipulating one variable in an RCT, be it exogenous or endogenous, will change other variables and factors in the classroom which, in turn, affect the RCT, e.g. changing the context of the RCT: it no longer operates in the original, same context and with the same causal probabilities (Kvernbekk, 2016, pp. 133–134).

The RCT does not operate in a vacuum, nor does it confine its effects to the RCT alone. To think otherwise is the optimism of over-simplification and the neglect of how causality operates in multiple, mutually informing, recursive webs of influence. An RCT in a classroom or classrooms has a knock-on effect on the context; it changes the context, 'causal webs', 'causal cakes' and connections and the influence of these on the effects. As complexity theory tells us, we should regard systems holistically rather than as an atomized constellation of discrete, isolated and isolable elements.

Where is context really taken into account in the RCT (i.e. not just conducting an RCT in a classroom)? How does context affect outcomes? Which contextual factors are important, which are not, and how is 'importance' decided, and by whom? Classroom-based RCTs purport to take account of contexts, but how are these controlled and faithful to the standard procedures of the RCT, how do they avoid simply paying lip-service to context, how do they affect causality? How are classrooms any more than the arena for the RCT? Which contextual variables matter, which is/are essential for establishing generalizability and causality? Koutsouris and Norwich (2018) make a powerful argument for the inclusion of context in interpreting RCTs, commenting that it is preferable to replace asking whether somethings 'work', with how they 'work' or do not 'work' for particular parties in the conditions, contexts and circumstances of the RCT in question, not least as RCTs in education operate in situations where multiple and high-density, complex factors are present and in which the interventions themselves are complex (p. 940). They argue that it is these contextual, 'real world' factors that affect whether the results are generalizable. As Pawson (2013) remarks, the driving questions concern the factors that make an intervention 'work', for whom, in what conditions and contingencies, over what period of time, and in what respects (p. 167).

Sullivan (2011) suggests that education, being a highly complex system, fits poorly with an RCT, as the latter requires clear criteria for including and excluding variables, together with interventions that are assuredly administered identically (e.g. by teachers), which may be impossible (p. 285). Frueh (2009, p. 1079) remarks that excluding and including variables, often focusing on a single variable of interest, overlooks broader contexts and applicability. Wrigley and McCusker (2019) comment that the procedures of RCTs might render inactive other factors present which exert a negative, distorting, strengthening or weakening influence on the matter being investigated (p. 115).

How do the operation and interaction of multiple causal mechanisms in specific contexts feature in identifying which features of 'context' are important? Many RCTs actively build out and exclude key elements of context, regarding them as 'contaminators', yet it could be these very factors that are important, and which contribute to overcoming Type I and Type II errors (false positives and false negatives respectively). What other things are happening in classrooms at the same time as the RCT, which might help, hinder, over-determine or under-determine the outcomes of the RCT? Without *using* (rather than simply reporting) process data, RCTs are weak for identifying causes (plural), causal mechanisms and causal processes; educators need more than simply knowing *if* something does or does not 'work'; they need an understanding of causal mechanisms – 'why' and 'how', not simply 'what' – for them to work in specific contexts.

Connolly et al. (2017, 2018) oppose suggestions that RCTs build out context, arguing that they take place in the real world of classrooms and that they draw on both qualitative and quantitative data. Along with them, Julnes and Rog (2009) argue for mixed methods approaches in understanding complex and interacting causal mechanisms (p. 104). But how are such contexts *really* taken into account; how do they affect the way in which the RCT operates, and with what effects; how do they make a difference to the RCT and its outcomes; how to they affect causality? Just because they take place in a context is not the same as showing how the context affects the RCT. And how do contexts feature in meta-analysis, meta-meta-analysis and systematic reviews (Chapter 12); they appear to be discarded here. Whilst quantitative methods might suggest the supposed magnitude of an effect or impact, qualitative data might suggest the causal processes at work, and their complexity, and this might be important for policy decisions (Julnes and Rog, 2009, pp. 105–106). But, as Greene (2009) remarks, whilst simplicity and certainty are attractive to governments and policy makers, by contrast, research and evaluation typically deal with uncertainty and complexity (p. 158).

Pawson and Tilley (1993) argue that striving to control the influence of extraneous factors, by random assignation of participants to control and experimental groups and controlling out variables, risks preventing researchers from identifying those very factors that might be contributing to the success or failure of a program or intervention, i.e. precisely the sort of information that might be useful to policy makers. Clarke and Dawson (1999, p. 54) observe that it is the *people* in a program that cause it to work, not simply the program itself. This may be important to policy makers, for it may enable money to be allocated more efficiently and effectively. For example, if it is the participants' motivation rather than the actual contents of a program that are the critical factors in a program's success, then chan-nelling money, let us say, into material resources rather than into human resources and human resource management (e.g. increasing the number of teachers of students with special needs) might be misplaced.

Added to this, Cohen et al. (2002) note that teachers use the same resources in different ways and with considerable variation in the results of using them differently; what teachers and students do with resources has consequences that are just as important as what the resources actually are (p. 86), and some teachers are much more effective than others in using resour-ces to promote learning (p. 91). How teachers use resources also varies according to their philosophies of teaching and learning (p. 93).

An RCT might fail to catch, or ignore or over-ride, the complexity and significance of teacher–student interactions, and education comprises an ongoing, dynamic interplay of systems, contexts and people that may not be captured in a single RCT. Whatever the justification offered (reductionism in order to gain clarity), RCTs over-simplify the 'real world'. Contamination and the Hawthorne effect may occur in the RCT, and other factors operate, like it or not. This presents a problem for RCTs: if they ignore, over-ride or take no account of classroom factors, then they can be accused of being unfaithful to the real-world setting of the RCT; however, if they include and take account of classroom-related factors then they can be accused of build-ing in contaminating factors and reducing generalizability.

Outcomes of RCTs and judging 'what works'

A single intervention does not produce only one outcome; it produces sev-eral, even though the RCT might only measure one outcome. What if out-comes vary by schools, in, for example, a cluster RCT, and these differences cannot be attributed to implementation differences (Julnes and Rog, 2009, p. 104)? And what if the measurable outcomes overlook other important out-comes? 'What works' is neither absolute nor unambiguous; a treatment for cancer can remove the cancer but it might also bring several side-effects, e.g. hair loss, amputation, sickness and gross lethargy. In other, perhaps non-life-threatening cases, the 'treatment' might be worse than the illness.

Judging 'what works' in RCTs should require pre-specifying the intended goals or outcomes of a program or intervention (e.g. to avoid 'dredging': searching for any relationships or findings that were not the initial concern of the RCT). In an RCT, the intended outcome might be expressed singularly (e.g. raising student achievement in mathematics, as measured in examination grades), but this belies the fact that educational programs have *several* aims in different domains, and, therefore, several outcome measures, metrics and qualitative data may be necessary. Identifying which effects are consequences of which elements of the program may be difficult. Further, recognizing that there are several outcomes of an intervention or program requires a judgement to be made about the relative importance or priority to be given to each outcome. RCTs neglect this. Focusing on one outcome alone, and neglecting others, is arguably unethical.

An outcome measure must demonstrate validity, measuring not only what it is intended to measure, but ensure that this is interpreted *contextually*, even though some RCTs have a very limited focus. A simple, narrow measure might be possible in an RCT that is examining the effects of a particular fertilizer on crop yields in the natural sciences (as in Fisher's (1966) seminal work), or the action of a particular drug on the human body in medical science, but, in interpersonal and personal situations, notions of improvement are ethical and much more wide-ranging. This is to suggest that outcome measures should catch actual outcomes, and that outcome measures will necessarily have to be interpreted comprehensively and in context (Rossi and Freeman, 1993). RCT's outcome measures, however, may focus on the easily quantifiable instead of the important outcomes (Manzi, 2012, p. 80). Indeed, Major and Higgins (2019) note that simpler outcomes are easier to show improvement than more complex outcomes (p. xxiii).

Concerns about RCT's resonate with Pawson's (2013) comment that, considering implementation, an intervention would be well advised to use such-and-such a method, targeted to such-and-such a group, and aware of the pitfalls of such-and-such (p. 190) (see also Healy et al., 2014). This is echoed by Pearce and Raman (2014) in their comment on the relation between RCTs and policy making, suggesting that advocates of RCTs could help institutions more by putting evidence from RCTs into their 'proper context' by clarifying the conditions under which such interventions do or do not work, and why (p. 398).

Conclusion

Context is an indisputable element in the 'what works' agenda; its role must be elevated beyond simply process data to issues of causality, and RCTs operate a restricted view of causality and its mechanisms.

Context requires attention to causality, what and how causality is operating. This harks back to Chapter 3, and it is taken up again in Chapter 12: context affects generalizability. Further, context is not simply 'noise' that must be controlled out of the RCT; it is an essential ingredient in 'what works' and is intimately connected to matters of validity, reliability and utility. For RCTs to operate within and across given contexts that may differ from each other, standard procedures and protocols for the RCT must be operating. However, these risk understating the significance of human behaviour since, as professionals, people 'do something' with standard procedures, modifying them for the situation in hand. It is impossible, even undesirable or unethical, to expect standard, uniform procedures for an RCT in education to be followed slavishly in differing contexts, with different participants. Whilst the extent to which this undermines the reliability of the RCT may be an open question, it is surely incumbent on researchers to ensure that sufficient uniformity of procedures obtains. However, this, too, is a challenge: even the same word, in the same sequence, with the same emphasis and intonation, spoken by the same single person, means different things to different people. 'No' in native English speakers, means 'no'; in first-language Spanish speakers it can mean 'yes'.

All of this calls out the banality of 'what works'.

Chapter 8

Design issues in randomized controlled trials

Introduction and overview

The design of RCTs in education poses serious challenges. Whilst, at first sight, an RCT might appear to be straightforward, in practice it is not so. The chapter:

- raises ethical issues in RCTs, which might be partially but never completely soluble;
- indicates that timing and duration of an RCT and its outcome measures are problematic;
- suggests that, whilst it is important to pre-specify intended outcomes and success criteria of the RCT, in practice this is complex because it begs many questions, e.g. 'for whom'; 'in whose terms does something "work"'; 'under what conditions'; 'in what circumstances'; 'using what criteria'; 'at what cost/benefit';
- notes that pre-specifying outcomes risks overlooking other outcomes that might eventuate;
- notes that specifying outcomes might be simplistic and/or highly selective;
- argues that 'what works', being a valuative judgement, varies according to the values and perceptions of different parties;
- suggests that the rigour of an RCT must be built into its design, and that this raises questions such as: how clearly the intended purposes, research questions and outcomes of the RCT are stated; how appropriate and practicable is the design of the RCT; how acceptable are the criteria for judging the RCT's success and whether the intervention has 'worked'; how true to 'real life' is the RCT; what safeguards and supervisory oversight of the RCT operate, and how suitable and effective these are; and what actions are taken to enable the control group to have access to the benefits of the intervention if the RCT turns out to be efficacious.

The chapter argues for the importance of including teachers' views in judging 'what works' from an RCT, together with how it works, as they draw on a wider field of concern than simply an RCT in judging 'what works'.

Ethical issues

The perhaps seductive simplicity of the desire to find 'what works' by using RCTs disguises a range of complex factors, ethical as well as empirical. With regard to ethical questions one could not say that the end justifies the means, and in practical terms it might be unclear exactly how to judge 'what works' (Levačić and Glatter, 2000, p. 11). I might find, for example, that constant negative harassment of teachers by a school principal increases the amount of time they spend on lesson preparation, which might (or, indeed might not) improve lesson quality. However, it might be difficult to defend such behaviour ethically. The results might be effective in the short term, but such behaviour might also be counter-productive, as the poor interpersonal relations, the hostile atmosphere, the 'blame culture' and the demotivation of teachers caused by the principal's behaviour might lead to rapid staff turnover and the reduction in teachers' commitment to their work. Ethical behaviour involves not exposing participants to hazardous situations or materials (see Chapter 6 on risk assessment and risk management).

Concerns have been raised about the questionable ethics of randomization in denying control groups access to potentially positive interventions (e.g. Burtless, 2002; Cook and Payne, 2002). The immediate answer to this is that, in fact, underpinning an RCT is the view that the researchers simply do not know if a treatment is or is not beneficial or more beneficial than an alternative ('equipoise'), and that, indeed, the purpose of the RCT is to answer this. Assigning participants to a control group may spare them from exposure to a damaging treatment (though this should have been ruled out in development and prior approval of the RCT). This also raises the necessity of avoiding doing harm to participants: the principle of *primum non nocere*. Indeed, this is used as a justification for an RCT, *viz.* to discover whether, in fact, an intervention does harm, with safeguards (risk analysis and risk management) built into the RCT, or compensation arrangements being made.

There are other ethical issues, too. Gueron (2002) notes that money spent on RCTs should not be taken from what would otherwise go into normal service provision, and Boruch et al. (2002) note that, for an RCT to be conducted requires that a serious, rather than trivial, matter should be under investigation (p. 65), and that: (a) the results would not be discoverable by other, non-RCT methods; (b) results should impact on policy making; (c) participants' rights not to participate are respected (pp. 65–67); and (d) needs analyses must be conducted before a decision is taken on whether to run the RCT (p. 73).

Added to these issues is the matter of informed consent. Whilst informed consent is important, it is not only often breached (Oakley, 2000, p. 288), but it is also complex (Cohen et al., 2018, pp. 122–127), as it raises a lengthy list of concerns, e.g.:

- Should consent be an individual, family, institutional or communitarian decision?
- Who gives consent, and for whom, for what and for how long (e.g. longevity of data storage)?
- What constitutes 'consent'?
- Who is competent to give consent, and on whose behalf?
- Can children over-ride parents' wishes?
- What pressure (deliberate or not) on people and institutions is there to give consent?
- What does 'voluntary' really mean in 'voluntary consent'?
- In whose interests is consent given or withheld?
- How is consent given in different cultures?
- How to protect vulnerable people in giving consent?
- What degree of informality and formality is appropriate in consent giving?
- What are the possible consequences (and to whom) of consent or non-consent?
- How do power differentials affect consent giving?
- Is biological age of consent 'good enough' for giving consent?
- What are the relationships between consent and confidentiality?
- How much information is necessary to give or withhold from participants when asking for informed consent (what does 'fully informed' mean and require)? ... .
- How can consent be given when what happens may not be fully known in advance of the research (e.g. in exploratory research)?

(Cohen et al., 2018, p. 125)

What starts out as a simple label – 'informed consent' – raises a long list of concerns. Arguments can be raised against informed consent (*ibid.*, pp. 126–127), e.g. in the interests of not disturbing a situation, enabling access to be achieved, and as gaining informed consent might affect outcomes and data.

Cook and Payne (2002) and Connolly et al. (2017) note that, if something 'works', then the control group can be exposed to it at a later date after the RCT; however, this may not be good enough. For example, let us say that I want to try out an intervention to improve language learning in a group of students; in the first semester I can give the intervention to the intervention group, and then give the intervention to the control group in the second semester. However, the language skills that the first-semester students have learnt are able to help them in the second semester and thereafter, whilst those in the second semester group miss that opportunity for one semester's benefit, i.e. the time available might raise ethical issues. Further, to say that the premise of the experiment is that we don't know whether something will 'work' may not be good enough, as, for example, in clinical research, an experiment is typically not permitted to be undertaken unless there are good reasons for believing that it will be efficacious and bring benefit (Chapter 6).

Ethics are also related to sampling. In medicine, ethical questions are raised if participants might be subjected to potentially hazardous treatments. Further, Fitz-Gibbon and Morris (1987) report drawing the sample from 'borderline cases' only for the control group; patients in greatest need of treatment/intervention are not deprived of it, and it is only those patients who are at the borders of needing treatment who are randomly assigned to control or experimental groups (Clarke and Dawson, 1999, p. 29). Whilst the borderline method might make for ethical practice, it limits the generalizability of the results. Further, if informed consent is to be obtained from participants, then this might skew the sample to volunteers, who may or may not be representative of the wider population.

Ethical issues are raised in terms of the limits of the RCT. RCTs which are concerned with outcome measures have been criticized for being elitist (Julnes and Rog, 2009) in that the voices and values of the participants are either not included or are subordinated to a simple outcome measure. In such circumstances, the authors ask, how are respect for persons, beneficence, risk reduction, and justice (the fair distributions of benefits and burdens of the research across different participants and stakeholders) addressed (pp. 117–118)?

Further, outcome measures, whilst attractive to policy makers and accountability enthusiasts, risk furthering the preoccupation with testing and measurement in high-stakes and low-stakes testing, both in terms of the validity of measuring education against such impoverished criteria and in terms of the backwash effects in narrowing education to test performance on prescribed, pre-determined, uniform outcomes: standardized minds (Sacks, 1999). RCTs all too easily fall into the trap of the agendas of the accountability and testing lobby, occasioning high levels of stress in students and the sheep/goats view of education: some succeed whilst other are consigned to failure. Who decides outcomes, why are RCTs designed to address them, and what side effects can these have on children and young minds?

This ethical concern extends to the use of evidence and beneficence, as those who provide the evidence may not be the ones who take the decisions on its uses and consequences, raising questions of the obligations of the researchers to those who provided the evidence. As Willard Whyte observed in his study of 'street corner society' (Whyte, 1955), the local community had helped many researchers to become famous and get their doctorates, but they had left the locals' quality of life with no improvement. Similarly, Willis and Saunders (2007, p. 96), reporting on indigenous groups, commented that they had been incessantly and minutely interrogated, poked and prodded by outside 'experts' but had been left impoverished.

Duration and timing of RCTs

The duration of the RCT is critical; indeed, Chapter 12 notes that meta-analyses and meta-meta-analyses which combine studies of different duration overlook the important issue of the duration of each RCT. A short-term RCT may have a significant short-term impact but no lasting impact, or indeed the opposite may be true – the RCT has only a delayed, long-term impact. An RCT over a longer period of time may encounter severe problems of attrition, contamination and changes of contextual factors over the duration of the trial. We need to know whether shorter or longer interventions make for smaller or larger effects (Higgins, 2018, p. 24).

How long does it take for an RCT to 'work', i.e. to have an impact? Three weeks, three months, six months, a year? Gueron (2002) argues for the need to have a suitably large sample and to run the RCT for a sufficiently long time for potential impacts to be detectable and reliable: too short a time, or too small a sample, and emergent impacts may go undetected. In education, treatment may need to last for years (p. 19).

Duration is one of the key variables, yet it is understated in planning and reporting RCTs. How did the researcher decide how long the intervention would last? How was that decision reached? Was the decision evidence-based, or a hunch, or time available, or based on what? Would the RCT have 'worked' or 'worked' better or worse if it had run for longer? What is the optimum time for the intervention? We don't see such concerns or justifications appearing in the RCT literature, yet it is akin to the importance of the dose–response in clinical trials: over how long a period of time, and with what frequency and intensity, must the intervention last for it to be effective?

There is no single one-size-fits-all duration of the RCT, as: (a) the deeper the intervention, the longer it might take to become embedded; (b) the number, frequency, intensity and duration of each of the sessions of the intervention have an impact on outcomes; (c) the timing of the pre-test and the post-test influence the assessed outcome; (d) the duration of the post-test affects the assessed outcome (if the post-test is long then students' concentration may flag or, by contrast, it may enable a fuller picture to be obtained of their performance). At issue here is the need for the RCT to justify its duration, decisions on the number, frequency, intensity and duration of each intervention session, the timing of the pre-test and post-test (or, indeed post-tests (plural) over a time period), but it is rare to see such justifications appearing in studies – they report but do not justify. Funding agencies may not be prepared to wait for years for an RCT to show results, yet some outcomes may need such a time scale for a valid result to appear.

It might take time for an effect to manifest itself. As Morrison (2009) writes, students might hate studying Latin, considering it to be a worthless, dead language, but then, after, say, 30 years, they see its usefulness in understanding the English language and its etymology, or even other languages (p. 49).

At what point does the post-test occur? The timing of the post-test rehearses the concerns raised by curvilinearity: in the short term, raising stress can improve performance but in the longer term it is detrimental to health. Drinking copious amounts of coffee can bring temporary stimulation but in the long term can be damaging. A short, sharp stay in a harsh prison regime might show a brief decline in recidivism (e.g. the 'Scared Straight' programme, which turned out to be a failure), but, in the longer term, it might make no difference to rates of recidivism (see also Prigogine's and Stengers's (1985) discussion of dissipative structures and the movement towards entropy).

Whilst it might be useful for an RCT to find a short-term result, Morrison (2009) argues that taking measures too soon overlooks the long-term effects and whether effects are ephemeral and short-term: '[t]oo early an evaluation may find no effect; too late an evaluation, and the effect may have petered out … . [E]ffects may be short-lived' (p. 49).

A cause may not reveal itself immediately. There may be an 'induction period' (the time taken to develop, for example, as in a disease), and the last point in the causal chain is not the entire cause, even though its induction time is zero in the sense that it is contiguous with the effect. As Morrison (*ibid.*) argues: cancer may take a long time to develop (i.e. a long induction period), and may have a long 'latency' period (i.e. present but undetected) (p. 51). In the context of an RCT, can we really assume that the cause only commences when the RCT commences, or whether several supporting causal factors and conditions in the intervention group have existed prior to the intervention but have not existed in the control group, which controlling out variables is unable to detect?

Here the trajectories of groups may not be the same: let us imagine that the measured performance in mathematics of the control group members happened to be on a downward trajectory over time (e.g. months) before the RCTs took place, whilst that of the treatment group was upward (see Figure 8.1). At the point of the RCT ('the pre-test time') the pre-test scores of the two groups were the same, but the post-test scores were very different because of the different trajectories of the groups. The trend line for the control group (thin dotted line) is downward, whilst that of the treatment group (thick dotted line) is rising. This could present a Type I error: a false positive, as the trend was happening anyway, regardless of the RCT.

In conducting RCTs, how is account taken not only of the measures, but of the timing, the duration of the intervention, and the presence or absence of causal conditions which may not be the same for the control and intervention groups?

Pre-specification of outcomes in an RCT

Whilst RCT's might identify and pre-specify their indicators of success and the kinds of evidence to be used to measure or evaluate success, there are larger issues of clarifying the terms and criteria for judging 'what works'. 'What works' has to be qualified in terms of: (a) 'what works for whom'; (b)

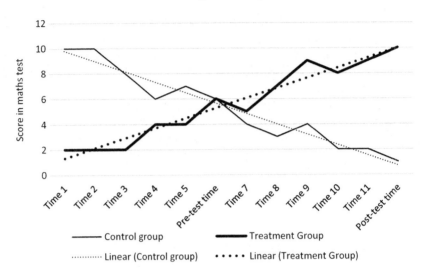

Figure 8.1 Trajectories of mathematics performance of control and treatment groups

'in whose terms "what works" is being judged'; (c) 'under what conditions, in what circumstances'; (d) 'using what criteria "what works" is being judged'; (e) 'compared to what'; and (f) 'at what cost/benefit "what works" is being judged'. The argument turns to these matters.

For example, imagine an RCT concerning the school principal's behaviour: an intervention might be judged a success in the principal's eyes, but, in the eyes of the staff, the intervention is a dismal failure; 'what works' for one party does not work in the eyes of another. Witness the debate about 're-engineering' the company (Nissan in the 1980s). Whilst for managers this made for a lean, efficient, profitable company, it was also a euphemism for massive job losses (Micklethwait and Wooldridge, 1997). In Japanese management practices, company officers saw a 'virtuous circle' of flexibility, quality and teamwork, whereas the same practices were seen by other (junior) participants as a vicious circle of exploitation, control and surveillance respectively (Wickens, 1987; Garrahan and Stewart, 1992). It is not that one party was correct and the other incorrect; both parties were correct but they had different perceptions of the same phenomena. This argues for the need to adopt a multi-perspectival position on observed phenomena and for a clearly stated set of pre-intervention-specified criteria for judging whether the RCT has 'worked', using what indicators and evidence, and how reliability and validity are addressed. It is difficult to see how RCTs can catch this spread of perceptions in judging 'what works', unless they include a range of outcome measures which, in turn, require comprehensive success criteria. Increasing homework may be effective according to a school principal, but may demotivate students from lifelong learning – clearly a failure in the eyes of students.

'What works' is a matter of judgement which is informed by data from RCTs; the data alone do not speak for themselves. As Chapter 2 indicated, 'evidence' is not neutral. Data have to be interpreted, weighed, judged, and considered. As with notions of worthwhileness or success, what works is a matter of discussion and debate, not simply of data; 'what works' is a value statement, not simply an empirical statement, and to neglect this is to commit a category mistake. This argument seriously undermines the putative 'value neutrality' of RCTs. As Nietzsche (1973) remarked, there is a point at which the philosopher's 'conviction appears on the scene' (p. 20). Behind the apparent autonomy of all logic there stand evaluations (*ibid.*, p. 17) – what we see is influenced by how and where we look (paradigmatic behaviour); it is value-based, and this risks bias.

The problem of bias (a threat to objectivity) lurks everywhere in an RCT. Jadad and Enkin (2007) identify bias in many areas:

- Selection bias (who is included in, and excluded from, the RCT).
- Ascertainment bias before and after the data collection (lack of blinding).
- Choice of question bias.
- Measurement bias (using measures of the *intervention* alone, thereby giving an unfair advantage to the intervention group).
- Regulation bias (e.g. over-restrictive or over-permissive review boards).
- Wrong design of researchers bias.
- Population and sample choice bias (e.g. non-random or selective).
- Recruitment of the participants.
- Selection of researchers bias.
- Allocation bias.
- Intervention choice bias (the timing of the pre-test and post-tests, e.g. testing at the time when chances of finding a result are at their optimum).
- Control group bias (poorly chosen control group).
- Outcome choice bias (unreliable, invalid, selective, simplistic measures).
- Withdrawal bias (attrition, violations of protocols and procedures).
- Selective reporting (cherry-picking positive results and not including negative results in the same study).
- Fraud bias (making up results).
- Publication bias (only publishing studies which report positive results).
- Language bias (publication in favoured languages).
- Time lag bias (speed of publication – positive results appear more quickly than negative results).
- Uptake bias (writer bias; reader bias) (pp. 29–47).

In total the authors identified 80 types of bias. Echoing Jadad and Enkin, Feinstein (1995) notes that believing that randomization alone prevents bias is simply dogma, as bias can arise at very many stages of an RCT (p. 78).

The pre-specification of outcomes, whilst important, risks missing catching unintended – and perhaps unmeasurable – effects of a program; it also assumes that outcomes can be operationalized and measured comparatively straightforwardly. But measures may only catch superficiality or highly selective outcomes (though Connolly et al. (2017) suggest that the inclusion of qualitative data may attenuate this). Further, Ayres (2007) argues that, whilst RCTs might provide information on the 'causal impact' of an intervention on a treatment group in comparison to a control group, human judgement is still required to interpret the data and their significance (p. 126).

An RCT may be entirely rigorous but, maybe as a consequence of meeting the canons of rigour by isolating and controlling out important factors of the experiment, leave only a 'trivial' or limited range of factors in the experiment; they yield little worth knowing. Indeed, Cartwright (2019) questions the whole notion of 'rigour', as conventionally conceived in RCTs, arguing that, at best, RCTs apply to a named population, including problems of using averages, but, beyond that, they are based on questionable principles of induction and might not apply to individual cases. Further, simply piling up studies commits the enumeration error of assuming that the more studies there are, the greater the degree of confidence that can be placed in what they show for an individual case, but they neglect important contextual and causal matters (*ibid.*). Whilst this is the same for any kind of research data, *viz.* they are retrospective and always in principle falsifiable, such that prediction is not absolutely certain, nevertheless, the predictive claims of RCTs underplay the limits of induction in a 'what works' agenda.

Even if causality is shown, it might be in such restricted, local, specific terms as to be non-transferable to other contexts. Whilst a single RCT may not expose 'hidden conditionals' that influence the effectiveness of a treatment, there is no guarantee that further RCTs will guarantee certainty that all the conditionals have been found (Manzi, 2012, p. 86). As Manzi argues, RCTs, on their own or in combination, do not 'self-generalize' (p. 89), and they may rely on other kinds of data to support their case and to explain why a program works better for some groups than for others (p. 172). Though constructing appropriate measures may be a technical matter, this is unlikely to be the sole resolution of the problem, as the judgement of adequate construct and content validity is not decided by measures alone; rather, it is deliberative and often requires the 'thick descriptions' (Geertz, 1973) of qualitative data.

RCTs operate with pre-specified goals; in the bigger picture of everyday classrooms, what works in an RCT may be incompatible with other factors that are taking place in the classroom. A reading intervention might raise students' measured achievements in reading but may provoke an intense dislike of books or reading for pleasure. Alternatively, if an RCT 'works', then it may have positive effects beyond its original, intended limits. An RCT which, for example, simply focuses on student achievement in X, is operating in an artificial, sealed world; this is blinkered, tunnel vision which conceals rather than clarifies effective practice. Interventions must be judged not only in their own terms but in terms of their compatibility with the overall conditions, contexts, programs, practices, purposes, operations, effects and values of the education of students.

What is being suggested here is that RCTs should be concerned not only with which interventions 'work', but, more specifically, in what ways, with what consequences, and with which people and, of course, which interventions do not 'work'. At one level, this is a matter of sampling and clarifying the parameters of generalizability, avoiding homogenizing disparate populations. At another level, the more one recognizes the uniqueness of situations, people, conditions and interactions, the less likely it is that replicability or generalizability are attainable. The question, then, becomes less about 'what works' and more about 'what works' with and for whom, in what conditions, and in what and whose terms. Recognizing this reinforces the importance of the teacher using RCTs only in her/his own unique context. As Winch et al. (2015) note, teachers are unlikely to accept a recipe for 'what works' that derives from research, as, inherently, research in education does not provide a definite, unequivocally usable outcome. At best, research can provide a 'reasonable warrant' for decision making by teachers, conditional on the particular circumstances that obtain in a situation (p. 210).

Simply providing *ex cathedra*, handed down recipes to teachers seriously misrepresents the nature of education and unworthily discredits teachers, however attractive such moves might be to policy makers. Of course, this occurs with other types of research, but the present argument concerns RCTs only.

Conclusion

Design issues in RCTs in education face serious challenges. These concern, for example, ethical issues, timing and duration, pre-specification of outcomes and too narrow a focus on these alone or largely. The problems extend to judging 'what works' in terms of outcomes, as this is conditional not only on a range of subtler factors than simply 'what works' in terms of pre-specified outcomes, but is also a matter of *judgement*, with different parties having different criteria and values.

A range of factors feature in terms of design: e.g. data collection, instrumentation – its size and scope – reliability and validity, sampling and sample size, statements of research purposes and intended outcomes, success criteria, representativeness of 'normal' everyday life in classrooms and contexts, ben-efits and costs, and modifications made to the RCT by participants in the RCT. The chapter has argued for the importance of including teachers in judging 'what works' from an RCT, together with their responsibilities in ensuring that an RCT runs according to plan. The design of the RCT affects the interpretation of the effect size – a frequently used statistic in deciding whether an intervention 'works' (Chapter 10). A key element of the design of the RCT is the sampling, and it is to this that the next chapter turns.

Chapter 9

Sampling in randomized controlled trials

Introduction and overview

Sampling in an RCT is critical, i.e. it can 'make or break' the reliability, validity and usefulness of the RCT and what can be taken from it. Representativeness of the sample is significant, and ensuring it is challenging. Measures of sampling error are insufficient here, as the characteristics of the target population must be known. Even if generalizability to a wider population is not intended, then this does not absolve the researcher from taking great care with sampling. Such care extends to:

- addressing randomization; though random *selection* might be impossible, random *allocation* is necessary though not always achievable;
- reviewing the appeal to *ceteris paribus* clauses in randomization;
- questioning whether randomization is preferable to matched samples;
- ensuring that sampling is fair to the homogeneity and heterogeneity of the population from which it is drawn;
- questioning how to handle outliers;
- addressing challenges raised by contamination and blinding;
- considering the benefits of, and challenges in, using cluster samples;
- respecting the importance of sub-sampling;
- considering ethical issues in sampling;
- addressing problems of attrition;
- recognizing that sample size is critically important but problematic.

Whilst random sampling is central to an RCT, ensuring that it occurs is not the panacea for the range of challenges facing RCTs, and randomization does little to assist an understanding of causality.

Samples, sub-samples and populations

To be credible, useful and generalizable, sampling in RCTs requires careful attention to the nature, size, access to, representativeness and nature of the sample and of the population from which it is drawn. The RCT's sample must fairly represent the target population in terms of key, relevant characteristics and the causal interplay and causal relevance of these; without this it is unlikely to generalize findings securely to the wider population. This means that the characteristics of the wider population and their causal inter-relationships must be known and fairly represented in the sample, otherwise the average effects calculated in the trial may not reflect the average effects obtaining in the population (Joyce, 2019). This requires any skewness in the population to be represented in the sample (Cartwright, 2019, p. 70), which, in turn, requires a knowledge of distributions in the population, and, indeed, a move away from randomization. It is important to represent not only the population in terms of demographics, but in terms of their causal characteristics, i.e. to demonstrate that demographics are *causal* and not simply the theatre or arena within which the actions of other causal factors take place (Goldthorpe, 2007).

Whilst random sampling (random selection and random allocation to the control or treatment group) is held up as most useful, in practice it is not always achievable (Deaton and Cartwright, 2018), and samples might be drawn from volunteers, or might be simply a convenience sample. Whilst it may be possible to randomly allocate to control or treatment groups, it is almost impossible to ensure that there is initial random selection of the sample (Cartwright, 2019). Many RCTs are conducted with biased sampling (Joyce, 2019).

If the population is heterogeneous then this should be reflected in the sample, but, even if it is, this might not guarantee that the sample fairly represents the population. If outliers are present in the population then account has to be taken of these in the sample, and this may lead to false positives or false negatives in calculating outcomes of the RCT. This is not to say that outliers should be removed, discussed below. We cannot assume that, simply because the distributions in the population are reflected in the distributions of the sample, this means that it is safe to calculate average treatment effects (which is what RCTs typically calculate). What may be true for the sample in an RCT may not be true for the wider population, discussed below.

Clarke and Dawson (1999), taking the example of RCTs in clinical practice, suggest that, in order to ensure that causality is clear, patients suffering from more than one illness (comorbidity) might be deliberately excluded from the RCT. This results, characteristically, in small or very small samples, and, in this case, there are limits to generalizability, typicality and representativeness. The same problem applies to education: in order to establish clear causality, the reduction of the sample to a subset might lead to very small samples. The results of the RCTs may, then, be 'true' but trivially so, i.e. unable to be generalized to any wider population or circumstance. The simple accretion of results from RCTs through meta-analysis is one approach to validating them, as is the prolongation of the duration of the RCT, but this is blind to other consequences and activities taking places all around the RCT, and, indeed, meta-analysis and meta-meta-analysis are not without their critics (Chapter 12).

Sampling bias may manifest itself in selection bias (Burtless, 2002), e.g. systematic differences in the sample, such as in volunteer samples. For example, a teacher may choose which students to be members of the control or experimental groups in an RCT (Henry, 2009), and such selection may not be random. Whilst blind, double-blind or triple-blind randomization may be possible in clinical trials, in the world of classrooms and schools, such blinding may be impossible (Bickman and Reich, 2009; Didau, 2015). Unlike in clinical trials, participants in educational research are likely to know if they are in the control or treatment group. When combined with differences in how the procedures of the treatment are carried out by teachers, i.e. how, when and where treatment and control groups operate in, for example, different classrooms, then caution must be exercised in suggesting that the results really demonstrate what is being claimed for them. This raises the issue, too, that, if an RCT in education is to avoid selection bias, then the sampling, in order to be random in selection and allocation (to treatment or control groups) should be controlled by the researcher, not the teacher, hence the teacher has to relinquish control over what happens in the school, classroom, curriculum, pedagogy and so on, which could be seen as compromising his/her professional responsibility for the students in his/her care.

For RCTs in educational research, benefits often come from analysing sub-sampling and sub-group targeted treatments with varied outcomes, as in personalized medicine, and researched in differentiated trials in the 'real world' (Goodman, 2009). This is a far cry from the relatively crude, undifferentiated RCTs that appear in education, which typically report statistical significance and a single, overall effect size. Connolly et al. (2018) comment on the importance of sub-group analysis in RCTs in education (with the caution advocated by Styles and Torgerson (2018) to avoid 'data dredging' for findings in sub-groups); Styles and Torgerson suggest that evidence from sub-groups 'should be a spur for a future trial of the intervention *on that subgroup* rather than viewed as a definitive conclusion' (p. 257).

Contamination and blinding

The teacher may be unable to avoid the problem of the control groups and experimental groups coming into contact with each other and, thereby, 'contaminating' the RCT. Having control and experimental groups in different schools or clusters of school can be one way of overcoming this (Torgerson and Torgerson, 2008; Hutchison and Styles, 2010; Connolly et al., 2017). However, running clusters for RCTs often involves very many schools, as each school is seen as a single unit (rather than the number of students participating in the RCT in that school). Cluster trials might have, for example, 5,000 students, but only 20 schools ($n = 20$): 10 schools in the control group and 10 in the treatment group; cluster trials are greedy.

The intention may be to operate single blind experiments (where students in the control group and the experimental group do not know to which group they belong), double-blind experiments (where none of the participants knows to which group they have been assigned or who is receiving the treatment or intervention), or triple blind experiments (where the data are coded in such a way as to prevent those processing the data from knowing to which groups the participants have been assigned). However, how realistic is this? Nash (1973) shows how quickly, accurately and insightfully students and teachers are able to appreciate exactly what is happening in classrooms. Some RCTs are impossible to blind, such as those in which the treatment itself prevents blinding (e.g. a new pedagogy in Mathematics teaching), or because of side-effects that were not present before the treatment, or adherence to procedures of the treatment make it obvious which is the treatment group. Blind RCTs in education are often impossible (Didau, 2015; Thomas, 2016; Wrigley and McCusker, 2019). Students and teachers notice if their practices are being changed. This can compromise reliability and validity.

Sampling and ethics

Sampling also raises questions of ethics (Chapter 6). For example, as in medicine, ethical questions can be raised about the randomization, wherein control groups might be denied access to treatment (e.g. the teacher's attention or access to resources) or where participants might be subjected to potentially hazardous treatments. Chapter 6 set out a range of ethical principles, underpinned by: beneficence (bring about the good of individuals, groups and society); *primum non nocere* (first, do no harm) and non-maleficence, with due diligence in matters of risk analysis and management; informed consent and avoidance of coercion, stress or duress; don't tell lies; avoid bias; ensure that the RCT is sufficiently rigorous; ensure rights to withdraw at any time or for the researcher to stop the RCT; justice (the RCT's outcomes do not exclude those who might benefit from the subsequent intervention, and Chapter 7 discusses the issue of students in the control group subsequently being given the intervention after the experiment has finished); and respect for people (e.g. Meinert, 2011; Cohen et al., 2018). The RCT proposal should also be reviewed and approved before commencing.

If informed consent is to be obtained from participants, then this might skew the sampling to volunteers, who may or may not be representative of the wider population. As Deaton and Cartwright (2018) note, people who choose to take part may do so because they feel they may benefit from it, i.e. it is in their interests, for whatever reason, and those who perceive no benefit from participation may decline to participate. Either way, this leads to a biased sample and affects the 'intention to treat' analysis.

Attrition

Sampling bias might occur through attrition. Heckman and Smith (1995) note that relying on results from RCTs can be dangerous if there has been a significant decline in the number of participants who actually complete the experiment.

Clarke and Dawson (1999, p. 130) draw attention to attrition, commenting on the fact that, in health care, treatments may produce adverse reactions, in which case patients are withdrawn from the experiment. Others might simply leave the experiment. That this contributes to 'experimental mortality' or attrition rates has been long recognized (Campbell and Stanley, 1963). Less clear in education, however, is how the problem has been, or might be, addressed (Rossi and Freeman, 1993), not least as it turns a random sample into a non-random sample. This might undermine putative parity between the control and experimental groups, a parity which, from arguments earlier about the range of participants and characteristics within and between groups, is already suspect. As the constitution of the groups changes, however slightly (and chaos theory reminds us that small changes can have massive effects), so the dynamics of the situation change, and the consistency and comparability of the research protocol and procedures, conditions, contexts and contents are undermined. To address this involves identifying not only the exact factors on which assignation of the sample to control and experimental groups will take place, but also identifying significant ways in which the two groups differ. The judgement then becomes about how far dissimilarities between the two groups outweigh their similarities. It also raises the question of whether matched pairs might be preferable to randomization.

Randomization and the *ceteris paribus* condition

RCTs raise questions about the *ceteris paribus* condition, discussed in Chapter 3 and below. Randomization is designed to prevent one kind of bias from entering into the trial from systematically assigning participants to control or treatment groups, and to hold approximately evenly balanced or evenly spread the distribution of potential, unknown sources of bias between the control and treatment groups. The larger the sample, the greater is the chance of balancing the effects of such factors (Manzi, 2012, p. 76). A random stratified sample is designed to improve the chances of reducing bias by identifying known confounding factors, as way to achieve control in 'a causally dense environment' (*ibid.*, p. 172). Randomization, rather than sampling size, increases sampling precision (Mayer-Schönberger and Cukier, 2013, p. 22).

Randomization requires samples to be drawn randomly from a population and then, in an RCT, for that random sample to be randomly assigned to either a control group or an experimental group. Gueron (2002) argues that random assignment cannot be a half-hearted affair; it must be an 'all-or-nothing process' (p. 26), as without this, bias is built into the RCT. Random allocation to either the treatment or control group is intended to balance out both the 'known and unknown factors' in an RCT (Joyce, 2019, p. 45). It is designed to draw, distribute evenly and balance across the control and experimental groups the effects of the myriad of small factors, enablers, confounders, inhibitors, variables present in a population, such that they cease to exert different effects (i.e. to compare like with like) (Angrist and Pischke (2009) note that this was not observed in the celebrated STAR experiments on class size (p. 18)).

Heckman (1991), Boruch et al. (2002) and Cook and Payne (2002) comment that randomization is designed to ensure that an RCT avoids systematic bias, even though differences may exist by chance between the control and treatment groups (p. 51). This is an argument for large rather than small samples (Morrison, 2012), to overcome the variation caused by random or 'extraneous variation' (see also Cook, 1999, p. 28; Connolly et al., 2017, p. 52).

However, as Manzi (2012) observes, 'all else is never equal' (p. 81). For example, in clinical trials, patients have a range of co-morbidities, life styles, ages, needs, home factors etc., and doctors take these into account when taking decision on how to treat patients (ibid.). Indeed, complex matters do not always respond to straightforward cause-and-effect algorithms (Jadad and Enkin, 2007, p. 26).

Randomization constitutes a response to Holland's (1986) 'fundamental problem of causal inference' (p. 947), in which a person cannot be in both a control group and an experimental group in the same experiment. However, even if Holland's 'fundamental problem of causal inference' is addressed (e.g. through repeated measures experimentation or randomization), it remains the case that potentially key drivers of causal change – the unique combination of small variables and conditions that are specific to individuals – are, in effect, excluded, controlled out by being accommodated and relegated to having no appreciable effects in an RCT. That, surely, is misconceived.

Cook (1999) notes that 'the better we can randomize', the greater the reliability that can be placed in the results (p. 29), and Fisher's seminal texts *Statistical Methods for Research Workers* (1925) and *The Design of Experiments* (1966) place great emphasis on randomization. For them, randomization is essential for a true RCT which seeks to generalize, to address the *ceteris paribus* condition, to over-ride the difficulty in isolating and controlling the many variables in a causal situation, and to eliminate bias in estimating treatment effects by randomizing sources of possible bias which balance the effects of many small variations amongst the control and experimental groups.

Randomization is a cornerstone of RCTs, and care must be taken to include sub-groups in the sample. Despite there being large samples in the experiment, and despite randomization in an attempt to ensure even distribution of small factors, problems of random selection and allocation remain, in that small differences may occur between the control and experimental groups in an RCT, even if measured performance at the start is the same between the two groups. Whilst those who suggest that randomization overcomes these, the appeal is to an *assumption* rather than a proof in the specific RCT in question. We can ask 'what if there is random assignment and there no difference on the pre-test of two groups, but if the *ceteris paribus* assumption is, in fact, wrong?' Randomization is a statistical convenience only, and it does not necessarily equalize the two groups and does not balance all the relevant variables in the same way in each of the two groups; the 'causal cake' in one group may differ from the causal cake in another group, even if the ingredients are the same – their weighting in the control group may be different from their weighting in the treatment group, producing different causal chains and impacts.

Randomization in educational RCTs might be difficult, e.g. in classrooms, students are already allocated to classes and there might be contamination if the control and experimental groups are in the same school, thereby risking violating a principle of the RCT which is that participants should not influence other members' responses to the intervention (Joyce, 2019, p. 46). In cluster samples it may not be possible to match clusters sufficiently. Further, Heckman (1991) argues that advocates of RCTs implicitly assume that randomization does not affect the program in question, but this assumption is questionable, and randomization does not guarantee that bias is impossible (p. 3) as agentic humans may react to randomization (p. 32).

Randomization may not be appropriate in some circumstances, indeed Worrall (2004, 2007) argues that there are many limits of randomization. He contends that, from its inception, Fisher's (1925) argument for randomization was suspect (that it underpins significance testing and that it somehow magically controls for all possible 'confounders') (Kvernbekk, 2018), and that Bayesian affiliates see no justification for randomization. Worrall (2004) remarks that randomization cannot be trusted to 'control for known confounders' (p. 24), and Cartwright (2019) notes that randomization does not ensure that causal factors are balanced, even at the moment of randomizing (p. 70). She gives the example of the false expectation that, in any series of coin-flipping, it is highly unlikely that there will be exactly half heads and half tails. Randomization may work well in a perfect world, with large-scale data and endlessly repeated flips of a coin, but real life is not like this. The nearest we can get is to suggest that, the larger the sample, the greater is the chance of obtaining balance, but this is not absolute (Davies et al., 2000, p. 259). Further, many discoveries and methods of investigation, including experiments, are not premised on randomization; many prefer to use matched samples/paired samples, in which each pair of participants (one in the control group and one in the treatment group) share every characteristic except for the particular one being investigated.

The orthodoxy of randomization being able to eliminate bias is only a statistical article of faith in RCTs, and Worrall (2007) argues that it would be 'a miracle' if all the factors operating in a situation happen to balance each other out simply by being based on a single random division. He suggests that the potential elimination of bias in having control and experimental groups can be obtained by stringent requirements in other forms of research, (e.g. matched samples and stratification), i.e. RCTs have no privileged position here. In answering this however, La Caze et al. (2012) argue that Worrall misrepresents the purposes of randomization, noting that, for making a probability statement, it is not necessary to know the values of those covariates that are not measured; rather, it is enough to know their distribution, and randomization provides a clear distribution in its experimental distribution on which statistical inferences can be based (p. 1).

Researchers must take account of error factors in the control and experimental groups, and this is challenging, as the size of the error term might, in reality, be unknown, even though it might diminish as sample sizes increase (Deaton and Cartwright, 2018, p. 4). Error factors can be different in the control and experimental groups, i.e. they can be 'unbalanced', and this can skew the average effects or undermine their usefulness (*ibid.*). This can have dangerous consequences, as 'the causality that is being attributed to the treatment might, in fact, be coming from an imbalance in some other cause in our particular trial' (p. 5), which differs within and between the control and experimental group.

It is important, they aver, to strive for identical error factors in the two groups, taking account of the contribution of other possible causes excluded from the study, in order to ensure that average effects are reliable and valid. However, they argue that this is rarely achieved. The implication here is that, in an RCT, the researcher should conduct a *post hoc* examination of the covariates to ensure that these are balanced between the control and experimental groups, and that 'if we suspect that an observed variable x is a possible cause, and its means in the two groups are very different, we should treat our results with appropriate suspicion' (*ibid.*, p. 6). Not to conduct this is to risk finding a false positive.

They note also that whilst, in a laboratory experiment, there is often considerable prior knowledge of other possible and actual causes (*ibid.*, p. 4), such that it is possible to control these out of the experiment, this might not be the case outside the laboratory. To address this, they suggest that matching might be used, where each subject in each of the control and experimental groups is matched as closely as possible in terms of all the 'suspected causes' (p. 4), a method that is frequently used in non-randomized medical case-control studies and in econometric studies. They note, however, that if there are 'unknown or unobservable causes that have important effects, neither laboratory control nor matching offers protection' (p. 4).

Deaton and Cartwright (2018) comment that 'in any single trial, the chance of randomization can over-represent an important excluded cause(s) in one arm over the other, in which case there will be a difference between the means of the two groups that is not caused by the treatment' (p. 4), i.e. there is 'random confounding' or 'realized confounding'. They report that Fisher was aware of this, and that he showed how randomization can provide the basis for calculating the error size (p. 4). They note, however, that Gosset (alias 'Student') rejected Fisher's argument for randomization in his field trial, preferring his own non-random designs, as they yielded greater precision in estimates of the effects of treatment (p. 5).

Banerjee et al. (2016) argue that a non-randomized case study can be more useful than an RCT. They give an example of a school superintendent who wishes to investigate whether it is the type of school that a student attends or whether home background (poor or privileged) is the decisive factor. Here the best design involves a double-intervention: sending a poor child to a private school and a privileged child to a public/state school (p. 10), and that this gives the lie to the point that research should balance treatment and control groups.

Deaton and Cartwright (2018) suggest that randomization can be used when the researcher has insufficient knowledge to be able to control out variables: observed and unobserved factors in the control and experimental groups (p. 5). However, they draw attention to the important difference between the actual and expected – hypothetical – balance of such variables in the two groups, and the importance of having a large sample size in order to reduce the impact of such factors. Although, as the sample size increases, so does the balance between the standard error of the control and experimental groups, it does not follow that having a large sample size automatically increases the net balance of errors, as this depends, also, on the number of possible causes that have been included and which might affect outcomes, and the sampling strategy; the researcher needs to know these in order to judge the validity and reliability of the claims being made from the experiment (p. 6). Larger samples tend to increase the precision of the findings, and, thereby the confidence that can be placed in the results (Lortie-Forgues and Inglis, 2019a, p. 159), though this can be financially expensive in recruiting large numbers of participants.

Randomized stratified sampling can also be useful in reducing imbalance. However, as Deaton and Cartwright (2018) indicate (p. 6), if stratification is to be useful, then the researcher needs to have some prior understanding of which background factors or causes should be included in stratifying, and this undermines the appeal of RCTs to require no prior knowledge. Further, they note that stratification is impossible if too many covariates are present or if there are too many values in each of them (p. 6).

The argument for or against prior information exposes different views at work. On the one hand, non-random methods which use prior information are useful in avoiding waste, increasing precision, building in safeguards, and behaving ethically. Deaton and Cartwright (2018) contend that refusing to use prior knowledge, related to RCTs 'are recipes for preventing cumulative scientific progress' (p. 7). On the other hand, using prior information is argued to be running counter to the credibility, disinterestedness, neutrality and fairness of the research, and, in fact, expert prior knowledge is not always as expert as it is believed to be (Ayres, 2007, p. 108). Indeed, using large-scale data processed by computers might make more accurate and reliable predictions than humans, and unemotional regression equations are more reliable than emotion-informed human judgement or opinion (*ibid.*, pp. 115–122).

The appeal of randomization here is to the *ceteris paribus* condition: all other things being equal. However, as mentioned in Chapter 3, this is dangerous territory, as it is impossible to know whether and how far all other things in fact are equal. The assumption of *ceteris paribus* overrules or rules out, the importance of central features of some educational activities and interventions, contexts, personalities, contingencies, constraints and key elements of the defining principles of education – the human factor. Indeed, the human and interpersonal sides of education, together with contextual factors, *must* be taken into consideration when judging 'what works' and the evidence for or against this, which derives from RCTs.

The question is not whether there are differences between the control group and experimental group, as it goes without saying that there are; it is whether these differences matter, whether, even though they are not the same in the control and treatment groups, they balance out each other; that is a matter of judgement, not simply of a statistic. Goldacre (2013) remarks that there are sufficient similarities between children to outweigh the differences between them (see also Cook and Payne, 2002, p. 157). So what? What if there is no *ceteris paribus*, i.e. that the two groups are not the same, but an outcome has been observed (which is probably the real situation)? How sceptical or rigorous must the user of the research be?

Given the argument for including apparently small variables and context, it seems perverse to operate the *ceteris paribus* condition which feature in randomization's attempt to override a multitude of confounding variables (Stone, 1993, p. 461), as to do this is to cast to the wind the very factors which might be exerting a causal effect on an outcome. The fact that there may be a hundred different causal influences operating for every hundred people, and that randomization is seen as a way of balancing out the distributions of uncontrollable differences in an uncontrollable myriad of variables, seems to miss the point, which is that the tiny, individual, different causal variables and conditions *do* make a difference, and that all other things are *not* equal, even if randomization seeks to overcome these and distribute them evenly.

Very small conditions – be they *initial* as in chaos theory or *emergent* as in complexity theory (Chapter 5) – can cause major, unpredicted changes. Whilst it might be convenient to over-ride these through randomization, nevertheless this is to marginalize the very factors that could bring about the changes consequent on the intervention or the causes. Gildenhuys (2010) argues that, whilst causal laws in science only hold true if the *ceteris paribus* condition is met, nevertheless if we do not possess any means of determining when or whether everything else is actually equal, then making generalizations such as *ceteris paribus* is simply hedging our bets and empty (p. 608). Indeed, *ceteris paribus* clauses are vacuous if interpreted as meaning little more than 'all things are equal, except when they are not' (Strevens, 2012, p. 18).

Randomization may impede an understanding of causality; frequencies and large samples may not prove causality; and the small variables excluded from, or over-ridden in, or evenly distributed in an RCT might exert a significant causal influence on effects. Cook (1999, p. 10) suggests that, on its own, random allocation is 'irrelevant' in providing explanations, and that it simply helps to *describe* the effects an intervention, and RCTs speak to an 'oversimplified theory of causality' (p. 11). Further, complexity theory and chaos theory frustrate attempts at meeting the counterfactual requirement of causation, since it is impossible to predict what would have occurred if the intervention had not happened (p. 49), and they frustrate the attempts to rule out the effects of small differences between the control group and the experimental group.

Fisher's (1966) comment that randomization, intended to overcome individual differences, 'will suffice to guarantee the validity of the test of significance, by which the result of the experiment is to be judged' (p. 21) is self-condemning, as: (a) contextual factors, as complexity theory tells us, can affect outcomes in ways that cannot be overcome by randomization; and (b) significance testing has limited value, telling the research only about the likelihood of the result occurring by chance rather than by how much participants might or might not benefit (Clay, 2010); one cannot read off from a general result or a significance test what will be the result for an individual.

Conclusion

Whilst sampling is a key element of an RCT, its demands are immense and are rarely met. This extends beyond recourse to the *ceteris paribus* clause, random selection and allocation, and representativeness, to consideration of whether matching samples might be more useful than random samples. Whilst contamination is a potential problem if the control and treatment groups come from the same institution(s), it can be addressed through cluster samples, but then the unit of analysis is the cluster, not the number of individuals or groups within the cluster, and this brings with it issues of the homogeneity, heterogeneity and spread of characteristics within and between the samples, sample size and costs.

Whilst the power of randomization is augmented by having large samples, as these can help to address the balance of the myriad of small differences between control and treatment groups, many RCTs operate with small samples, such that the statistical power of the sample is undermined and their generalizability is attenuated or compromised.

The chapter argued for the importance of embracing the spread of characteristics of the sample, that sub-sampling is important and that consideration must be given to outliers – whether to include or exclude them. The chapter argued that it is dangerous to exclude outliers, but this raises challenges in terms of how to include them whilst overcoming their potentially distorting effects (e.g. in terms of calculating averages of pre-test and post-test scores). The chapter also suggested using matched samples. Finally, the chapter suggested that randomization cannot address the gamut of challenges facing RCTs, and it does little to assist an understanding of causality.

Chapter 10

Data analysis in randomized controlled trials

Introduction and overview

Whilst Connolly et al. (2017) set store on regression analysis for RCT data, other approaches are also available to researchers, e.g. null hypothesis significance testing (NHST) and effect size calculations. However, these are problematic, and the chapter introduces several concerns about these and other concerns in data analysis in RCTs:

- statistical power;
- averages in data analysis;
- distributions and clustering in regression analysis;
- outliers;
- null hypothesis significance testing (NHST);
- effect size;
- what effect size really measures.

The chapter argues that NHST makes many assumptions which are unlikely to be met in RCTs, and that, even if they are met, NHST tells us very little. Further, even if large samples are used, with considerable statistical power, researchers must be cautious and fair in the claims that they make from effect sizes.

Statistical power

Statistical power is the probability that a study will detect a true effect, separating this from random chance, and correctly reject a false hypothesis (false positive) and a false null hypothesis (false negative) (Cohen et al., 2018, p. 211). Statistical power is a function of four elements: effect size; sample size and nature; the alpha (α) statistical significance level (typically set at 0.05 or lower); and the setting of an acceptable β level (overcoming the probability of a false negative).

Statistical power is influenced by sample size: the larger the sample, the greater the potential power. Cohen et al. (2018) suggest that, for statistical power, it is important to have a large sample, to set a large effect size, to keep the alpha (α) low (reducing the chance of a false positive), to have a homogeneous sample (or to increase the sample size in order to embrace the heterogeneity of the sample), to use a one-tailed test (which predicts the direction of the findings, e.g. a positive correlation), to ensure high reliability coefficients (e.g. the Cronbach alpha), and to use parametric measures (p. 752). They indicate that, for the frequently used alpha (α) setting of 0.05 and beta (β) setting of 0.20, yielding a power level of 0.80 (p. 751), small samples (e.g. below 100) may attenuate the claims made for the research.

For a power level of 0.80 with an alpha of 0.05, Lehr (1992) suggests that, for a pre-specified effect size of 0.8 (a comparatively large effect size), the sample size should be 25 in each group (the control and treatment groups), giving a total of 50 participants. For a pre-specified effect size of 0.5 (a moderate effect), the sample size should be 64 in each group, giving a total of 128 participants; for a pre-specified effect size of 0.3 (a small effect), the sample size should be 178 in each group, giving a total of 356. The smaller the pre-specified effect size, the larger is the sample size required in order to detect it (Torgerson and Torgerson, 2008, p. 128). (See Cohen et al. (2018) for a further analysis of Lehr's work.)

Cohen et al. (2018, pp. 211–212) also note that statistical power varies according to the test and measures used, echoing Simpson's (2018b) comment that effect size varies relative to the design of the research, including the design and contents of the data collection instruments used. Cohen et al. (2018) caution that, as statistical power is affected by effect size, alpha levels and beta levels, if one changes any one of these then the required sample size changes (p. 212).

Statistical power and its relationship to sample size and pre-specification of effect size, call into question those RCTs which have any one or more of small samples, high alphas, low betas and small effect sizes, and yet which make bold claims for showing 'what works'. Many RCTs, particularly small-scale RCTs, are underpowered, such that it is dangerous to place too much store on what they claim to show. Indeed, Lortie-Forgues and Inglis (2019a) report that, of the 141 trials that they reviewed, only 6 per cent of these had statistical power at 0.80 and the average statistical power was 0.23, with a median of 0.17, i.e. considerably lower than the commonly set power metric of 0.80 (p. 162).

The limits of averages

The measures used in RCTs typically focus on average results rather than outliers or important sub-sample differences (discussed below), and, unlike medical trials (Chapter 6), there are very few replication RCTs in education

(Makel and Plucker, 2014). Wrigley (2018) remarks that statistical averaging is not a suitable proxy for a broad base of evidence (p. 359), and that it neglects the 'accumulated experience' of practitioners, the wishes and needs of students, and understandings deriving from cultural and social contexts (p. 359). Mark (2009) suggests the need to identify the conditions under which the average effect should be given greater or lesser priority (p. 222). RCTs typically use aggregated and averaged data, rather than individual or grouped data, which overlooks the distribution and spread of data or the possibilities of following up on individuals or sub-groups.

Feinstein (1995) raises the disturbing question of who benefits from RCTs that only show average treatment effects (p. 73); educators want to know what works for individuals, not average people, whatever that latter means. Averages violate scientific precision (p. 76), an irony when RCTs claim to be 'scientific'; indeed, Lortie-Forgues and Inglis (2019a) comment that many large-scale RCTs have very limited precision and, therefore are uninformative (though Simpson (2019c) questions the premises of 'informative' and 'uninformative' used in their study, to which Lortie-Forgues and Inglis (2019b) respond by arguing for a wider derivation of these terms than that used by Simpson).

The usefulness of averages depends, in part, on how homogeneous the group is; it is difficult to see how useful they are when the spread of the population and/or the sample is wide. Phillips (2019) notes that, in fact, it is very rare, if at all, for an RCT to find that an intervention produces exactly the same effect on all the people in the intervention group; rather, it is more likely that some members of the intervention group will derive a lot from the intervention, others only a 'modest amount', others no benefit, and others might even sustain harm from it (p. 21).

Wiliam (2019) draws attention to those advocates of evidence-based education who argue that an average positive effect trumps individual negative effects (e.g. even though some people are killed in a traffic accident *because* they are wearing seat belts, overall the wearing of seat belts saves thousands of lives) (p. 135), though such arguments might overlook consistently negative effects in some contexts.

Averages risk violating the scientific principle of genuine homogeneity. Feinstein (1995) gives the example that if all entities weigh approximately the same, then, on this principle, large cats, small dogs, babies of 6 months, and huge fish can be designated as belonging to the same homogeneous groups (p. 76), which is clearly a nonsense. Kvernbekk (2019) notes that negative results obtained by some parties in the treatment group exist within an overall positive effect (p. 28). One member of a treatment group might be given a 'fail' grade whilst the average group grade is a 'pass'. The calculation of an average (in an RCT, in meta-analyses and meta-meta-analyses) can all-too-easily overlook the point that some students may have negative/failure scores and/or some RCTs may fail to find a positive result. This violates one of Bradford Hill's (1965) requirements for demonstrating causality, which is consistency, i.e. the results of RCTs should go in the same direction. As Feinstein (1995) wrote, no notice is taken of inconsistencies that are buried in the 'statistical agglomeration' (p. 76).

Similarly, Deaton and Cartwright (2018) note that if average effects are low, this might conceal sub-group results which are high; conversely, if average effects are high this might conceal sub-group results which are low. Researchers might be interested in the sub-samples and the marginal distributions, not only average effects (p. 3). Goodman (2009) and Clay (2010) note that averages – the calculation used in RCTs – may disguise which sub-group(s) benefited from, did not benefit from, or was/were endangered or harmed by, the treatment. Standardizing treatments for, or across, a whole population may be risky or suboptimal for some individuals or sub-groups. Indeed, as Healy et al. (2014) observe, clinical practice seeks to discover and respect heterogeneity rather than obliterate it (p. 81).

Averages do not let us comment on individuals. The intervention may have a zero effect on some individuals in the experimental group and a massive effect on others in the same group, but this is lost in the overall average.

The null hypothesis assumes that the treatment has a zero effect on *all* the individual members of the treatment group, and Deaton and Cartwright (2018) mention that the use of difference tests (e.g. the *t*-test, which uses NHST) raises problems where inequality and asymmetry of variances obtain between the two groups, i.e. the requirements underpinning the t-distributions may be violated. For example, there may be asymmetric, skewed distributions such as high numbers of high-scoring members of the control or treatment groups or the presence of outliers in either or both groups.

The presence of even one outlier can distort an average. Outliers frustrate the reliability and trustworthiness of averages, leading to questionable results and spurious statistical significance, e.g. a false negative or a false positive (Deaton and Cartwright (2018) provide evidence of this widespread problem). Nor is it acceptable to simply remove outliers; that is for statistical rather than actual convenience; outliers are outliers and they cannot simply be discarded because they happen to be inconvenient. To remove them may be unethical. Outliers may be the very parties that do or do not benefit from the treatment (e.g. the Rand studies of health provision); as Deaton and Cartwright (2018) note, the outliers, in effect, are the sample (p. 9).

The issue also concerns whether the outliers are in the control or the treatment group. If the outliers are in the treatment group and the distribution in that group is wide and the standard error is large, this may lead to rejecting the null hypothesis. If the outliers are in the control group, and the distributions are small, the *t*-values can be large, negative and statistically significant (p. 9) and this, too, may lead to rejecting the null hypothesis. This problem is not solved by replication experiments, blinding or double-blinding, as the same asymmetries may obtain in replication studies, or may be compounded by paying insufficient attention to ensuring the exact replication of the detailed protocols for the treatment, thereby replicating the same 'spurious findings' (p. 9). Indeed, replication comes at the price of 'working according to manuals', which questions the professional judgement of teachers working in specific contexts (Jensen and Kjeldsen, 2014, p. 35; see also Wiberg, 2014). Hence, caution, even suspicion, should apply in considering the value of significance testing and reliance on averages.

Wrigley (2018) suggests that, whilst averages might be useful for making large-scale analyses, this entails: a 'smoothing out' of differences; standardization which both distorts and approximates; using proxies as indicators; and inventing categories, all of which are frequently 'misleading' (p. 361). They unacceptably oversimplify the complexity of the 'real' world, however benevolent their intent and however much teachers may support them. Indeed, he argues that they 'change the reality' that they purport to measure (p. 362).

Averages conceal individual differences. An average might understate or overstate the difference that the RCT makes for an individual student or a sub-sample. It is wrong-headed to believe that an average treatment which shows no statistical significance or only a tiny effect size does not 'work' for some sub-groups or individuals; conversely, just because something 'works' for many people on average, this does not mean that it will work for you. As the opening of this book mentioned: 'The research said that this would work. I tried it. It didn't.' Just as it is improper to commit the ecological fallacy (inferring individual behaviour from a group result), so it is improper to commit the exception fallacy (inferring group behaviour from individual behaviour).

Where and what is the wisdom of applying educational research derived from RCTs which only deal in averages, to students whose uniqueness, diversity, humanity, make-up and differences are to be celebrated rather than suppressed or overlooked, despite claims that might be made for the similarity between people (e.g. Goldacre, 2013)? So much for Goldacre's (2013) remark that in the world of education, even though every child is different, 'we are all similar enough that research can help find out which intervention will work best overall, and which strategies should be tried first, second or third, to help everyone achieve the best outcome' (p. 7). The slide from an 'is' to an 'ought' is conspicuous here. An average score is not the same as an average child, and, indeed, the latter does not exist except in the contrived world of a statistic. As Greene (2009) observed, human action is characterized by contextual diversity and multiple perspectives, personalities and varied behaviours; these have little place in RCTs. As such, RCTs may not fulfil the requirement of evidence set out in Chapter 2, of being 'actionable' (Mark, 2009, p. 230) or of ensuring that RCTs in education respect what it means for research to be 'educational'.

Deaton and Cartwright (2018), comment that randomization, despite claims to the contrary, 'does not automatically deliver a precise estimate of the average treatment effect (ATE), and it does not relieve us of the need to think about (observed or unobserved) covariates' (p. 2). As they note, the average treatment effect is only as strong as the sample from which it was obtained (p. 5), and that there is a threat posed to significance testing if there is an 'asymmetric distribution of individual treatment effects in the study population' (p. 3).

In clinical trials, it is not sufficient to have a single outcome measure, an average (e.g. Goldacre, 2012); rather it is important to differentiate by sub-sample and by dosage, e.g. amount, quality, strength, frequency, duration of the treatment. So it should be with education, yet currently many RCTs in education are content with a single average measure, a single dose amount measured in a single time frame, a single measure of effect size or statistical significance, overlooking dose–response differences, within-group differences, between-group differences and sub-sample differences (which factorial designs may not catch). Average difference conceals within-patient variation, between-patient variation and patient-treatment interaction. Whilst stratification attenuates this, it increases the sample size in each stratum, in order to retain statistical power.

Given the problems of averages in RCTs, Clay (2010) advocates supplementing findings from RCTs with evidence from other methodologies, e.g. the educational equivalent of epidemiological studies, case studies, historical studies and clinical experience in clinical trials. Similarly, Frueh (2009), discussing clinical RCTs, argues for case-control and non-random cohort studies in tandem with careful observational studies, non-random and retrospective analyses of data, i.e. methods that have been used long before RCTs came into vogue (p. 1079).

The use of regression analysis

Linear regression analysis is widely used in analysing data from RCT's. This plots a graph of the results of a pre-test and a post-test, comparing the control and treatment group, and conforms to the advice from Gene Glass, a seminal figure in meta-analysis, which states that 'the result of a meta-analysis should never be an average; it should be a graph' (Robinson, 2004, p. 29). For example, here are two instances of the same experiment.

Instance One: imagine that an RCT has been conducted with 60 students, 30 in each group (control and intervention groups), to ascertain whether implementing a new pedagogy in mathematics teaching improved students' mathematics performance. The students in both groups were given a pre-test and a post-test; the results are presented in a graph (Figure 10.1).

Here the line of best fit for the distributions of the scores of the intervention group (the thicker line) is higher than that of the control group, i.e. the scores of the intervention group are noticeably higher than those of the control groups, and the scores on the post-test have risen quite evenly (the fit line of the intervention group is nearly parallel to that of the control group). The rise in scores for each member of the intervention group was around 3 points; the average mark on the pre-test was 61.9 and on the post-test was 65.1.

The gradient of the line of best fit (i.e. for every measured unit on the pre-test, by what percentage fraction of a unit did it raise the commensurate measured unit on the post-test) for the control group was 0.973, whilst for the intervention group it was 0.932. There was close to 1 to 1 rise in the gradients for the lines of best fit for the two groups; in other words, the calculation of an average rise might be justified.

However, this time, Instance Two, imagine that the RCT has been conducted with 60 students, 30 in each group (control and intervention groups), to ascertain whether implementing a new pedagogy for mathematics teaching improved students' mathematics performance. The students in both groups were given a pre-test and a post-test; the results are presented in a graph (Figure 10.2).

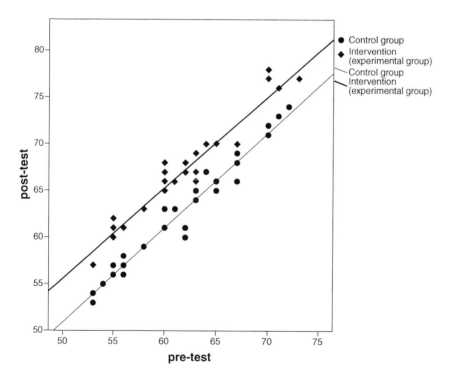

Figure 10.1 Pre-test and post-test scores for control and experimental groups (*n* = 60)

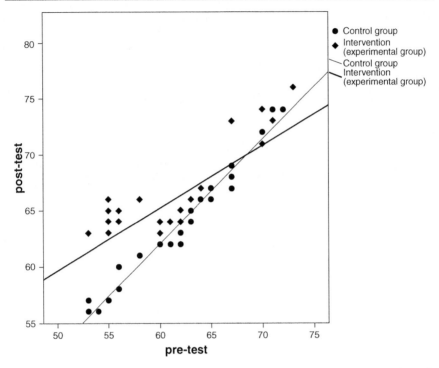

Figure 10.2 Revised pre-test and post-test scores for control and experimental groups (*n* = 60)

Here the line of best fit for the distributions of the scores of the intervention group (the thicker line) is not always higher than that of the control group, and indeed there is a cross-over in the upper levels of the distributions, i.e. the intervention gave much more 'added value' to the pre-test lower scoring students in the intervention group than to its higher-scoring students. Here the average marks on the pre-test remain exactly the same as in Figure 10.1 (61.9) and the post-test (65.1). Whilst the averages for the pre-test and post-test for both Figures 10.1 and 10.2 are identical, the distributions are very different.

Here the gradient of the line of best fit (i.e. for every measured unit on the pre-test, by what percentage fraction of a unit did it raise the commensurate measured unit on the post-test) for the control group was 0.973, whilst for the intervention group it was 0.665. The gradients of the lines of best fit for the two groups were very different; in other words, the calculation of an average rise is misleading as it conceals substantial differences.

This suggests that it is essential not only to look at the averages but at the distributions, skewness and sub-groups of participants. The reader of research should ask whether, in fact, the results of sub-groups are presented; this argues that simply reporting standard deviations is insufficient. In the two instances here, the standard deviations are set out in Table 10.1.

Table 10.1 Standard deviations for two sets of results for the same RCT

	Pre-test Standard Deviation	Post-test Standard Deviation
	Control group	Intervention group
Instance One	5.36	5.84
Instance Two	5.36	4.64

The standard deviations on the post-test for Instance One are larger than for Instance Two, i.e. suggesting that relying on standard deviations can be misleading. This argues for regression analysis to be faithful to the graphical nature – the spread of scores – of the within-group and between-group clustering of results by sub-groups. Averages tell us very little.

Null hypothesis significance testing

Data analysis in RCTs is often conducted by significance testing and effect size calculations. This raises the issue of how one judges 'success', i.e. compared to what something is judged to have 'worked'.

Though statistical significance features in educational research, it has serious limitations and, indeed has been widely discredited in the social sciences for many reasons, discussed below (e.g. Carver, 1978; Falk and Greenbaum, 1978; Thompson and Snyder, 1997; Wilkinson and the Task Force on Statistical Inference, 1999; Krueger, 2001; Thompson, 2002; Wright, 2003; Kline, 2004; Ziliak and McCloskey, 2008; American Psychological Association, 2010; Ellis, 2010; Cumming, 2012; Gorard, 2016; Cohen et al., 2018). Greenhalgh et al. (2014) comment that benefits arrived at by significance testing might, actually, be 'marginal in clinical practice' (p. 2).

Significance testing is silent on what many researchers and users of research want to, or need to, know: how much of an effect an intervention has, and on whom (which groups and sub-groups), under what conditions and contingencies, with how much 'treatment' (e.g. quantity, quality, intensity, strength, frequency, duration), at what cost, and compared to what. Null hypothesis significance testing (NHST) only hints at whether an intervention makes a difference by chance or not by chance, not by how much, and even this is questionable, as the 'null' is a dangerous assumption to make. Even if the assumption of the 'null' is defensible and proven, NHST says nothing about the size of the difference made, and it is the size of the difference made that the 'what works' agenda may wish to know. Nor does it tell us *why* an intervention has worked, and this is what users of research often need to know (i.e. causality, Chapter 3).

NHST (Kline, 2004; Cumming, 2012) is a test of the statistical 'rareness' of chance alone (i.e. not certainty) (Carver, 1978, p. 381), assuming that all the protocols of randomization and the requirements of the null hypothesis have been observed. However, NHST has been questioned so much that many researchers and journals (e.g. Torgerson and Torgerson, 2008, p. 128; Cumming, 2012, p. 28; Cohen et al., 2018) rule it out of court for several reasons:

- It commits the 'fallacy of the transposed conditional' (Ziliak and McCloskey, 2008), where, given the hypothesis, the probability of the data is such-and-such, is falsely transposed to read as given the data, the probability of the hypothesis is such-and-such (p. 41). For example: the probability of obtaining a dead person, given that the person was hanged, is extremely high (e.g. 0.97 or higher) whereas the probability that a person has been hanged, given that he is dead, is extremely low (e.g. 0.01 or lower) (Carver (1978).
- Assuming the null hypothesis is unfounded, questionable, dangerous, unsafe, false, untenable and illogical; it is extremely unlikely that the null hypothesis exists or is a safe assumption to make in social science; it is unsafe. NHST usage frequently violates the assumption of the null hypothesis and the protocols of randomization, rendering it invalid to use correctly.
- Statistical significance is wrongly confused with importance and wrongly confused with the size of an effect or a relationship.
- Statistical significance is highly susceptible to sample size: the larger the sample, the more likely it is to be statistically significant; indeed, it is almost impossible not to find statistical significance with a large sample (Cumming, 2012). Statistical significance can be reached by having a large coefficient together with a small sample, or having a small coefficient together with a large sample (Coe, 2000, p. 9).
- Statistical significance risks a Type I error (false positive) and a Type II error (false negative) (Torgerson and Torgerson, 2008; Ziliak and McCloskey, 2008; Ellis, 2010).
- Statistical significance does not tell researchers what they often want to know: how much of a difference an intervention makes: the size or amount of an intervention's effects or difference.
- Statistical significance has somewhat arbitrary cut-off points, even though a significance level of 0.05 corresponds to approximately 2 standard deviations above or below the mean and a significance level of 0.01 corresponds to approximately 3 standard deviations above or below the mean (Cohen et al., 2018, p. 743; see also Ayres, 2007, p. 200).
- Significance testing risks encouraging dichotomous thinking, i.e. a finding *is* or *is not* statistically significant (Kline, 2004, pp. 76–79).

In short, statistical significance testing is no guarantee that an intervention in an RCT 'works'. Abandon it.

Effect size

A widely used alternative to significance testing is effect size, a metric purporting to denote the size of a difference. However, it is dangerous to believe that effect size tells us objectively whether something 'works' or that a difference really is such-and-such. Effect size is all-too-frequently misinterpreted. It is not a measure of the effectiveness an intervention or of the unconditional size of a difference; rather, it is a measure in relation to the study as a whole, not solely the intervention, and to treat effect size as a measure of only the intervention's effect is to commit a serious category error (Simpson, 2018a, 2018b, 2019b, 2020). Many factors come into play in understanding of what an effect size is evidence; it does not speak for itself, nor is it self-evident.

Effect size, whilst attractive, is only a metric, and whilst this may appeal to many researchers and, indeed, is used to judge 'what works' in meta-analysis and meta-meta-analysis (e.g. Hattie, 2009; Major and Higgins, 2019), it is questionable. Further, it sacrifices the importance of context and conditions to a single, somewhat simplistic statistic, demeaning the complexity of class-rooms and interventions to a single computed figure; it is an impoverished view of the 'real' world of classrooms, even if the RCT takes place in a nat-ural classroom setting.

Effect size operates at the group level (averages) rather than the individual level, thereby overlooking individual differences. Small samples may not be able to detect a small effect size (a Type II error: a false negative) (Torgerson and Torgerson, 2008, p. 128), but a large sample may overlook substantial sub-group differences in distributions, by focusing on averages only.

Effect size is often purported to be a measure of the amount – the size – of a relationship, correlation or difference between a control and intervention group in a given piece of research. However, effect size is not as clear as this. It is relative, not absolute, and relative to the comparison group in question and to the conditions and clarity of the study in distinguishing the 'signal' from the 'noise' (Higgins, 2018; Simpson, 2017, 2018a, 2018b, 2019a, 2019b, 2020). Simpson (2017, 2018b, 2020) demonstrates that effect size is not a measure of effectiveness but 'is a property of the whole study, not just the intervention' (Simpson, 2018b, p. 910), a measure of how well the 'signal' in an RCT stands out from the 'noise' of other confounding factors (Simpson, 2020). Simpson (2019b, 2020) notes that it is a measure of the *clarity* of the difference (how clearly the 'signal' is separated from the 'noise') between control and treatment groups on a particular outcome measure, given, and only given, the features of the study in question, i.e. it is highly conditional on the study's design and operations, rather than simply being an unequi-vocal amount of difference or of the educational importance of an interven-tion; to confuse these is to commit a category error.

Effect size is not, on its own, a measure of the effectiveness of an intervention; rather, it is a measure conditional on a range of circumstances, processes, variables and factors. Effect size is sensitive to the designs of the RCT and the measures used (Simpson, 2019c, p. 383; 2020). Simpson (2019b) demonstrates the fallacy of thinking that effect size is a measure of the effectiveness of an intervention, or, indeed, that higher effect sizes are automatically related to bigger influences (p. 101), as effect size is relative to the specific context, to the proportion of the whole picture and the whole RCT.

A homogeneous sample creates less 'noise' than a more heterogeneous sample; the more that outcome questions are unrelated to the RCT, the more 'noise' is created; using open questions creates more 'noise' than multiple choice questions; multiple choice questions with many choices create less 'noise' than those with few choices; and the longer the period of time elapsing between the outcome and the treatment, the greater is the 'noise' (Simpson, 2020). Further, the greater is the variation in the intervention group's treatment, the smaller the effect size might be, and the greater is the variation in what is happening in the control group, the smaller the effect size might be (ibid.).

Effect size is relative to, and conditional on, many factors, and it must be interpreted by taking into account, for example: the research design; sampling; instrumentation; timing of the measures; comparison treatments; statistical power of the study; sample characteristics; test construction and characteristics; data analysis, distributions of scores; variances within and between the groups; control group activities; and so on. Effect size is affected by: the homogeneity/heterogeneity of the sample and the similarity of the distribution of characteristics of the sample; instrumentation, e.g. the scope, length and types of item included in the data collection; the types of intervention and other factors (e.g. in conducting meta-analyses of several studies) (Simpson, 2018b).

Effect size might also be influenced by the timing of the post-test, e.g. if there is a delay in post-treatment measurement (Simpson, 2018a, p. 9; 2020). Many factors and conditions operate in a situation (e.g. resources, teacher expertise, time spent, student characteristics, school characteristics, class size and make-up) and these influence effect sizes. The instruments used for testing and measuring (their contents, size and number of questions and their nature, selection from a bank of questions, scope, alignment with the material of the intervention) also influence effect sizes (Simpson, 2018a, 2020).

When reporting an effect size in a piece of research, then, it is essential, though often neglected, to note that, in this instance, with this design, sample, instrumentation, duration of the intervention, comparison treatments, statistical power, sample characteristics, test construction and characteristics, control group activities, distributions of scores, the effect size is such-and-such. But how often do we see this? Further, sample size is often taken to influence effect size, but Simpson (2020) indicates why this is not the case. Too often, what the effect size is taken to show is presumed to be self-evident, when it is not.

Effect size, both *per se* and in meta-analysis and meta-meta-analysis, raises several concerns. For example, Simpson (2017, 2018b, 2019b, 2020) notes that: (a) what the control group is doing is unclear; (b) if the sample is limited, such that it reduces the heterogeneity of the sample, this can enlarge the effect size; (c) RCTs risk using outcome measures that are more sympathetic to the treatment group rather than the control group. Reported effect sizes may reflect the sensitivity of the intervention being measured, rather than the educational significance of the intervention itself (Simpson, 2017). Huge effect sizes can be found even if, objectively speaking, the interventions are trivial (Simpson, 2020).

Effect size is susceptible to simple changes made to any of the basic elements of an RCT (Simpson, 2019b, p. 101), the measures being used and the activities of the control group (even if the treatment group receives identical treatment) (p. 102). Simpson cites examples of where, even with the same sample, the same intervention, and all other features of the design held constant apart from the test being used, 'radically different effect sizes' can result; in other words, effect size is not the same as the intervention's 'educational influence' (pp. 102–103) or its 'educational effectiveness' (p. 106). He adds that design choices can increase effect sizes, i.e. effect size is not independent of the research design. Indeed, he notes, that, for meta-analyses, it is fair to combine effect sizes from a range of studies if, and only if, the same intervention was undertaken in those studies with the same sample being compared to the 'same control activity' (i.e. what the control group did showed no variance), with the same study design, with outcome measures and statistics used being the same (p. 106), all of which, he avers, are 'vanishingly rare' (Simpson, 2020).

Effect size purports to reframe 'what works' as 'how well' or 'how much' something 'works'. It seeks to be more meaningful than NHST (Cohen, 1988; Kline, 2004; Ellis, 2010; Cumming, 2012; Cohen et al., 2018) as it overcomes NHST's 'sizeless stare' (Ziliak and McCloskey, 2008). However, it, too, has drawbacks (Maher et al., 2013). Interpreting effect size risks simplistically 'reading off' effect sizes into categories of 'small', 'medium' and 'large', or 'weak', 'modest', 'moderate', 'strong', 'very strong', and this falls into the trap of adhering to the same 'benchmarking' and 'cut off' mentality as statistical significance, whereas a subtler, more sophisticated interpretation is often wiser (Thompson, 2001, 2002; Maher et al., 2013, p. 350). Further, some effect size statistics (e.g. Cohen's *d*) over-estimate the 'breakpoints' between small, medium and large effects (Paterson et al., 2016). Indeed, measures of effect size (in terms of standardized units, original units or unit-free measures), vary according to which statistical tests are used to calculate them.

Bakker et al. (2019) call into question the meaning of 'small', 'medium' and 'large' effect size. As Cohen (1988) remarked: terms such as 'small', 'medium' and 'large' are relative to each other and to the specific contents and research methods being used in an investigation, and that, given this relativity, there is an inherent risk inherent in using simplistic terms (Cohen, 1988, p. 25).

There are 'good reasons' to be sceptical of figures and categories in effect size, when working in RCTs in education (Sanders and Chonaire, 2015, p. 5), not least as effect sizes are influenced by unequal or different types of comparison groups, range restriction and measurement design (Simpson, 2017, 2018b, 2020; Wrigley 2018). For example, effect size can be inflated if the sample contains less variation than exists in the population (Coe, 2018). Further, changes are age-related: an RCT conducted with young children may find a greater change than if the same RCT is conducted with older teenagers (Didau, 2015, p. 131) (see also Major and Higgins, 2019, p. xxiii). Effect sizes can be age-dependent (the older the students, the smaller the effect size), and time dependent (e.g. duration and intensity of an intervention) (Wiliam, 2016). Morrison and van der Werf (2014) comment that effect size plays only a limited role in the 'theatre of causality' (p. 251).

Wiliam (2016) notes that sub-group differences might be overlooked in studies which only focus on overall effect size for the entire sample rather than its sub-groups, and this may distort the fairness, applicability and usefulness of such studies. Further, he notes that teacher-devised measures tend to show larger effect sizes than standardized tests; effects vary by age group, teacher input and formative feedback and assessment. He notes that it is invidious to suppose that it is fair to compare interventions of different duration and intensity. Further, teachers may be less concerned with the short-term nature of effect sizes and more concerned with longer term effects on students – they are in it for the 'long haul' rather than the 'short sprint'. Wiliam (2019) also draws attention to the file drawer problem (publication bias and 'confirmation bias', in which positive results are published more than negative results and where researchers themselves shelve findings that have small and/or statistically insignificant results (see also Cheung and Slavin, 2016)).

Simpson (2018b) demonstrates that effect size is relative to the context in which it is located. He uses the analogy of a collection of photographs of princesses, which take up, on average 0.24 of the photo-size, and for a collection of photographs of elephants, which take up, on average 0.18 of the photo-size. The conclusion – that 'princesses are bigger than elephants' – is absurd, as an object's physical size is being calculated relative to the photo-size, not to the actual size, and to confuse the two is to commit a fundamental category error. For any semblance of fair comparability, the photographer, for every photograph, would have to use the same camera, the same lens, and be standing the same distance away from the subject in every photograph. As he comments, when comparing studies (e.g. as in meta-meta-analysis), use of effect size is fair only under certain very limited conditions, including where all the other factors which affect effect size are held equal, and where the distribution of all other factors which impact on effect size is equal across the groups of studies in question (p. 898). This is rarely the case in meta-meta-analysis, even if such analysts assume that they are. Lovell

(2018), too, notes that comparing which of two educational approaches is better, based on effect size, can only be only justified 'if all relevant factors are controlled for' (p. 7), and this is missing in meta-analyses and meta-meta-analyses. A salutary warning, strongly stated.

Effect size can change without changing the intervention itself, and effect sizes are susceptible to many influences (Coe, 2000; Cohen et al., 2018; Lovell, 2018; Simpson, 2018b, 2019a, 2019b), for example:

- *Restricted range*: using a sub-section of the data might yield a different effect size than looking at the entire population, hence comparing effect sizes without first checking the range restriction can lead to 'highly unreliable conclusions' (Lovell, 2018, p. 5). The smaller the range of scores (their distribution and spread), the greater is the possibility of a higher effect size (Cohen et al., 2018; Simpson, 2018b). The closer the match is between the choice of sample and the inclusion of those for whom the mechanism of the intervention is effective, the larger is the mean difference in a 'before and after' comparison (Simpson, 2018b, p. 902). Therefore, it is important to use the pooled standard deviation in calculating effect size, and to report the range or sampling here, e.g. the inclusion of a group of high achieving students rather than, for example, the whole ability range (Simpson, 2017).
- *Non-normal distributions*: effect size calculations often assume a normal distribution, which may not be the case, so non-normal distributions should be reported.
- *Measurement reliability*: the accuracy, validity, stability and robustness of the instrument being used, e.g.: the longer the test, or the more items used to measure something, the more reliable it might be; the closer the measure being used aligns to the intervention of the treatment group alone, the larger (and less valid) the effect size is likely to be. For example, in an intervention to improve algebra scores, measuring algebra alone might yield a higher effect size than if one embeds algebra within a test of many areas of mathematics (Simpson, 2017, 2018b). Indeed, Simpson (2018b) comments that even with the same intervention, the same sample and the same 'comparison treatments', effect sizes will differ according to the test being used (p. 903). He notes that effect sizes for researcher-designed tests could be double those of standardized tests and that the closer the test is to the curriculum of the intervention, the larger are the effect sizes (*ibid.*). Effect sizes from rigorous, standardized, objective measures in RCTs are considerably smaller than researcher-devised measures in the same field (Cheung and Slavin, 2016; Malouf and Taymans, 2016; Styles and Torgerson, 2018), so it is important not to overstate claims or to 'cherry pick' from or amongst studies. Indeed, the sounder the technical rigour of an RCTs is, the less likelihood there is of finding a positive result (Oakley, 2007, p. 100; Cheung and Slavin, 2016).
- Having unequal comparison groups (Lovell, 2018).

- Individual differences.
- Differences in calculating and using the standard deviations in the studies (Glass, 1977).
- Sample heterogeneity/homogeneity: the greater the heterogeneity, the lower might be the effect size, and heterogeneity is sensitive to sample attrition (Simpson, 2018a, p. 8; Lortie-Forgues and Inglis, 2019a, p. 159).
- Neglect of small effect sizes.
- Experimenter and experiment effects.
- The duration of the intervention, particularly if it is brief (Slavin, 2018b, p. 2).
- Scope of the data collected.

Experimenter-designed tests of interventions often produce larger effect sizes than standardized tests (Cheung and Slavin, 2016; Malouf and Taymans, 2016; Lovell, 2018; Slavin, 2018b; Lortie-Forgues and Inglis, 2019a) (though Li and Ma (2010) report the opposite in a standardized measure of an RCT on mathematics using computers). Effect sizes in meta-analysis are prone to problems caused by differences in experimental design; aggregating effect sizes commits a category error.

Effect sizes are often inflated in studies with small sample sizes and of short duration (Cheung and Slavin, 2016; Slavin, 2018b), i.e. false positives. Cheung and Slavin (2016), comparing published and unpublished studies of mathematics, science and reading, report that effect sizes were twice as large or more (up to 2.75 time higher) for (a) small-scale trials, (b) researcher-made measures and (c) published articles than for large-scale, 'independent'/standardized outcome measures (i.e. those which were not biased towards the contents of the treatments to which only the experimental group was exposed and which were not created by the researchers for the particular RCT in question) and published articles respectively. Similarly, Malouf and Taymans (2016) report that interventions using researcher-developed tests found average effect sizes of 0.39, compared to effect sizes of 0.08 on 'broad-scope standardized tests' (p. 456) (see also Lortie-Forgues and Inglis, 2019a, p. 159).

The larger the sample, the smaller the effect size; small samples had effect sizes of up to twice as large as those with large samples. Cheung and Slavin (2016) suggest that this might be because small-scale research can adhere more closely to fidelity to the research treatments than large-scale research. Cheung and Slavin (2016) and de Boer et al. (2014) also found that effect sizes were appreciably higher in quasi-experiments (e.g. with matched samples) than in RCTs. All of this questions the confidence that can be placed in published RCTs which report effect sizes.

Cheung and Slavin (2016) also suggest that the effect sizes calculated for large-scale RCTs which use independent measures might be closer to the truth, and that researcher-generated measures should be eliminated. They comment that this is a 'sobering perspective' for those who fund and abide by large-scale RCTs.

Malouf and Taymans (2016) found that the more rigorously conducted interventions reviewed in the What Works Clearinghouse (WWC) had effect sizes that were of 'questionable magnitude' in terms of sufficiently meeting the policy goals of education (they report that out of 550 studies, only some 30 per cent of studies met the WWC standards; Malouf and Taymans, 2016, p. 455). Lortie-Forgues and Inglis (2019a) note that, in their analysis of 141 trials, the average effect size of large-scale studies that had been rigorously investigated, was only 0.06 SDs, i.e. considerably smaller than those often found in the literature, and that effectiveness trials produced lower effect sizes than efficacy trials (p. 165); a salutary pair of findings. Once one winnows out poor quality and under-powered RCTs, how far the remaining few studies are actually useful is questionable.

As effect size is 'a relative metric', comparing how well an intervention group performs *relative* to a control group; the worse the performance of the control group turns out to be, the better the intervention appears for the control group (Simpson, 2018a, p. 2). Therefore, it makes little sense to combine or compare effect sizes when two different studies have two different control groups, as in a meta-analysis (p. 2).

As effect sizes can experience biases from sampling quality (Maher et al., 2013, p. 349), the statistical power of the research design, specific design features and measures being used (Sanders and Chonaire, 2015, p. 1), they may lack practical significance and generalizability, and they depend on both the context of the research and the researcher's judgment (p. 350). On the one hand, teachers may find them unhelpful and of little practical use. However, on the other hand, even a small effect size (0.1) may be useful, e.g. sufficiently useful to save lives in disease reduction (Maher et al., 2013). It is not only large effect sizes that are useful. What if the researcher only wanted a particular intervention to have a small effect, not a large effect, but found that it had a large effect, or *vice versa* – does that mean that the intervention did or did not 'work'? Or what if the effect size is large for an outlier subpopulation but small overall?

Effect sizes are also affected by blinding (Simpson, 2018a). Simpson, citing Howick (2011) suggests that up to seven different groups may need to be blinded in an RCT: 'allocators, participants, treatment implementers, data collectors, assessors, analysts, and authors' (p. 3). This echoes the identification of many sources of bias indicated by Jadad and Enkin (2007).

What does effect size actually tell us? Does it tell us that something 'works'? No. It tells us that if we subtract the mean of one group from the mean of another group and divide it by the pooled standard deviation, we obtain such-and-such a figure in the context of such-and-such a research comparison group and comparison activities, such-and-such a research design, such-and-such a sample size, with such-and-such instrumentation, with such-and-such an amount or duration of intervention, measured at such-and-such a point in time and with such-and-such a power size in a power analysis. It is a measure of an average difference between a given control and treatment group, under multiple conditions, not a measure of 'what works' or the claimed size of the intervention unaffected by design features. 'What works' is a human judgment and it is not possible to simply read off from an effect size, RCT or a series of RCTs (e.g. in a meta-analysis) that the same result will obtain in other contexts. It is a highly limited, highly contingent statistic.

Whether one uses significance testing and/or effect size, these are immensely reductionist: all the sparkling complexity of an intervention, its conditions and settings, its peoples, its multiple channels and directions of webs of causality and 'causal cakes', are reduced to a single figure; how demeaning; what a travesty of inclusive education and, indeed, education itself.

Conclusion

Researchers should consider the statistical power of the research undertaken. However, even if large samples are used, with appropriate statistical power, analysis undertaken has limitations and conditions. The chapter has indicated concerns about the use of averages, regression analysis, null hypothesis significance testing and effect size calculations and what they show. Even if the RCT in question uses a large sample with considerable statistical power, researchers must still include conditional statements in the claims that they make from such analyses. Averages have their limitations, as do regression analysis, NHST and effect size calculations. Hence, claims made from them must demonstrate fidelity to the limitations of their uses, assumptions underpinning their uses, and statements of the conditions affecting what they show and do not show. NHST has little worth; effect size is subject to a panoply of conditionals; what do they show? How useful are they? Not much, and nowhere near as much as is often claimed for them.

Chapter 11

Reporting and evaluating randomized controlled trials in education

Introduction and overview

Reporting and evaluating RCTs and what they show must address several key requirements, such as:

- caution in claims made for what RCTs show and do not show;
- what to include in reporting RCTs;
- questions in evaluating RCTs, to be addressed in the planning as well as the reporting stages.

The chapter provides examples of what to include in reporting RCTs and argues that many of these are neglected in reports of RCTs. It argues for greater rigour and inclusion in reporting RCTs, and this has a backwash effect on the planning and design of RCTs in education.

Standards for reporting and evaluating randomized controlled trials

There are several examples available of what to report and what to consider in evaluating RCTs. The CONSORT (Consolidated Standards of Reporting Trials) Group provides a checklist of 25 items to include in reporting trials (CONSORT, 2010), with several sub-areas:

Title and abstract
Introduction

   Background and objectives

Methods

   Trial design
   Participants
   Interventions
   Outcomes
   Sample size

Randomisation:

> Sequence generation
> Allocation and concealment mechanism
> Implementation

Blinding
Statistical methods

Results

> Participant flow (a diagram is strongly recommended)
> Recruitment
> Baseline data
> Numbers analysed
> Outcomes and estimation
> Ancillary analysis
> Harms

Discussion

> Limitations
> Generalisability
> Interpretation

Other information

> Registration
> Protocol
> Funding

At the time of writing, the UK's Education Endowment Foundation provides guidance on what and how to report an RCT:

- https://educationendowmentfoundation.org.uk/projects-and-evaluation/evaluating-projects/evaluator-resources/
- https://educationendowmentfoundation.org.uk/projects-and-evaluation/evaluating-projects/evaluator-resources/writing-a-research-report/
- https://educationendowmentfoundation.org.uk/public/files/Evaluation/Writing_a_Research_Report/EEF_evaluation_report_template_2019.docx
- https://educationendowmentfoundation.org.uk/public/files/Grantee_guide_and_EEF_policies/Evaluation/Writing_a_Protocol_or_SAP/EEF_statistical_analysis_guidance_2018.pdf
- https://educationendowmentfoundation.org.uk/public/files/Evaluation/Setting_up_an_Evaluation/IPE_guidance.pdf

Its *Report Template* (Education Endowment Foundation, 2019a) includes:

Costs
Impact
Introduction

>Background
>Intervention
>Evaluation objectives
>Ethics and trial registration
>Data protection
>Project team

Methods

>Trial design
>Participant selection
>Outcome measures
>Sample size
>Randomisation
>Statistical analysis
>Implementation and process evaluation
>Costs
>Timeline
>Impact evaluation results
>Participant flow
>Attrition
>Pupil and school characteristics
>Outcomes and analysis

Implementation and process evaluation

>Compliance
>Fidelity
>Usual practice

Cost
Conclusion

At the time of writing, the What Works Clearinghouse (2017) (WWC) provides guidance on what and how to report an RCT in terms of procedures and standards:

- https://ies.ed.gov/ncee/wwc/handbooks
- https://ies.ed.gov/ncee/wwc/Docs/ReferenceResources/wwc_gsa_v1.pdf
- https://ies.ed.gov/ncee/wwc/Docs/referenceresources/wwc_procedures_v2_1_standards_handbook.pdf

- https://ies.ed.gov/ncee/wwc/Docs/referenceresources/wwc_standards_ha ndbook_v4.pdf
- https://ies.ed.gov/ncee/wwc/StudyReviewGuide
- https://ies.ed.gov/ncee/wwc/Docs/ReferenceResources/wwc_gd_guide_ 022218.pdf

Its *Reporting Guide for Study Authors: Group Design Studies* (U.S. Department of Education, 2018) has three main areas and several sub-areas:

1   Study Characteristics and Context

   Intervention and comparison conditions
   Study sample
   Setting

2   Study Design and Analysis

   Measures
   Design
   Analytic Approach
   Missing data

3   Study Data

   1   Provide values for key pre-intervention measures and characteristics if the study collected these data.
   2   Review relevant WWC review protocols to understand what pre-intervention measures or characteristics the WWC may want to examine. Examples include other pre-intervention measures that may be related to the outcome measure, student age, and race or ethnicity.
   3   How many individuals are in the analytic sample? … .
   4   What is the mean value for each measure or characteristic for the analytic sample? For outcome measures, the means may be adjusted for pre-intervention measures accounted for in the analysis.
   5   What is the unadjusted standard deviation for each measure or characteristic for the analytic sample? … .
   6   Provide the statistic used to estimate the effect of the intervention (e.g., a regression coefficient or difference in means) and the associated p-value.
   7   Provide the effect size, if available (the WWC reports Hedges' g; see the *WWC Procedures Handbook* for more information).
   8   RCTs that assign individuals to the intervention and comparison groups, to allow WWC reviewers to assess attrition.
   9   Designs where clusters of individuals were assigned to the intervention and comparison groups, to allow WWC reviewers to assess

baseline equivalence of clusters (as opposed to individuals) and the extent to which the sample is representative of clusters.

10 RCTs where clusters of individuals were randomly assigned to the intervention and comparison groups, to allow WWC reviewers to assess cluster-level attrition and non-response within clusters.

11 Pre-intervention measures for which any observations are imputed or missing, to allow WWC reviewers to assess baseline equivalence in this special case.

12 Outcome measures that are imputed, to allow WWC reviewers to determine whether the study limits potential bias from imputed outcome data.

(U.S. Department of Education, 2018, pp. 3 & 4; reproduced with permission of the US Department of Education)

Furlong and Oancea (2005) set out standards for *Assessing Quality in Applied and Practice-based Educational Research* (including non-RCT studies) (pp. 11–15):

Methodological and theoretical robustness – the epistemic dimension

Trustworthiness
Contribution to knowledge
Explicitness in designing and reporting
Propriety (conforming to legal requirements and ethical principles)
Paradigm-dependent criteria

Value for use – the technological dimension

Salience/ timeliness
Purposivity (fitness for purpose)
Specificity (how the research responds to the needs of the users and to their specification), and accessibility (to relevant audiences)
Concern for enabling impact
Flexibility and operationalisability

Capacity building and value for people

Partnership, collaboration and engagement
Plausibility (from the practitioner's perspective)
Reflection and criticism
Receptiveness (to the practitioner's viewpoint)
Stimulating personal growth

The economic dimension

Cost-effectiveness
Marketability and competitiveness

Auditability
Feasibility
Originality
Value-efficiency

The US National Library of Medicine at the National Center for Biotechnology Information (2018) sets out several quality rating criteria for
RCTs and observational studies (Table 11.1).

Evaluating and reporting RCTs in education raises a perhaps formidable
list of questions, set out below.

Table 11.1 US Preventive Services Task Force quality rating criteria for randomized controlled trials and observational studies

Criteria
- *Initial assembly of comparable groups: RCTs – adequate randomization, including con-
  cealment and whether potential confounders were distributed equally among groups;
  cohort studies – consideration of potential confounders with either restriction or measure-
  ment for adjustment in the analysis; consideration of inception cohorts*
- *Maintenance of comparable groups (includes attrition, cross-over, adherence, contamination)*
- *Important differential loss to follow-up or overall high loss to follow-up*
- *Measurements: equal, reliable, and valid (includes masking of outcome assessment)*
- *Clear definition of interventions*
- *Important outcomes considered*
- *Analysis: adjustment for potential confounders for cohort studies, or intention-to-treat
  analysis for RCTs; for cluster RCTs, correction for correlation coefficient*

Definition of ratings based on above criteria

Good: Meets all criteria: comparable groups are assembled initially and maintained
        throughout the study (follow-up at least 80%); reliable and valid measure-
        ment instruments are used and applied equally to groups; interventions are
        spelled out clearly; important outcomes are considered; and appropriate
        attention to confounders in analysis.

Fair: Studies will be graded 'fair' if any or all of the following problems occur,
        without the important limitations noted in the 'poor' category below: gen-
        erally comparable groups are assembled initially but some question remains
        whether some (although not major) differences occurred in follow-up; mea-
        surement instruments are acceptable (although not the best) and generally
        applied equally; some but not all important outcomes are considered; and
        some but not all potential confounders are accounted for.

Poor: Studies will be graded 'poor' if any of the following major limitations exists:
        groups assembled initially are not close to being comparable or maintained
        throughout the study; unreliable or invalid measurement instruments are
        used or not applied at all equally among groups (including not masking out-
        come assessment); and key confounders are given little or no attention.

Reproduced with permission of the National Center for Biotechnology Information (NCBI)

Planning of the RCT

1 How clearly stated were the intended purposes and outcomes of the RCT?
2 How clearly stated were the research questions of the RCT?
3 What was the intervention, and how clearly and fully was it described and justified?
4 How appropriate and practicable was the design of the RCT?
5 How acceptable were the criteria for judging the success of the RCT, and whether the intervention had 'worked'?
6 How true to 'real life' was the RCT?
7 What safeguards and supervisory oversight of the RCT operated, and how suitable and effective was this?
8 How were the ethics of the RCT addressed?
9 What actions were taken to enable the control group to have access to the benefits of the intervention if the RCT turned out to be efficacious?

Randomization and sampling in control and treatment groups

1 Was there random selection and random allocation? If not, was the alternative acceptable, and on what grounds?
2 How representative of the population (and what population) was the sample?
3 How was the sampling undertaken?
4 How acceptable was the application of the *ceteris paribus* condition in the RCT?
5 How well were the demographics and other key characteristics matched between the control and experimental groups?
6 Were the control and treatment groups sufficiently matched on pre-tests?
7 Were suitable and sufficient controls adopted in the RCT?
8 How homogeneous/heterogeneous were each of the control and experimental groups?
9 How convincing a counterfactual was the control group?
10 Were the RCT's group sizes sufficiently large to enable safe conclusions to be drawn?
11 Was there attrition/equal attrition in the control and treatment groups, and with what effects?
12 Were cluster samples used to minimize bias and contamination?
13 What steps were taken to address the sample power?

Controls, conditions, contexts

1 In the case of more than one control group and more than one treatment group, were the control groups doing the same activities and were the treatment groups doing the same treatment?
2 What notice was taken of contexts, conditions and contingencies in the RCT?

Causality

1 How secure was the attribution of causality and the identification of causes and their interaction?
2 How acceptable were the ingredients of the 'causal cakes', 'support factors', and their relative amounts and strengths in the RCTs?
3 What were the 'webs of causality', and how did they differ at each stage of the RCT?

Conduct of the RCT

1 Were the treatment protocols and procedures sufficiently detailed to rule out differences in treatments and operations in the treatment groups?
2 Was the timing of the post-test suitable, too soon or too late?
3 Were ethical issues in the RCT sufficiently addressed in practice?
4 What notice was taken of the 'human factor' in the RCT: agency, creativity, personality, intentionality, interactions, imagination, spontaneity, responsiveness, activity, volitions etc.?
5 Were sufficient steps taken to avoid 'contamination' between the control and treatment groups?
6 What was the control group doing: 'business as usual' or something else, and what was 'business as usual'?
7 How far were differences in frequency, quality, intensity, strength, duration and timing of the treatment addressed?
8 What blinding, double-blinding, triple-blinding operated in the RCT?
9 How far were the measures – the 'what' – used in the RCT complemented by process data concerning the 'why', 'how', 'where' 'by whom' in the RCT?
10 What were the side effects – intended and unanticipated – of the RCT, and how positive/negative/acceptable were these?
11 What risk analysis and risk management were conducted before the RCT?

Data analysis

1 Was the data analysis appropriate and correct?
2 Were the standard deviations of the control and treatment groups sufficiently similar in the pre-test?
3 Were the distributions of results in the control and treatment groups normally distributed, skewed, and if they were skewed, were the skews in the same direction?
4 Were sub-sample analyses conducted for different sub-groups, and, if so, what did they show?

5 How safe and useful were the averages in terms of normal and non-normal distributions, and were outliers exerting a strong effect?
6 What steps were taken to ensure that averaging was fair to the spread and distributions of the data?
7 What attention was given to outliers and sub-groups?
8 Why and how was null hypothesis significance testing used?
9 How far did the assumptions underpinning null hypothesis significance testing really obtain in the RCT?
10 How sufficiently were proportionality and multiple conditionality addressed in the claims made from effect sizes?
11 Were the claims made for the effect sizes justified, given the challenges faced, and multiple conditionality in using effect sizes and what they show?
12 What steps were taken to reduce false positives and false negatives?
13 What criteria were used to judge whether the RCT 'worked'?

Reporting

1 What results were reported?
2 How complete and sufficient was the reporting of the RCT?
3 Were all the key elements of the RCT included and addressed in the report?
4 Did the report acknowledge the limits of validity and reliability of the RCT?
5 Did the report make clear the boundaries, limits, strengths and weaknesses of the RCT?
6 Did the report contain sufficient information for researchers to understand and evaluate the RCT?
7 How easy to understand was the report?
8 Was bias addressed at all stages of the RCT?
9 Were the language and register of the report appropriate for the intended readership?

Generalizability, external validity and utility

1 What claims were made for generalizability, on what grounds, and with what degree of security, validity and acceptability?
2 How useful and usable were the results of the RCT for classroom practice?
3 What steps were taken to reduce false positives and false negatives?
4 Did the RCT demonstrate 'what works', and on what grounds?

It goes without saying that the RCT report should be fit for purpose and audience. The question here is whether the report provides the reader with sufficient information to judge whether this requirement has been met.

Gorard et al. (2017) and See (2018) comment that RCTs are open to criticism for failing to address sufficiently questions such as those set out above, for committing errors in the RCT, and for having weaknesses that undermine the power, reliability, validity of the RCT and the credibility of the reported results. In short, many RCTs are not robust.

Conclusion

Reporting and evaluating RCTs and what they show must meet high standards in terms of the claims made – what they do and do not show – and in terms of including key items of the RCT. References were made to examples of such items and to a substantial list of questions to be asked in evaluating the report of the research and the research itself. Strict adherence to reporting demands exposes weaknesses in published examples not only in reporting RCTs but in their design, with weaknesses in the trial itself.

Chapter 12

Generalizability and generalizing in randomized controlled trials, meta-analysis and meta-meta-analysis

Introduction and overview

Generalizability is often regarded as the 'Achilles heel' of RCTs (Connolly et al., 2017, p. 27). Whilst RCTs may be strong on internal validity (though the previous chapters have indicated some of the demands placed on them here), external validity/generalizing from, and generalizability of, RCTs is questionable. There are many limits on generalizability, and many conditions to be met if they are to be generalizable. This chapter raises several concerns and issues in generalizing from, and generalizability of, RCTs:

- The limits of generalizability in RCTs.
- The limits of induction.
- The need for considerable similarity of causes, 'support factors', conditions and contexts for generalizability to be possible.
- Scaling up from RCTs.
- Concerns about generalizing in meta-analysis, meta-meta-analysis and systematic reviews.

The chapter raises many concerns and criticisms that have been levelled at meta-analysis and meta-meta-analysis, and argues for greater limits to be placed on claims for what they really show and how secure are the results. It concludes by throwing down the gauntlet to advocates of generalizability, to ask whether, in fact, generalizability is as possible, desirable or acceptable as its advocates suggest. Indeed, Norman (2003) makes the wry, ironical comment that an 'understanding of how difficult transfer is, and what can be done about it, did not result from large randomised trials' (p. 583), but from 'small, tightly controlled studies' (to establish causality), with 'many replications' and 'driven by theories of the process' (pp. 583–584).

Generalizability and transferability

A major concern of RCT's is their generalizability and transferability out of their initial contexts. A context-specific RCT may be useful in that context alone (Buck and McGee, 2015, p. 8), telling us simply that an intervention did or did not work in that one place, not in all places. The Agence Nouvelle des Solidarités Actives (2017) reported that not only were there insufficient numbers of robust RCTs available but that the applicability to the UK context of RCTs conducted abroad could not be assessed (p. 12). Replicability, as Krathwohl (1985) notes, is at the heart of external validity (p. 123). However, local and cultural conditions make a difference to generalizability, e.g. drill and practice pedagogies are supported in some cultures and berated in others. Cronbach (1982b) commented that internal validity is relatively trivial when compared to external validity. Some RCTs may have limited external validity (generalizability), and findings in one context may not work in another context (Cartwright and Hardie, 2012).

Just as generalizability is problematical in clinical trials (Clarke and Dawson, 1999, p. 31), so it is in education and other branches of social science, as contextuality has such a large hand in everyday behaviour. As Krogstrup (2011) remarks: we cannot study social phenomena 'independently of their context' (p. 140). Cowen (2019) remarks that, perhaps paradoxically, it is exactly that which makes RCTs attractive within a given context that reveals the limits of their usefulness outside that context (p. 83). Deaton and Cartwright (2018) contend that demanding external validity is asking too much from an RCT (p. 2). They argue that extrapolating and generalizing from RCTs are dangerous as it cannot be assumed that average treatment effects are generalizable, what they find in one context may not be found in another context, and external validity requires reliance on much more than average treatment effects (p. 3).

Findings from RCTs undertaken in one location or situation may not transfer to another location or situation (Oakley, 2007; Cartwright and Hardie, 2012; Kvernbekk, 2019). Just because research has shown that such-and-such 'works' in a such-and-such a research setting, be it contrived or naturalistic, this is no reason to believe that it will work in a different temporal, locational, causal, contextual setting, or even the same setting, a second time. What 'works' with Form A is a disaster with the parallel Form B, even with the same teacher, curriculum, pedagogy, timing, resources and similar, but not identical, students. What 'works' once with Form A once is a disaster the second time with the same students, teacher, curriculum, pedagogy, timing and resources. The same teaching works wonders with student A's learning, but for his partner sitting next to him in the same class there is little or no learning taking place. That is the challenge, frustration and delight of teaching. If only there were simple recipes, but there are not. To think otherwise is an exercise in self-deception.

Too often we confuse efficacy with effectiveness: what 'works' for a specific instance, purpose or ideal condition (efficacy) may not be effective in a larger, more general context (effectiveness); efficacy and effectiveness are not the same. What has happened in one piece of research may be a poor predictor of what might happen if repeated elsewhere or at another time. This is the problem of induction. As mentioned in Chapter 1: '[i]nferring from efficacy to effectiveness is induction on a wing and a prayer' (Cartwright, 2010, p. 203) with very little similarity between them (p. 204). Major and Higgins (2019) note that the Education Endowment Foundation report that only around one quarter of its studies warrant scaled-up trials.

The need for similarity of causes, conditions and contexts

Cartwright and Hardie (2012) argue that, for something to work 'there' when it has worked 'here' requires the 'causal principles', 'causal cakes' (combinations of causal factors, ingredients, triggers and weights), 'causal roles' (how the principles operate) and causal conditions ('support factors') – Mackie's (1993) INUS factors (groups of factors: time, manner, context, conditions) – to be in place and similar (pp. 56–57) (Chapter 3). 'Causal roles' do not 'travel' well (Cartwright and Hardie, 2012, p. 88), and 'support factors' and their relative strengths differ. For transferability, all of these factors must obtain, not only in their presence but in their same relative strengths and operations, as this affects the causality at work here. In this respect the 'evidence' to be provided must be 'relevant' – important – in both the originating context and destinations, but what is 'relevant' may differ across two or more contexts.

The conditions, contingencies, constraints, and relevant factors 'there' are not the same as those 'here'; populations, personalities, values, cultural practices may be similar but not sufficiently similar for something to work when moved from 'there' to 'here', even if the same causal factors are present in the two situations. Indeed, as Rømer (2014) notes, the teacher's personality is a critical component in the evidence-based movement (p. 108). As Chapter 3 indicated, how factors are combined might differ between 'there' and 'here' in terms of strength, combinations, intensity, weightings, causal impact, even if the enablers, qualifiers, inhibitors, causal pathways, contingencies and conditions, and side-effects are similar (Kvernbekk, 2016, pp. 140–147). The user of the evidence, then, has to determine whether these are sufficiently similar for 'what works' to transfer securely. This is a powerful argument for local research and locally relevant research, and, indeed, for RCTs not to strive for, or claim, external validity. Indeed, Cartwright (2019) observes that there are 'unknown unknowns' with regard to causal factors, even if we have strong background knowledge (p. 71).

Deaton and Cartwright (2018) note that:

two populations will have the same ATE [average treatment effect] if and only if they have the same average for the net effect of the support factors necessary for the treatment to work ... . These are however just the kind of factors that are likely to be differently distributed in different populations. Given that support factors will operate with different strengths and effectiveness in different places, it is not surprising that the size of the ATE differs from place to place.

(Deaton and Cartwright, 2018, p. 12)

The 'support factors' may differ between locations, hence the question becomes 'are the same causes present in the new location, in the same strengths, weighting, and same combination, and in the absence of new countervailing support factors, and operating in the same ways, with the same circumstances, nature and conduct of the population and participants, as in the original location?' This is unlikely to be the case.

Scalability

How far is it possible to scale up the findings from one situation to a wider, bigger situation, and how safe is it to move from a pilot study to a larger scale RCT (Garcia et al., 2014, pp. 228–232)? Though aggregating RCTs on the same topic from different parts of the world may go some way to addressing this (e.g. Hattie, 2009; Major and Higgins, 2019), e.g. in meta-analyses and meta-meta-analyses, whether the outcome is simply an artefact of those who engage in this kind of exercise is questionable, discussed below.

Causality is context-dependent, and causes operating in one context may differ from those operating in another, by process, outcome, effects and strength. Hence, users of research evidence have to be circumspect about how well an RCT from one context will work in another. This argues for the exercise of the user's professional judgement in determining whether the causes, how they operate and the conditions in which they are operating, are sufficiently similar to their own for the similar intervention to 'work'. Such conditions are not only empirical, material and physical; they concern, for example, values, purposes, agendas, persons and personalities.

Given the concerns about RCTs' generalizability, it is maybe wiser to confine them to a limited context than apply them to new locations and contexts. This argues for local rather than more widely applicable RCTs, or for sub-group analysis rather than looking at average treatment effects, an argument that, in turn, challenges the usefulness of meta-analyses and meta-meta-analyses.

Scaling up to a wider or different population is problematical. This suggests the need to conduct RCTs in other contexts and contingencies, and it is important for researchers to find where and why they do and do not 'work' in contexts and conditions other than those in which they were first conducted. If an RCT has 'worked' in one set of contexts, it is important to see where else and how it 'works' or does not 'work'. Conversely, if it has not 'worked' in one context that does not mean it will not 'work' elsewhere. In both cases there is a requirement for the careful identification of the causal conditions, causal webs, and Cartwright and Hardie's (2012) 'causal cakes' and 'support factors' at work, and operating in the same ways and to the same extents, with what nature and degrees of variance and invariance, in both sets of contexts, before such replication studies are conducted, to avoid wastage of time and resources. Indeed, recognizing that strict replication is likely to be impossible (Tilley, 1993), it is prudent to identify the contexts, causal mechanisms and 'causal cakes' that led to the original outcomes, rather than to simply conduct the same RCT in a different context and 'hope for the best' (Nutley et al., 2007, p. 56).

Cartwright (2009) questions any assumption that a cause which might 'work' in an efficacy RCT will 'work' outside it, e.g. in a wider setting (p. 186); we are wrong to believe that a measure of one quantity in a particular setting will be the same as in another, new setting (p. 190). The challenge, as she puts it, is to identify what it is about the causes operating in an RCT in one setting that will produce the same results in another (p. 192).

In considering scalability, once findings are put onto a large stage, new additional factors come into play that were not present in the original RCT. As Buck and McGee (2015) observe, when a program is scaled up, this might bring about a new, different equilibrium of effects (p. 9). New factors may appear, facilitating, obstructing or having no effect on the scalability of the RCT; in each case, the reasons for this have to be identified, as these, too, concern the presence of new causal webs, 'causal cakes' and 'support factors'. For example, imagine that external examination results in one school are very positive, and the school attracts many new students. As the school grows, the factors that contributed to the positive examination results (e.g. small classes, human-centred dialogical teaching, individualized programs, close attention by teachers) are attenuated, and success is turned into failure when findings from a small-scale RCT are scaled up.

Deaton and Cartwright (2018) give the example of cocoa farmers whose use of a fertilizer improves yield and the farmers' income but, as more and more farmers use the fertilizer, i.e. the use of the fertilizer is scaled up, the price of cocoa falls and, along with it, because demand for 'cocoa' is 'price inelastic', incomes fall (p. 16); market scarcity increases income for the farmers, whilst market saturation overall reduces their income, so a positive correlation becomes a negative correlation. Scalability brings it costs as well as it benefits.

Generalizing from meta-analysis, meta-meta-analysis, research syntheses and systematic reviews

Generalizing from RCTs is often addressed through meta-analysis, meta-meta-analysis, research syntheses and systematic reviews, and their growth over the last two decades is enormous. However, their results are not guaranteed to be secure. Simpson (2017) notes that meta-analyses, meta-meta-analyses and systematic reviews take insufficient account of the differing quality of the contributing research. See (2018) reports that many RCTs used in meta-analysis are of poor quality; Major and Higgins (2019), strong proponents of meta-analysis and systematic reviews, note that gaps and errors exist in what is known, that perfection is chimerical, and that 'what works' for some groups does not 'work' for others (p. xii).

Higgins et al. (2011) used a 'star' rating scale for systematic reviews and meta-analyses:

* Quantitative evidence of impact from single studies, but with effect size data reported or calculable. No systematic reviews with quantitative data or meta-analyses located.
** At least one meta-analysis or systematic review with quantitative evidence of impact on attainment or cognitive or curriculum outcome measures.
*** Two or more rigorous meta-analyses of experimental studies of school age students with cognitive or curriculum outcome measures.
**** Three or more meta-analyses from well controlled experiments mainly undertaken in schools, using pupil attainment data with some exploration of causes of any identified heterogeneity.
***** Consistent high quality evidence from at least five robust and recent [within the previous ten years] meta-analyses where the majority of the included studies have good ecological validity and where the outcome measures include curriculum measures or standardised tests in school subject areas.

(Higgins et al., 2011)

The Education Endowment Foundation (2018) has a 'padlock' rating for judging how robust 'evidence' is, based on: 'the number and types of research studies available; the outcomes measured in those studies; the quality of the studies and whether they enable researchers to draw conclusions about impact; the consistency of the impact estimates in the different studies' (p. 1). There are five 'padlock' levels, from weak to strong:

🔒 = **Very limited evidence**: No evidence reviews available, only individual research studies.

🔒 🔒 = **Limited evidence**: At least one evidence review. Reviews include studies with relevant outcomes, and studies with methods which enable researchers to draw weak conclusions about impact.

🔒 🔒 🔒 = **Moderate evidence**: At least two evidence reviews. Reviews include studies with relevant outcomes, and studies with methods and analysis which enable researchers to draw moderate conclusions about impact.

🔒 🔒 🔒 🔒 = **Extensive evidence**: At least 3 evidence reviews. Reviews include studies with highly relevant outcomes, and studies with methods and analysis which enable researchers to draw strong conclusions about impact. Impact estimates are broadly consistent across studies.

🔒 🔒 🔒 🔒 🔒 = **Very extensive evidence**: At least 5 evidence reviews. Reviews are recent, and include studies with highly relevant outcomes, and studies with methods and analysis which enable researchers to draw strong conclusions about impact. Impact estimates are consistent across studies.

(Education Endowment Foundation, 2018, p. 1)

The 'padlock' approach uses quantitative data, reporting effect size and impact evaluation; at the time of writing it does not ask for whom it 'works', under what circumstances, how, and the ratings do not appear to take account of whether or how far the intervention itself was successful. This raises questions of its ability to really identify causality or to judge worthwhileness.

Meta-analysis

Meta-analysis is much favoured by the Department for Education (2016) in setting out 'what works' and what does not (p. 37). Meta-analysis is a statistical procedure which combines findings from many studies in seeking generalizability. It is the analysis of other analyses, usually RCTs, making generalizations from a range of separate, disparate studies, aggregating and combining their results into an overall account to discover main effects (Higgins, 2018; Joyce, 2019). This is typically done statistically, computing and combining effect sizes. Meta-analysis combines large-scale and small-scale studies into an overall effect size. It is an attempt to overcome the problems of small samples (see Maynard and Chalmers's (1997) review of the Cochrane Collaboration in medicine). Glass (1976, 1977), Glass et al. (1981), Hedges and Olkin (1985), Rosenthal (1991), Higgins (2018), Major and Higgins (2019) indicate how to conduct meta-analysis, involving the quantification and synthesis of findings from separate studies on some common measure, typically an aggregate of effect size calculations, i.e. *how much* difference a factor of interest purports to make overall.

Meta-analyses have the worthy intention of addressing the concern that single RCTs, on their own, are unreliable (Hammersley, 2013, p. 3). They occupy a prominent position in educational discourse. Higgins et al. (2011), for example, drew on thousands of studies in their first 'Toolkit of Strategies to Improve Learning'. Since then the Toolkit has gone through many versions and is now a major website (https://educationendowmentfoundation. org.uk/evidence-summaries/teaching-learning-toolkit/), and Higgins and his colleagues (e.g. Higgins, 2018; Major and Higgins, 2019), together with the Education Endowment Foundation, have produced a multiplicity of studies. Major and Higgins (2019) report that, by 2015, some two-thirds of teachers in England had used the Toolkit and different versions were operating in different parts of the UK and the world (p. ix). Major and Higgins's (2019) study of 'what works' draws on more than 200 summaries of some 8,000 studies of interventions (p. xii). Importantly, they state clearly that their work indicates 'good bets' rather than certainties about 'what works', not least as within-group variation and between group-variation can confound attempts at certainty (p. xxii). The Education Endowment Foundation's Teaching and Learning Toolkit (Education Endowment Foundation, 2019b) includes questions such as 'How effective is it?', 'How secure is the evidence?', 'What are the costs?', and 'What should I consider?', in addition to a Technical Appendix for each entry.

Meta-analyses have their supporters and their critics, discussed below. At one end of the spectrum of support for meta-analyses is assembled a formidable group of protagonists, e.g. Glass, Hedges, Hattie, Higgins; at the other end comes the title of Feinstein's (1995) paper that meta-analysis is simply 'statistical alchemy for the 21st century' and Meinert's (1989) questioning of whether meta-analysis is science or religion.

The two most frequently used indices of effect sizes are standardized mean differences and correlations, and assume that meta-analysis can only be undertaken for RCTs, rather than for all types of research. Glass et al. (1981) suggest that 'meta-analysis is particularly useful when it uses unpublished dissertations' (Cheung and Slavin's (2016) terminology of 'gray literature', e.g. technical reports, dissertations, other papers), as these contain weaker correlations than those reported in published research, and hence act as a brake on misleading, more spectacular generalizations (Cohen et al., 2018), though unpublished research may be difficult to locate, and ownership and release of data may be prohibited or restricted.

Glass et al. (1981, pp. 226–9) argue that it is necessary to counter gross claims made in published research with more cautious claims found in unpublished research. Added to this is the file drawer problem, i.e. publication bias and 'confirmation bias', publishing studies only with large effect sizes, and this raises questions against meta-analyses that over-estimate overall effect sizes; hence, comprehensive searches for, and inclusion of, studies that represent the range of findings are required. Wolf (1986) suggests the need to report the limitations of the meta-analyses conducted. The Education Endowment Foundation (2017) in the UK and the National Center for Educational Evaluation and Regional Assistance (2017) in the USA insist that their RCTs publish the findings regardless of the outcome and that this prevents publication bias by requiring RCTs to conform to a standard format for reporting.

If meta-analysis is to be fair, then, in the traditions of natural science, as standard practice it should gather and evaluate alternative, rival explanations and data that might disconfirm the hypotheses under investigation. Further, meta-analyses must be tempered with cautions, which as Major and Higgins (2019) argue, are often lost in headline-grabbing statements; meta-analyses are not unassailable truths; rather, they deal in 'best bets' rather than certainties (p. ix). Major and Higgins recognize that statements of 'what works' risk oversimplifying reality (and the title of their book is a question ('*What Works?*') rather than a certainty).

Higgins (2018) suggests that meta-analysis is useful in considering whether to accept option A or option B in, for example, a pedagogical approach – a teacher would be more advised to use an option with a higher overall effect size than one with a lower effect size, aware of the need to check the limits of the inferences that have been stated (p. 51).

Meta-analysis is claimed to be a means of avoiding Type II errors (failing to find effects that really exist: false negatives) (Cooper and Rosenthal, 1980), though Hedges and Olkin (1985) and Cook et al. (1992, p. 297) dispute this, showing that Type II errors become more likely as the number of studies included in the sample increases.

The confidence that can be placed in meta-analysis is a matter for judgement. For example, Cohen et al. (2018) report that meta-analysis has many critics (e.g. Wolf, 1986; Thomas and Pring, 2004; Elliott, 2007). Wolf (1986, pp. 14–17) suggests six areas of concern:

1   It is difficult to draw logical conclusions from studies that use different interventions, measurements, definitions of variables, and participants.
2   Results from poorly designed studies take their place alongside results from higher quality studies.
3   Published research is favoured over unpublished research.
4   Multiple results from a single study are used, making the overall meta-analysis appear more reliable than it is, since the results are not independent.
5   Interaction effects are overlooked in favour of main effects.
6   Meta-analysis may have 'mischievous consequences' (p. 16) because its apparent objectivity and precision may disguise procedural invalidity in the studies.

RCTs currently are placed at the top of the status tree in meta-analysis, in judging 'what works'. Nevertheless, errors of omission, commission and bias, e.g. combining different designs, data, analysis and presentation factors which risk leading to questionable research findings (Ioannidis, 2005, p. 0697), are such that, for the majority of research designs and their settings, a research claim is more likely to be false rather than true, and the claimed findings from research may often be no more than accurate measures of the bias present in the study (*ibid.*, p. 0696). Whilst Ioannidis argues that large-scale studies or low-bias meta-analyses can help to improve the quality of the meta-analysis, Paterson et al. (2016) note that many studies employed in meta-analysis are statistically underpowered, leading to excessive numbers of Type I errors (false positives). Coe (2002) notes that, if effect size derives from experiments, each of whose outcomes measures differ significantly, then the result 'may be totally meaningless' (p. 9).

Makel and Plucker (2014) make copious references to problems concerning meta-analysis, including, for example: publication bias; low reliability between reviewers; creating hypotheses after the results have been found (i.e. 'dredging'); using and misusing statistics and data; the file drawer problem (e. g. not submitting papers that have small effect sizes); and over-reliance on null hypothesis significance testing (Chapter 10).

Slavin (2018b) notes that a meta-analysis can be deceptive, in that it might be based on very few studies (he gives the example of a meta-analysis in which the effect size hinged on one study of practising tennis) (see also Shanahan, 2017). See (2018) references a study which was of a single participant. Gersten and Hitchcock (2009) note that limits on the value of meta-analysis might depend on the number of studies used: a meta-analysis containing only a small number of studies may be of limited use. If the evidence is so small, so slight, and derived from so few studies, how much trust can be put in the meta-analysis? Having a small number of studies undermines claims to generalizability. Further, individual studies themselves might be weak; this argues for the careful scrutiny of these before any meta-analysis is considered (Feinstein, 1995). As Feinstein argues, poor-quality RCTs may be lumped together with high-quality studies.

In a 2004 interview, Gene Glass, one of the originators of meta-analysis commented that:

> Medicine enjoys the advantages of a simpler domain [than education]: Treatments are packaged in standard form, outcome measures are generally agreed upon; success and failure tend to be counted on the same metric. Education research enjoys none of these. Our biggest challenge is to tame the wild variation in our findings not by decreeing this or that set of standard protocols by describing and accounting for variability in our findings. The result of a meta-analysis should never be an average; it should be a graph.
>
> (Robinson, 2004, p. 29)

Wrigley (2018) notes that in meta-analysis: insufficient or no account is taken of how long each intervention lasts; disparate outcomes are muddled together (p. 369); little or no attention is paid to the fact that differences in effect size vary by age (e.g. as children grow older, the effect size becomes smaller); categories and terms used vary in their scope; and comparisons between the control and intervention groups are wrongly equated with gains by the same group of students over time (p. 369).

Jadad and Enkin (2007) note that meta-analyses may be suspect if they use RCTs which have small sample sizes, bias and biased designs, incomplete reporting, or answer questions that were not the main purpose of the meta-analysis itself (p. 82). See (2018) demonstrates that 'methodological flaws are common' in meta-analyses and that evidence is 'flawed', noting that some meta-analyses included studies that had attrition rates as high as 70 per cent. Referring to over 5,000 studies, she indicates many weaknesses:

- *Sampling problems*: volunteer sampling; unfair comparison groups; lack of comparison groups (therefore an inability to address the counterfactual condition); small, uneven and unequal samples; small sub-groups in samples; sample membership; different age groups of samples; lack of randomization.
- *Scope*: few studies included; limited attention to classroom variables.
- *Insufficient warrants for the conclusions drawn and claims made*: overstating generalizability; drawing unfair conclusions from the evidence presented; inapplicability to classrooms or practice; validity of outcome measures and claims made from them.
- *Data analysis*: questionable averaging of diverse effect sizes; misuse of statistics (e.g. applying statistics for random samples when no random sample was used); misinterpretation and misuse of statistical significance testing.
- *Conflicts of interest*.
- *Biased reporting*: failure to reports adverse effects and negative impacts.
- *Data quality*, e.g.: self-reporting; use of different measures in different studies.
- *Lack of trials*.
- *Non-experimental designs*.
- *Lack of clarity*: whether studies were or were not classroom based; outcome measures.

These are a formidable catalogue of challenges, which See backs up with many examples. She argues for much greater attention to be given by those reviewing, publishing and using research to key features in ensuring the quality of the research, by having large samples, using random assignment, with 'minimal attrition', conducting evaluation independently, and with standardized assessments being used in outcomes measurements (See, 2018, p. 54). Studies must demonstrate that claims to causality are defensible, that biased reporting is avoided, that published papers report their methods and designs, and that, for transparency and reader judgement, claims made must follow from the research itself, and truthfulness and transparency must be evident.

In addition to these can be added further concerns, for example:

- The research design does not fit the research purposes or the research questions.
- Causality is confused with correlation.
- Insufficient controls are placed on the data and the data analysis.
- Counterfactuals, comparison groups, counterfactual analysis are absent.
- Claims for causality are spurious.

- The contingencies of specific situations are excluded, overlooked or neglected.
- Studies are too small scale for statistical power, statistical analysis or secure generalization.
- Missing data and attrition bring about unreliability in the data analysis and claims made.
- Replication studies are few and unreliable (unrepeatable).
- Measurements are not as exact as they are taken to be.
- Conflicts of interest may suppress negative findings.

In conducting a fair meta-analysis, it is important to weight the studies according to criteria such as sample size, rigour and quality of the research, and to include studies which confirm and disconfirm a hypothesis (e.g. which find no, or small, effects, rather than simply those studies which include moderate or large effect sizes). It is important, also, to report the confidence with which calculations of averages are valid, reliable and useful. Further, what appears to be currently missing from meta-analysis is metadata, which would help in judging the quality of the data and the studies included.

Meta-analysis which uses RCTs should ensure that the samples really represent their target populations; without this it is dangerous to suggest that combining studies will ensure representativeness. Cohen et al. (2018) remark that, as much hangs on the quality of the results to be combined in the meta-analysis, there is a risk that the inadequacies of the data base and the limits of the sample might simply be multiplied, vainly trying to compare what are incomparable studies (p. 223). Dissimilar studies may simply be lumped together, regardless of sample size, duration of the intervention, sample characteristics and so on. Hence, sampling error and the influence of other factors should be addressed, and these should account for only a small fraction of the variance in observed effect sizes if the results are to be acceptable.

Meta-analyses might use studies that have included few controls. Cohen et al. (2018) and Slavin (2018a, 2018b) comment meta-analysis risks overlooking the differences between methodologically rigorous and poor quality, methodologically flawed research. It is little surprise, perhaps, that scepticism exists on how much meta-analysis is actually 'analysis' at all, that it is simply statistical processing with a cranked-out outcome (e.g. Wrigley, 2018).

Wrigley (2018) notes that a major weakness of meta-analyses in education, in contrast to medical research, is their lack of a 'theoretical explanation' (p. 368), i.e. that meta-analyses simply process data, regardless of their theoretical warrants or underpinnings. Cowen (2019) comments that, for a meta-analysis to provide a solution to the problem of generalizing from the results of an intervention, we need a *theory* of how the intervention works (which is extraneous to the RCT) and an understanding of the environment in which it can be applied, not simply additional RCTs (p. 83) (see also Cartwright, 2009).

Meta-analyses risk overlooking significant differences between the effect sizes of included studies: some effect sizes may be very small whilst other may be large, but these are lost in an overall calculation. Brown (2013) questions the use of averages: one study in a meta-analysis might have a very low (or even negative) effect size, whilst another study has a high effect size, but combining these in calculating an average loses this 'vital detail' (p. 3).

Wood (1995, p. 296), Pawson (2006) and Wrigley (2018) suggest that meta-analyses oversimplify the phenomena about which they are reporting, by aggregating studies, by omitting contextual factors and conditions, by overlooking irregularities, by removing studies, by focusing on averages, by concentrating on overall effects to the neglect of the interaction of intervening variables, thereby overlooking exactly those features which explain how an intervention works (Pawson, 2006, p. 43). Indeed, the statement of 'what works' overlooks the important question of how something 'works' (Wrigley, 2018, p. 374).

Borenstein et al. (2009) identify several further criticisms of meta-analysis. For example, a single number cannot fairly summarize a research field, therefore it is preferable to include comments on distribution and dispersions, rather than simply to provide a single figure. Hunter et al. (1982) suggest that sampling error and the influence of other factors must be addressed, and that sampling error should account for less than 75 per cent of the variance in observed effect sizes. Meta-analysis risks synthesizing studies which are insufficiently similar to each other for such synthesis to be tolerable (Cohen et al., 2018, p. 224), a charge which Glass et al. (1981) reject. Further, for meta-analysis to be defensible, there needs to be differentiation between methodologically rigorous and poorly constructed RCTs (Cook et al., 1992, p. 297), a point which has been addressed by Smith and Glass (1977), Glass et al. (1981), Slavin (1995) and Evans et al. (2000).

Simpson (2018b) comments that calculating an average overall effect size from studies which differ in comparison treatments commits a category error of reading effect sizes as if they indicated the relative effectiveness of the interventions included (p. 902). They do not; rather, they are measures that are highly conditional on the design and features of the study in question; they are indicators of the clarity of the difference between the 'signal' and the 'noise' (Chapter 10) rather than an objective index of success. He provides examples of meta-analyses in which the studies chosen for inclusion differed in terms of the tests used, the sample and the comparison treatments (p. 905). He argues that if one wishes to assess how effective different interventions are, using effect sizes that have been averaged, this can only be done fairly if all the other factors and items that impact on effect size are distributed equally (the same) across the meta-analyses and the meta-meta-analyses in question (p. 906). This includes the test (e.g. as the more test questions are included, the higher the effect size) (Simpson, 2017), the sample, and the comparison treatments. He adds that just because some interventions might be similar is no justification for the credibility of the meta-analysis, as small differences between studies can have large effect sizes, and, anyway, metrics do not currently exist for indicating the cut-off levels for accepting sufficient similarity between studies.

Whether studies vary so much that meta-analysis, in combining several studies, are an attempt to mix oil and water, apples and pears, apples and oranges, indeed other mixed fruits (including 'rotten fruits' (Feinstein, 1995, p. 72)), is problematic, though Higgins (2018) suggests that meta-analyses are useful at the level of 'fruit' rather than specific fruits (p. 42). How much sense does it make to combine and then calculate averages from entirely different studies? What is the average of an orange and an apple: an orple? Higgins (2018) understates this problem in his throwaway line that 'combining effect sizes of different kinds is risky' (p. 49).

Morrison (2001) identifies a key challenge here:

> How can we be certain that meta-analysis is fair if the hypotheses for the separate experiments were not identical, if the hypotheses were not operationalisations of the identical constructs, if the conduct of the separate RCTs (e.g. time frames, interventions and programmes, controls, constitution of the groups, characteristics of the participants, measures used) were not identical?
>
> (Morrison, 2001, p. 78)

We can learn from 'medical models' here, where pooling disparate groups of patients into a single meta-analysis has 'poor scientific quality' (Feinstein, 1995, p. 72). How far can the results of unique, context-specific, idiographic RCTs combine to make a legitimate meta-analysis? Meta-analyses must ensure that they are valid and reliable.

As a parallel example, say that I have conducted a meta-analysis comprising four different surveys of the size of the problem of school dropout, using different Likert scales, with data as set out in Table 12.1.

Overlooking the point that it is inappropriate to calculate the mean from ordinal data, given the considerable differences reported in Table 12.1, it would be ridiculous to combine these into a single result (e.g. an overall mean of 4.5), so why exempt meta-analyses using RCTs from such concerns?

Smith and Glass (1977), Glass et al. (1981, pp. 218–220), Slavin (1995, 2018a) and Evans et al. (2000) address such charges. Evans et al. (2000) argue that weak studies can add up to a strong conclusion (p. 221) and that the differences in the effect sizes between high-validity and low-validity RCTs are surprisingly small (p. 226) (see also Glass et al., 1981, pp. 220–226). Glass (2000) indicates that he was prepared for such criticism, writing that 'of course it [meta-analysis] mixes apples and oranges; in the study of fruit nothing else is sensible; comparing apples and oranges is the only endeavor worthy of true scientists; comparing apples to apples is trivial ... . No two

Table 12.1 Data from four surveys

	Sample size	No. of rating scale points	Mean	Standard deviation	Confidence level	Confidence interval	Statistical power
Survey 1	500	7	5.3	6.1	90%	3%	0.5
Survey 2	150	5	4.1	4.3	95%	5%	0.3
Survey 3	75	7	3.9	5.2	95%	5%	0.4
Survey 4	1000	5	4.7	4.1	99%	4%	0.8

things can be compared unless they are the same. If they are the same, there is no reason to compare them' (p. 6). It was a neat response but he also stated that 'I had a gnawing insecurity that the critics might be right' (*ibid.*). It side-stepped the issues of what makes some apples edible and others rotten and *why* we should concern ourselves with 'fruit' generally when, for teaching and learning, we should be looking at good apples and bad apples *and* at good oranges and bad oranges.

Meta-analysis risks the 'garbage in, garbage out' problem: those that include low-quality studies or studies with the same bias, challenge the validity and reliability of the meta-analysis. To address this, quality control and inclusion criteria must be rigorous, leading to careful selectivity in deciding which studies to include and which to weed out, with transparent eligibility criteria to enable bias to be reduced and relevance to be addressed.

To the charge that meta-analyses take insufficient account of the dangers of mixing high-quality and low-quality studies, Glass (2000) was resolute:

> I remain staunchly committed to the idea that meta-analyses must deal with all studies, good, bad and indifferent, and that their results are only properly understood in the context of each other, not after having been censored by some *a priori* set of prejudices.
>
> (Glass, 2000, p. 10)

Wrigley (2018) comments that meta-analyses:

- use studies coming largely from America and which can be up to 50 years old (p. 369) (a claim which the Education Endowment Foundation addresses by putting a ten-year limit on eligible studies);
- use measures which are so narrow as to fail to reflect 'important educational aims' (p. 369);
- under-represent certain areas of the curriculum, concentrating on basic numeracy and literacy (though the range of topics in the Education Endowment Foundation is wide);

- overlook the varying duration of each intervention included;
- combine several different curriculum areas and 'psychological gains' in drawing conclusions (p. 369);
- make no allowance for the observed tendency of average effect sizes to become significantly smaller as children's grow older (e.g. 5 to 9 years) (p. 369);
- make calculations based on categories which vary in breadth and specificity;
- do not indicate sufficiently clearly whether comparisons are being made between control and experimental groups or between the same students before and after the study.

Wrigley and McCusker (2019) note that: the direction of influence of factors is unclear; measures that use grades are mixed with the percentages of students who graduate; measures of self-esteem are mixed with measures of attainment (p. 119). To this they add that, with regard to the work of both Hattie and the Education Endowment Foundation's Toolkit (on meta-meta-analyses), there is a neglect of theories, contexts and the extent of similarity between the studies (i.e. again mixing 'apples and oranges') (p. 119).

Borenstein et al. (2009) comment that meta-analyses might be conducted poorly; meta-analysis is complex, and it is inevitable that errors will be made, therefore great care is needed to ensure that what is, in principle, a rigorous method, is conducted equally rigorously and carefully in practice. Also, results from a meta-analysis might yield results which differ from those of large-scale RCTs, therefore, like must be fairly compared with like, i.e. matched studies must disclose the criteria used, including fair and matched sample size and characteristics. Suri (2018) suggests that meta-analysts conduct sensitivity analyses to 'assess robustness and to bound uncertainty levels' and to 'make fair comparisons between what was found in a single study and a wider population' (p. 430).

Wiliam (2019) poses several questions to judge whether the results of meta-analysis 'are worth taking seriously':

- Are the studies included relevant?
- Are the effect sizes the result of interventions, or merely associations?
- Are the effect sizes comparing the same things (e.g. comparison with an alternative intervention or 'business as usual', rather than just before and after)?
- Are the effect sizes at the same level (e.g. individual, group)?
- Is there a check on publication bias, for example, through the use of a funnel plot?
- Are the interventions being compared of similar duration?
- Are the interventions being compared of similar intensity?
- Are all the outcome measures used all measuring the same thing?

- Is the dispersion of the measured attribute similar in the studies being compared?
- Are the outcome measures used equally sensitive to the treatment being investigated?
- Do the participants in the studies have equal aptitude for the treatment being investigated?

(Wiliam, 2019, p. 136)

He comments that if the answer to all of these is 'yes', then the meta-analysis can be taken seriously.

Attempts to ensure the quality of meta-analyses are manifested in reporting requirements. The QUOROM statement (QUality Of RepOrting Meta-analyses) (Moher et al., 1999) is designed to improve the quality of reporting meta-analyses. It includes 21 reporting requirements:

- *Abstract*: the objectives, data sources, review methods, results and conclusions.
- *Introduction*: a statement of the problem and a rationale for the review.
- *Methods*: the searching, selection criteria, validity assessment, data abstraction, study characteristics, quantitative data synthesis.
- *Results*: the trial flow, the study characteristics.
- *Discussion* section: a summary of the key findings, their inferences, potential biases, and suggestions for future research.

The QUOROM statement was superseded by the PRISMA statement (Moher et al., 2009) on *Preferred Reporting Items for Systematic Reviews and Meta-Analyses* (PRISMA), which includes 27 items:

- A *title*.
- A structured *abstract*.
- An *introduction* with a rationale and objectives.
- A *methods* section which includes a protocol and registration, eligibility criteria, information sources, search, study selection, data collection process, data items, risk of bias in individual studies and across studies, summary measures, synthesis of results, additional analysis.
- A *results* section which includes study selection, study characteristics, risk of bias within and across studies, results of individual studies, synthesis of results, additional analysis.
- A *discussion* section which includes a summary of results, limitations, conclusions.
- A *funding* section.

These steps are designed to insert rigour into the meta-analysis and to ensure that the limitations of the meta-analysis are transparent. The

QUOROM and the PRISMA statements are for clinical trials. The same rigour is being applied to meta-analyses in education as the What Works Clearinghouse and the Education Endowment Foundation play catch-up.

What we have, then, in meta-analysis, holds out the possibility of combining studies to provide a clear message about accumulated data from RCTs, but how much confidence can be placed in meta-analyses requires an evaluation of the contributing studies. The problems indicated above stem from flawed principles and conduct of the meta-analysis. Meta-analysis floats above the 'real world' and the lived experiences of participants; why give them such prominence? Meta-analysis can provide hints or 'best bets' (Higgins, 2018; Major and Higgins, 2019) but not much more. There are many ways of showing that something 'works', so why place your bet on only one horse?

Meta-meta-analyses

Meta-meta-analyses (combining meta-analyses into a single über-analysis) is a well-publicized attempt at generalizing, though it is not without its critics. Higgins (2018) notes that it is 'controversial' (p. 42) and he references key critics (p. 49) who argue that it is less like combining apples and oranges under the label of 'fruit' and more like comparing an apple with a chair (p. 49). An example of a meta-meta-analysis is Hattie's (2009) *Visible Learning*, which, when it was published, was hailed as teaching's 'holy grail'. However, opinions of the study were divided, some supportive and others critical. Here it is used as a worked example to indicate strengths of, and challenges to, meta-meta-analysis.

Hattie's study is massive, the number of meta-analyses and students featured in his study was immense, his methodology was explicit and he identified the point at which the study judged an intervention to have 'worked' (the hinge point) in terms of overall effect size. However, the study has received significant criticism, as introduced below, and such criticisms can be levelled at meta-meta-analyses more widely.

Hattie's *Visible Learning*, based on more than 800 meta-analyses of 52,637 studies and several million participants (Hattie, 2009), was later increased to over 1,500 meta-analyses. Hattie (2012) reports that since his original studies in 2008, he added 115 new meta-analyses, an extra 7,515 studies, and that these indicate negligible changes to ranking of issues and effect sizes. In other words, it seems as though his meta-meta-analyses had reached saturation point, beyond which studies did not make any further changes.

Berk (2011) draws attention to the possible bias in some of the studies Hattie used, as they were not RCTs (p. 199). Brown (2013) comments that Hattie's work, in averaging combined averages from meta-analyses, is highly questionable, as not only do the original averages in the meta-analyses combine studies which have varying effect sizes, but then, to average these averages yields a figure that is almost meaningless. Hattie averages averages of averages. Berk (2011) comments that Hattie unfairly mixes and combines studies, e.g. because: (a) some studies use pre-and post-testing of the same single group whilst others compare two separate groups (p. 4); (b) studies are of different duration; (c) differences within and between sub-groups in a study are lost (e.g. low-achieving students might be benefiting from an intervention whilst high-achieving students might not) (p. 4); (d) some studies are based on self-reported grades; (e) some studies use correlations rather than measures of difference (p. 5) (see also Wrigley, 2018; Kraft, 2019;); (f) studies average across age ranges, whereas effect size often decreases as students grow older. To this can be added Poulsen's (2014) comment that Hattie uses studies which have no control groups and Kraft's (2019) note that Hattie includes studies that use non-standardized measures.

Bakker et al. (2019) comment that Hattie takes insufficient account of: which effect size calculation is used in the studies and how such calculations are based on different variances found in the studies; different confidence intervals in the studies used; different comparison groups (e.g. between- or within-group differences); the effects of different research designs on the findings; the degree of alignment between the intervention and measures used; differences between groups who were *offered* the intervention and those who took up or did not take up the offer; differences in the duration of the intervention; differences in sample sizes in the studies used; differences in the characteristics and make-up of the samples in the studies used; differences in the ease with which the dependent variable could be influenced; and contextual differences.

When meta-analyses and meta-meta-analyses are conducted, the risk is that, because of averaging of averaging, and averaging of averaging of averaging respectively, out of the window go significant contextual factors – age, ability, gender, ethnicity, the subjects studied, socio-economic factors, duration of the intervention, class size, teacher behaviour, student characteristics, fidelity to the procedures required, different data collection instruments, different purposes and designs of the research, differences in populations and samples etc. – which are not only the exact points that teachers need to know but whose absence leads to bland generalizations of questionable utility.

Bergeron and Rivard (2017) argue that Hattie's work is 'pseudo-science' since:

- it does not clarify what it means by 'success';
- it relies too heavily on questionable effect sizes;
- it makes spurious inferences of impact;
- it lacks attention to negative probabilities: overlooking 'the presence of negative probabilities' (p. 3);
- it violates requirements for statistical analysis;
- it excludes important variables and makes illegitimate comparisons between data;
- it uses a formula for converting a correlation into Cohen's d without understanding the requirements for rendering this valid;

- he makes miscalculations in his meta-analyses;
- he uses 'inappropriate baseline comparisons' (p. 3);
- some of his descriptors of variables and proxies have questionable validity;
- the timescales of some of the studies reported were of questionable worth;
- he combines many different types of study into a single aggregated effect;
- he employs unfair averaging and 'averages that do not make any sense' (p. 5), e.g. if one's head is extremely hot and one's feet are extremely cold then it is a nonsense to say that, on average, we are 'comfortably warm' (p. 5);
- he falsely equates the comparison of a before-and-after treatment in the same group with comparing two independent groups;
- his interpretation of effects lacks objectivity and justification;
- he unfairly 'confounds correlation and causality' (p. 6);
- there are errors of calculation and interpretation (p. 10);
- the reduction of many factors to a single number 'is insufficient to represent reality' (p. 10);
- analyses fail to meet the required level of statistical sophistication (e.g. relying on averages and standard deviations).

As Bergeron and Rivard (2017) comment, the quality of a study and the validity of data trump numbers and large samples (p. 246). Quality trumps quantity. To Bergeron and Rivard's comments can be added: the inclusion of poor-quality or unknown-quality studies (Higgins and Simpson, 2011); insufficient attention being paid to the differing contexts of studies; different durations of studies and the reliability and validity of short-duration studies; skewness and non-normal distributions in the findings; neglect of the influence of moderating and other influencing factors; problems of different meanings and interpretations of the same words/labels being used (e.g. 'feedback', 'problem-solving', 'project-based teaching', 'cooperative work', 'small' and 'large' with reference to class size); and, when studies are combined, differences of control variables and which variables are included and excluded.

Schulmeister and Loviscach (2014) cast serious doubt over the methods used by Hattie and the results that stem from them, in that: (a) he uses studies whose methodology is questionable; (b) he groups together studies which do not have the 'same effect group' as is accorded to them (e.g. he mixes studies of teacher-to-student feedback with studies of student-to-teacher feedback); (c) he has not employed 'due diligence' in selecting studies (e.g. for the areas of 'concentration, persistence, and engagement' he included a meta-analysis that focuses on industrial power rather than mental power); (d) even though he grouped some meta-analyses correctly in terms of their independent variables (e.g. interventions), he mixed 'apples and oranges' in his dependent variables; (e) he presents misleading statistics (e.g. he draws on two meta-analyses that have an effect size of $d = 0.06$ and $d = 0.59$ to give an average effect size of 0.33); and (f) he provides an 'untenable ranking list' in that, if one addresses the problems indicated in (a) to (e) here, then their positions in his ranking list move significantly up or down (p. 2). The authors comment that the effect of a particular intervention is dependent on the circumstances of the individual case.

There are also problems of combining samples from small populations or abnormal populations (e.g. children with very specific learning difficulties) (Simpson, 2017; See, 2018; Kraft, 2019) as these may not be generalizable. Problems also exist in using the same studies in different meta-analyses, i.e. double-counting, such that these might affect weightings and reliability (Shanahan, 2017).

Arnold (2011) notes that Hattie did not use weighted averages, giving equal weight to large and small meta-analyses, despite Glass's (1977) noting of challenges in combining and weighting differently sized studies (very little to very large), raising the question of whether big is beautiful or monstrous.

Slavin (2018a) comments that Hattie:

- is simply 'shovelling' meta-analyses which contain massive bias into further meta-meta-analyses that have the same biases (p. 1), without sufficient questioning of the contributing studies and their differing quality and size (see also Snook et al., 2009; See, 2018);
- is misguided in using an effect size of 0.40 as a 'hinge point' (the cut-off point in his 'barometer'), as this overlooks the importance of smaller effects achieved by different groups;
- uses effect size studies that are correlational, with insufficient controls, or lacking in control groups, or which are pre-post designs; and
- uses studies without sufficient attention to their meaning or quality, i.e. does not screen them sufficiently, for example in using studies with no control groups and invalid measures.

The example of concerns about the work of Hattie suggest that great caution must be taken in determining what meta-meta-analyses really show and how reliable, valid and usable they are. Indeed, one anonymous reviewer of the present manuscript commented that when one compares Hattie's work and that of the Education Endowment Foundation (EEF) with the careful databases that one finds in medical evidence, Hattie and the EEF seem 'terribly crude'.

Hattie's responses are measured and careful (Lovell, 2018), stating that: he has taken account of many factors in his work; nobody has 'invented a different story' from his data; he himself has reworked the data but arrived at the same story; aggregating still makes sense; the claims for the importance of moderators are unproven; differences in effect sizes between individual studies and meta-analyses are over-stated; and overall, his results are preferable to having no results.

However, we perhaps should remain suspicious of meta-analyses and meta-meta-analyses in practice and in principle. As Wiliam (2019) remarks: '[a]ny claims about "what works" are necessarily local, in that they are limited to the participants and contexts actually studied, and judgement will be needed to apply them in other contexts' (p. 135). The pursuit of the general in the belief that it will surely 'work', is futile and unnecessary. 'Bullying by numbers' (Wrigley, 2015), however beautifully, dazzlingly and sensationally wrought, is still bullying.

A note on systematic reviews

This section is a footnote on systematic reviews rather than a full treatment of the topic, as many of the points made about meta-analysis and meta-meta-analysis apply here.

Systematic reviews are designed to maximize precision and minimize bias in reporting collated and combined responses of many RCTs (and other types of research) in a given field. The Alliance for Useful Evidence (Nesta), resonating with Goldacre (2012), makes a strong case for systematic reviews:

> Instead of unconsciously picking out papers here and there that support preexisting beliefs, [we] take a scientific, systematic approach to the very process of looking for scientific evidence, ensuring that evidence is as complete and representative as possible of all the research that has ever been done.
>
> (Gough et al., 2013, p. 4)

This is particularly apposite as the number of studies increases over time; a systematic review is one way of cutting through the 'voluminous literature of educational research' (Glass, 1976, p. 4).

Systematic reviews are designed to replace those literature reviews that are 'selective, opinionated and discursive rampages through literature which the reviewer happens to know about or can easily lay his or her hands on' (Oakley, 2007, p. 96). Gough et al. (2013) claim that systematic reviews:

> provide a meticulous way of finding relevant, high quality studies; and integrating their findings to give a clearer and more comprehensive picture than any single study can produce. Moreover, they are based on a clearly stated set of assumptions. Readers can base their judgments on a coherent set of studies encapsulated within a single report. Systematic reviews enable us to establish not only what is known from research; but also what is not known. They can inform decisions about what further research might be best undertaken, thereby creating a virtuous cycle.
>
> (Gough et al., 2013 p. 5)

A systematic review, Gough et al. aver, makes clear the following:

Need: Who is asking the question and what they will do with the answer.
Review question: What will the review do and what are its underlying assumptions.
Scope: Establishing the criteria used to select studies.
Search: Designing and running a search strategy to find promising sources.
Screen: Checking which studies are relevant and discarding those that are not.
Code: Collecting information for mapping, quality assurance, and on study findings.
Map: Describing the nature of the research.
Appraise: Judging the relevance, utility and quality of the studies.
Synthesise: Bringing together the findings of different studies to answer the review question.
Communicate: Describing how the review was done, its findings and implications for future decisions. (Gough et al., 2013, p. 11)

Similarly, the UK's HM Treasury (2011) has a clearly stated set of objectives with pre-defined eligibility criteria for a systematic review:

- has an explicit, reproducible methodology;
- uses a systematic search that attempts to identify all studies that meet the eligibility criteria;
- includes a formal assessment of the validity of the findings of the included studies;
- produces a systematic presentation, and synthesis, of the characteristics and findings of the included studies.

(HM Treasury, 2011, p. 61)

However, in examining systematic reviews, See (2018) notes that many are of poor quality, with weak methodology, flawed evidence (p. 40) and biased reporting, including conflicts of interest (see also Gorard et al., 2017). Simpson (2017) notes that, like meta-analyses, systematic reviews take insufficient account of the differing quality of the contributing research. Hammersley (2013) questions whether the studies used in a systematic review are all focusing on the same issue and whether they are sufficiently similar in focus, conduct and methodology to warrant being included (p. 105).

Slavin (2008) makes a strong case for exacting, rigorous standards of evidence in systematic reviews. He notes that the number of studies in some reviews is small, and that some research is conducted by parties with a potentially vested interest (e.g. commercial companies) with a risk of biased reporting and/or exclusion of negative findings in their advertising and reporting, where publication bias leads to the publication of 'successes' rather than 'failures', negative results or 'no difference' results. He notes that it is unsafe to assume that such flaws 'cancel each other out' (p. 7), and he sets out a range of challenges in research syntheses (pp. 7–11), including, e.g.:

- the strength of the evidence provided;
- the minimization of bias, and the use of large samples to address this;
- appropriate compromises between setting such a high bar that very few studies are included (therefore risking bias) and including poorer quality studies;
- being strict in ruling out bias and easier on factors which do not risk bias;
- insisting that research includes controls;
- adopting RCTs and random assignation;
- insisting on pre-test and post-test measures;
- avoiding small-scale studies, as these may have 'highly variable effects' (p. 8) and limited statistical power, can be prone to publication bias, may not be replicable, and may not be able to separate teacher effects from school effects;
- excluding studies which lasted for fewer than twelve weeks;
- using only those studies with low or no attrition;
- ensuring the validity of outcome measures;
- ensuring that studies are not so removed from everyday practice as to be artificial and unrealistic;
- using studies which include effect sizes;
- excluding studies where the pre-test differences are more than a half of a standard deviation;
- ensuring robust research designs;
- including several rather than few studies;
- ensuring that studies are of use to practising educators;
- excluding studies in which the outcome measures relate only to what the experimental group has been exposed to, as these will be biased (see also Lortie-Forgues and Inglis, 2019a), i.e. measures should be valid for both the control group and the experimental group (Slavin gives the example of the fault in testing geometry skills if only the experimental group had been taught geometry).

In judging 'what works' it is not only the *type* of evidence that it important; it is the quality – the rigour and security – of each of the studies themselves, separately and in combination, that must be addressed, and, as argued above, this is currently open to question.

Conclusion

For generalizability, many demands must be met in claiming that findings from RCTs in one context can transfer smoothly into another. For generalizability to be possible requires the existing and intended, new contexts to be similar, even identical, in terms of their causal make-up and how these causes operate together ('causal cakes', 'causal webs' and 'support factors'), socio-cultural and socio-political contexts, components and conditions, population characteristics, value systems and purposes, and decision-making parties. Induction places significant limits on what can be inferred when transferring findings from RCTs in one context to another context. The chapter raised concerns about scalability, arguing that this is not straightforward, since, as scale increases, this brings new factors into operation.

The chapter raised concerns about three widely used methods of generalizing from RCTs in the 'what works' agenda: meta-analyses, meta-meta-analyses, and systematic reviews. It reported criticisms of these on a range of criteria, and argued for greater attention to deciding which studies to include and what can and cannot legitimately be inferred from meta-analyses, meta-meta-analyses and systematic reviews. Despite claims to the contrary from leading advocates and practitioners of meta-analyses and meta-meta-analyses, there are many and severe problems with many existing meta-analyses and meta-meta-analyses. These argue for greater limits to be placed on which studies to include, deciding whether to include them, and what can legitimately and securely be claimed for what they really show. Indeed, the chapter questions the whole enterprise of meta-analyses and meta-meta-analyses as currently practised.

Generalizability might not be as important as its proponents and advocates might have us believe. RCTs might have limited generalizability, particularly if small-scale RCTs are the order of the day, but how much does this matter? Several researchers would argue that, in fact, it might not (e.g. Elliott, 2007; Oakley, 2007; Schofield, 2007; Hammersley, 2013; Pring, 2015; Cain, 2019; and the host of qualitative researchers). As Malouf and Taymans (2016) remark, single case designs and non-randomized trials might be better suited than RCTs to many school settings (p. 458). Of great concern is the need for research to catch the human-centred, individual and group focused, interaction- and relationship-based defining characteristics of education, i.e. what makes educational research truly educational. Idiographic and nomothetic research both have a part to play in improving education. Poor-quality meta-analyses and meta-meta-analyses don't offer much here.

Chapter 13

From evidence to policy to practice

Introduction and overview

Moves from evidence to policy making and decision making, and to practice by educationists, are complex, indirect and unstraightforward, as different parties:

- operate in different contexts;
- have different agendas, perspectives, priorities, needs, concerns, areas of focus and values, and make different uses of evidence;
- have different time scales;
- have different criteria for judging 'what works';
- pay differential attention to research;
- recognize the limits of evidence;
- use evidence in different ways.

The chapter identifies recent steps taken to bring research and research evidence into classrooms, but it notes that the links between research and policy making remain tenuous, and it provides suggestions for why this is the case.

Bringing research evidence into practice in education constitutes a major change for many parties, and this engages theories and practices of change and innovation, involving identifying and addressing barriers and facilitating factors in change, which are several.

Using evidence in policy and practice

To move from evidence to policy and practice is not simple, direct or straightforward. To suppose that what evidence 'shows' is unequivocal and straightforward misrepresents the nature of the relationship between evidence and policy. Evidence is not unequivocal; in most cases it is temporary, tentative, partial, incomplete, time-bound, locale-bound, sample-bound and design-bound; it might provide backing and support rather than proof. As Cartwright and Hardie (2012) and Nutley et al.

(2007) note, evidence plays an indirect rather than a direct role in policy making.

To move from evidence to practice, or from policy to practice, is fraught with challenges. Finding a result and then using that result are different: policy makers use evidence in different ways, as do educators and other practitioners. Research under-determines policy (Hammersley, 2013, p. 34). Further, interventions and their applications – the basis of evidence-based practice – involve change, but, as Morrison (1998) notes: 'just as people change change, so change changes people' (p. 145). Different parties extract what they want from research evidence and apply it as they deem fit in their own contexts, which typically differ from those that gave rise to the findings. This brings us into the vast realm of leading and managing change and innovation, which is outside the scope of the present volume. We cannot, indeed do not, simply read off pre-scripted recipes; rather, we exercise our judgement in deciding what works for us in our situations and contingencies, with our several parties involved.

What we find in the 'what works' evidence base is that it focuses on the substance of the intervention rather than on its management (other than protocols and procedures, for example, for conducting an RCT). If I wished to draw on evidence to implement an intervention in my policy making, decision making, school or teaching, I would hope to have guidance on how to manage it with my students, colleagues, parents and so on. Many interventions fail because of poor management of the intervention, but the evidence base in the 'what works' agenda pays scant regard to management. This is an important desideratum.

Taken more widely, where is the evidence that evidence-based education and RCTs are any more beneficial than other approaches to improving education and making education 'work'? And what are the counterfactuals here in establishing causation?

We live in many worlds: those of the researcher, policy maker, decision maker, classroom, teacher, learner, parents, and so on. Even though worlds might overlap, they still differ from each other; what policy makers want from the 'what works' agenda may differ from what teachers want. As Gorard (2018) notes, the relationship between policy, education and evidence from research is 'strange' (p. 213). The same educational practice may 'work' for one party whilst not 'working' for another party.

This takes us back to questions raised earlier in this book: how to decide at what point something does or does not 'work', and in comparison to what? Indeed, the uptake and impact of the research may depend in large part on its timeliness, relevance, and whether it can meet the deadlines for policy makers and practitioners, e.g. researchers often have longer time scales than policy makers (Levin, 1991) and research tends to make matters more, rather than less, complex, and this loses its attraction to policy makers (Nutley et al., 2007, p. 71).

204 Randomized controlled trials

Different parties want different things from research evidence and make different cases for how to use research. For example, policy makers might want a popular 'quick fix'; researchers might want evidence of causality; teachers might want evidence of what will work in their classrooms. Teachers who read research will almost automatically ask themselves 'that's all very well, but will this work with the students in my class?', 'what will I need to do to make it work here?', and 'what can I take from this research for my own work with these students?' Further, research uses do not operate in isolation; other things are happening at the same time and in conjunction with the research, i.e. research uptake and impact are contingent and conditional, not guaranteed.

It is rare for educational research, as for other kinds of social research, to provide definitive answers that policy makers seek or to be able to translate into immediate practice. Busy teachers who are under pressure from many sources, seeking definitive, action-oriented answers to the question 'what does this research tell me about what to do on Monday morning with my class of 15-year-olds?', may be disappointed. Research – like policy – is seldom so easily applicable; rather it is used in complex, unstraightforward, indirect, subtle, nonlinear, multidimensional, fluid, interactional, dynamical, changing and diverse ways (Nutley et al., 2007). We don't have, and never will have, enough evidence to say unequivocally that something 'works', and, anyway, it is far too simplistic a question. Indeed, questions can be raised about whether findings are as objective and neutral as they might claim to be, being paradigm-driven and contextually situated. Data contribute to 'evidence', i.e. to a case being made (Chapter 2).

People take a result of research evidence and do something *with* it and something *to* it; they have the sense to realize that it cannot simply be imported lock, stock and barrel without modification, and that to accept it without question is almost a guarantee that it won't work. Simply because something is published is no guarantee that anyone will take it up. People are not automatons, and they translate, adapt, modify, refine and reconstruct the research into their own or other contexts, and, in so doing, they adjust the research to those situations (Gorard et al., 2018; Cain, 2019). As Sheldon and Chilvers (2000) note, the effectiveness of evidence-based practice depends on the readers (p. 42). A Procrustean 'one-size-fits-all' approach is ill-judged as, at the risk of tautology, situations are situationally specific. As Nutley et al. (2007) remark, 'research use is highly contingent and context-dependent' (p. 303).

Research has many different kinds of impact, and this depends in part at the level at which it is pitched, e.g. conceptual, practical, valuative, political, economic, etc. and the parties and sectors at which it is aimed. For example, it may: 'shape values' (Nutley et al., 2007, p. 11); inform decisions (provided that it is fit for purpose); validate, reaffirm and challenge existing practice; influence conceptual and instrumental ways of thinking about, and reflecting on, practices; and impact on strategic as well as tactical policies and practices (p. 37). Research is often aimed at more than the 'what works' agenda.

Gorard et al. (2018) note that, in fact, the impact of research on practice is limited. They identify three problems here. Firstly, research that has the greatest impact might not be the highest quality research; high quality research may be used inefficiently yet claims made from, and the impact of, low quality research may be unwarranted (pp. 17–21). Secondly, it is misconceived to think that single studies have impact; there are few replication studies in education, and a 'best evidence summary' may include contradictory findings, e.g. from other high quality studies (p. 22). Thirdly, the progress made in 'generating good evidence' is not matched by a commensurate growth in understanding how to ensure that this evidence can best be handled to have 'appropriate impact' (p. 23).

Makel and Plucker (2014, p. 306) note that there are several disincentives to researchers conducting replication studies in education:

a   submission bias: researchers may consider opportunity cost and devote their time to other kinds of research;
b   funding bias: replication studies may not attract funding;
c   editor bias: editors may consider replication studies to be less prestigious than other kinds of studies;
d   publication bias: journals may decline replication studies;
e   hiring bias: researchers who have published replications may not be attractive to institutions;
f   promotion bias: replication research may not be attractive in the promotion stakes;
g   journal bias: some journals are less favourable to replication studies than others;
h   novelty bias: pressure for novelty reduces the attractiveness of replication studies.

Indeed, the authors note that, of 100 journals studied over a 5-year period, only 6 included over 1 per cent of replication studies and 43 published no replication studies.

The uptake of research (not only RCTs) depends on a range of factors (e.g. Anderson and Biddle, 1991; Zeuli, 1994; Rickinson, 2005; Nutley et al, 2007; Hammersley, 2013; Slavin, 2016; Gorard et al., 2018):

• the credibility accorded to the research (and the source/origin bodies of the research);
• the clarity, comprehensibility and user-friendliness of the research and its reporting;
• the complexity of the research: researchers raise and produce complex, detailed, qualified and contingent issues, whilst policy makers often want simple solutions and ideas;

- the nature of the work: researchers raise questions and problems, whilst policy makers want answers and solutions;
- the certainty of the findings: research is, in principle, fallible, whilst policy makers prefer certainty;
- the relevance of the research: researchers are criticized for being insufficiently issue-based and practice oriented;
- the 'acceptability threshold' (Hammersley, 2013, p. 33): researchers are judged by their peers in terms of the reliability and validity of their research and the theoretical warrants underpinning it, whilst policy makers are concerned with practical matters, cost, popularity, re-electability and practicality;
- the practicality of the research: some research is criticized for not focusing on practical matters, whilst practical matters are the 'bread and butter' of policy makers;
- the relevance of the research to the users' contexts, values and needs;
- the timeliness and perceived relevance of the research: researchers may take years to produce results, whilst policy makers want immediate results;
- the agendas and purposes of the several stakeholders;
- the characteristics and opinions of the users and adopters of the research;
- the background, experience and expertise of the readers of the research (e.g. their ability to understand the significance and meaning of the research);
- the time available to users of researcher to read the research and consider its implications;
- the effectiveness of the dissemination of, and access to, the research;
- the operations of 'knowledge brokers' (Nutley et al., 2007, p. 82) – those who act as the bridge between researchers, users of research and practitioners;
- the alignment and goodness of fit between the values implicit in the research and those of the users of the research;
- how far, and how well, the research meets the user's needs, agendas, purposes and situations;
- researchers may not judge what is good or bad for policy, whilst for policy makers this is a central issue;
- the channels for, and effectiveness of, communication;
- the support available for putting into practice the implications of the research, i.e. resource matters, e.g. human, temporal, material, managerial, financial, administrative, personal, technological etc.;
- the openness and commitment of the users of research to change and innovation;
- the power and autonomy of the users of the research;

- the ability of the participants to identify and overcome barriers and resistances to change;
- the absence of, or opportunity to overcome, resistance to change and innovation;
- the presence of users' cultures that promote or inhibit innovation, change and collegiality;
- responsiveness to feedback;
- ownership of the change and innovation (the 'buy in' factor);
- 'overcoming scepticism' (Cain, 2019, p. 207);
- perceived benefits and relative advantage of the research-based/research-informed innovation;
- the extent to which the research tells users 'what works' and confirms or matches their own pre-existing values, biases and experiences.

Research uptake and impact, then, are rooted in managing change and innovation, and Morrison (1998) and Garcia et al. (2014) comment that factors that facilitate and inhibit change reside in many fields. These include, e.g.: leadership; staff commitment; resources; support; determination; staff expertise, development and reskilling; workloads; time to read, digest and respond to 'evidence'; habits; support from outside parties; reduction in threat to people and practices; psychological matters: self-confidence, self-esteem and stress tolerance; trust between all participants; and overcoming reluctance to let go of the present situation. Nutley et al. (2007) note that the greater challenge is to persuade people to abandon their old ideas rather than simply to accept new ideas (p. 194).

It would be unfair and mischievous to argue that there is a dearth of practical recommendations that derive from research. Attempts have been made to ensure that research in education is rendered accessible and usable by teachers. For example, Hattie and his associates have taken many steps to address this (Hattie, 2009, 2012; Hattie and Yates, 2013; Hattie and Zierer, 2017; Hattie and Clarke, 2018). Further, at the time of writing, the Education Endowment Foundation's Teaching and Learning Toolkit (addressing 35 topics), its Early Years Toolkit (addressing 12 topic areas), and its focus on 14 Key Themes in its 'Big Picture', provide summaries and address issues such as how effective are the recommendations, how secure is the evidence, and what are the financial costs. Major and Higgins (2019), for each of their 21 areas of focus, provide indications of 'attainment gain', 'learning benefits', 'unexpected finding', 'teaching tips', 'leadership tips', 'principles', and 'key readings' (separated into 'academic' and 'practical' readings), though perhaps regrettably they confine their cautions and statements of limits only to the opening introduction rather than for each topic. Busch and Watson (2019) set out 77 topic areas, and, for each, address 'related research', 'classroom implications', 'studies that every teacher needs to know', and 'the main findings' of a particular study.

Whilst the link between research and educational practice is moving forward, the picture for research and policy is less clear and more tenuous (Hammersley, 2013; Gorard et al., 2018). This hiatus is not new; it stretches back decades (e.g. Anderson and Biddle, 1991). The reasons for this are several; the nature, amount and extent of the uptake and impact of research by policy makers depends on a huge range of issues: valuative, power-based, financial, comprehensibility, affirmatory possibilities, and many others. The issues set out in the papers in Anderson and Biddle (1991) are alive and well some thirty years later. Here the alignment of the research with policy objectives, agendas and values is vital, with research acting as affirmation rather than contradiction or challenge to policy makers and policies. The attractiveness of research to different policy groups and their powers is matched to the predicted policy situation and contexts in the near future, therefore the topicality and relevance of the research to policy agendas and priorities is of significant concern to policy makers. This includes the likelihood of the implications of the research being accepted by different interest groups and professionals, and the predicted consequences and possible fallout of the research where it affects policy making.

Further, policy makers are mindful of public reaction, public opinion, public interest and interests at work, whereas research might place such concerns less centrally in their agendas. This also concerns the nature of the research (e.g. 'pure' or 'applied') and how easy it is for the research to be applied in the 'real world': if it is too difficult, impractical or contestable then it might not be used. This includes matters of cost and investment needed to put policies into practice where they are informed by research (and, indeed, RCTs themselves can be very costly).

Policy makers are also concerned with the level of certainty of the research findings and of their practicability, which links to the specificity and focus of the research. This was raised earlier in relating the 'what works' agenda to the question in Part I, *viz.* 'compared to what?' and to comparison standards and references groups, criteria and threshold statements in deciding when something is 'working', not 'working', 'working' well or not well.

At a practical level, the language, terminology, jargon and accessibility of the research affects whether it is even read. Policy makers need to be clear on where the research can be useful (research dissemination, uptake, utilization and impact), e.g. in problem identification and solution, in tactical and strategic planning, and the target groups affected if the policy uses research evidence (e.g. indicating the benefit to the policy maker of acting on the research evidence, and how it will impact on public perception of the policies and policy makers).

The pessimistic point here is that it is probably fanciful to imagine that research evidence will have a prominent place in policy making and the decision making that flows from such policy making. There is more on the policy maker's palette than research evidence. Political positioning and consequences trump often research evidence. As Levin (1991) remarked some thirty years ago: policy makers and researchers live in two different worlds, with different cultures and goals.

Conclusion

Moving from evidence to policy making, decision making and practice by educationists, is challenging in many ways, as single interventions are embedded in a range of varying conditions, contexts, agendas, needs and priorities which impinge on uptake and impact. Whilst several attempts have been, and are being, made to render research evidence more accessible to teachers, the links between evidence and policy making are weaker. To understand how to enable evidence and decision making to coalesce, attention is required to leadership (and Major and Higgins (2019) provide tips for leadership) and to managing change and innovation, and this engages a vast range of issues. The chapter drew attention to a major obstacle in managing change, which is the need to persuade people to leave their comfort zones and existing practices, values and ideas. This is not new, and, indeed, harks back to Dalin (1978) who identified barriers to change lying in differences of values, power, psychological and practical concerns by the several parties involved in change.

The chapter sounded a cautionary note in thinking that policy makers will concern themselves with evidence, and that, even if they do, their attention to research evidence is conditional on a range of factors, since policy makers occupy different worlds, inhabit different cultures, and have different agendas from, researchers. Whilst much of the chapter did not refer specifically to RCTs, its implications apply clearly to them.

Chapter 14

Summary cautions and fifty theses on randomized controlled trials in education

Introduction and overview

Whether or not we wish to base our policy making and practices on 'what works' from RCTs raises several serious questions, including addressing the limits and possibilities of RCTs in providing useful evidence of 'what works', and in addressing a range of technical issues concerned with RCTs with regard to design, sampling, data analysis, reporting, generalizability, meta-analysis, reliability and validity. Context is important in interpreting and applying research in the practice of education; we neglect it at our peril.

RCTs alone cannot provide the sole source of evidence in informing an all-embracing view of evidence-based education (Levačić and Glatter, 2000, p. 19). To the charge that much practice and policy making are ill-informed by evidence from RCTs, one can offer a sharp *tu quoque*: where is the evidence that RCTs are any better or worse than other sources of rigorous data and studies in informing policy making? To the answer that this is simply a matter of time before the evidence appears, should be whether *only*, or how far, RCTs should inform policy making, because they are inherently a seriously incomplete picture.

Though teachers may use putative RCTs (and they do, in their thousands), they should judge the efficacy of their effects carefully and cautiously. Of course, evidence of supposed effects exists; that is not in question (e.g. Gorard et al., 2017; Connolly et al., 2017, 2018; Major and Higgins, 2019; Education Endowment Foundation, 2019b). The questions are, rather: (a) the extent to which we wish to use data from RCTs in formulating policy and in informing practice; (b) whether, in reality, RCTs in education are able to meet their own standards of rigour singly or collectively in meta-analysis and meta-meta-analysis; and (c) if so, at what costs as well as what benefits. RCTs may be costly in terms of time, money and implementation (though this is contested, e.g. Buck and McGee (2015)). Are the benefits worth the rigour that, rightly, accompanies them? At what point does the accumulation of a quantity of RCTs become sufficient to be converted to a qualitative shift in policy making, decision making and concluding that something 'works' – a tipping point? At what point does something 'work', who decides and based on what and whose criteria? The evidence that might answer these questions does not derive from RCTs alone, and this perhaps undermines their own status; RCTs are a means to an extraneous end and derive from a range of exogenous issues.

This is not to argue simplistically against RCTs *per se*; they have their place. Their potential to address teachers' self-generated problems should not be overlooked (Davies, 1999; Didau, 2015; Connolly et al., 2017). Indeed, the Education Endowment Foundation has thousands of teachers and schools involved in its projects. Rather, it is to suggest that, even if technical matters can be resolved (and this volume has suggested that this may not be possible), 'fitness for purpose' renders RCTs only one source of contributory data to evidence-based education, and not the sole or the unquestionably pre-eminent source. As Thomas (2016) remarks, rather than expending energy on 'eulogizing' one particular method, it is more fruitful to select the 'optimal mix' of methods for the required purposes (p. 407).

It is not the case that RCTs provide the *only* useful research data on 'what works', and this undermines the status currently afforded to them; as Bickman and Reich (2009, p. 71) argue, *pace* Churchill: the randomized design is the worst form of design except for all the others. Scriven (2009) contends that insisting on confining research to an experimental approach 'is simply bigotry'; it is neither pragmatic nor logical. Indeed, he states that it affronts scientific method and that it is absurd to pronounce that alternative methods compromise reliability of results or constitute 'unscientific' practices (p. 136).

I don't need an RCT to tell me that if I drop a brick on my foot, it hurts. Goodman (2009), like other researchers (e.g. Gersten and Hitchcock, 2009; Scriven, 2009), calls for RCTs to be supplemented by observational studies with a variety of sources (Goodman, 2009, p. 16), both prospective and retrospective. If, and only if, a sufficient set of information is provided in an RCT to enable one to judge whether it is transferable from its original locale to a new locale, then its contribution to evidence-based practice might be useful (arguably); without this, using that RCT is a shot in the dark.

This volume has suggested a host of problems with RCTs. Nevill (2019) notes that RCTs have several claimed attractions: they are 'currently the optimal and least-biased method for estimating, on average, whether something works, *when done well*' (italics in original); schools are willing to take part in them, including randomization; and they can provide 'powerful information' for those making decisions. However, in the same blog she notes that RCTs cannot answer all types of questions and that, in fact, there are some matters for which schools are unwilling to be randomized. She alludes to the well-worn comments that: (a) RCTs use averages, and that this does not help a school to know if it will 'work' for them; and (b) decision makers have shorter time scales – the here and now – rather than the longer time scales often required for an RCT to 'work' (*ibid.*).

Whilst identifying whether an intervention 'works' under carefully controlled conditions, RCTs should extend sub-group identification and inclusion, with careful and detailed stratification and analysis of differential treatment effects. For educational research, the argument put forward here is that RCTs should seek, only where appropriate, to abide by the rigours of clinical RCTs, to attend to careful and inclusive sub-group sampling and to the whole person in dynamical systems approaches rather than, or in addition to, the isolationist and reductionist approaches of RCTs in judging 'what works'.

If we wish to use RCTs in education, we could well benefit from bringing them closer to the rigour of RCTs in medicine, where applicable, but also recognize that, even with such rigour, RCTs in education might not give educationists the important information that they need, and they are unfit for many educational purposes. Here, advice on clinical trials might also be applied to education, where relevant:

> Data derived from narrowly defined, tightly controlled study populations in analytic validation studies and clinical trials is not always representative of the results that will be achieved with typical patients in real-world settings ... . Treatments or diagnostic procedures that seem promising in clinical trials may prove to be less effective in routine practice.
>
> (President's Council of Advisers on Science and Technology, 2008, pp. 8, p. 46)

Fifty theses on RCTs

Adopting a more polemical tone, the concerns about RCTs are set out here in a series of fifty summary statements which encapsulate key issues set out in this volume. They are intentionally polarized to clarify and crystallize the concerns that have been raised, and they deliberately omit the responses that can be made to these, as these have been set out already in the preceding chapters. They are organized into eight key areas; for 'they', read 'RCTs'.

Status

They are not the hackneyed 'gold standard'.
They have questionable priority and status in educational research.

Ontology

They are ontologically suspect, as they understate human agency and the action-orientation, humanity and intentionality of participants.
They adopt a limited view of what is 'educational' in 'educational research'.

They don't catch necessary complexity, contingency, contextuality, situatedness and conditionality.

They confuse mind and brain, biology and humanity.

Epistemology and methodology

They are epistemologically naïve.

They are based on suspect assumptions and premises.

They have an impoverished view of science and scientific investigations.

They overstate claims made for randomization.

They appeal to a relatively meaningless and worthless usage of *ceteris paribus* clauses.

They rely on questionable induction.

They neglect issues of timing and duration of interventions and associated measures.

They neglect the necessary implications of theories of complexity and chaos.

They neglect dynamical, unpredictable, emergent, nonlinear open systems.

They neglect the significance of interactions of multiple variables interacting in a situation and impacting on an outcome.

They cannot meet their own canons of reliability, validity and methodology.

They are indefensibly reductionist.

They neglect important elements of clinical trials that can be applied, either directly or in their educational equivalents.

They underrate the limits and boundaries of their design features.

They neglect side effects and knock-on effects.

They under-address risk analysis and risk management.

They yield questionable and exclusive outcomes.

They do not address sufficiently the question of criteria for deciding when something 'works' and 'compared to what'.

They are used for meta-analysis and meta-meta-analysis, but these are suspect, even unreliable, invalid and of little use or value.

They cannot guarantee to address ethical matters sufficiently.

They use treatment and control protocols and procedures which are open to variance in practice, being insufficiently standardized or standardizable.

They pay insufficient attention to what the control group is doing.

Their reliance on the isolation and manipulation of controls and variables is misguided and misrepresents what is occurring in a complex, holistic, multivariate system.

They use questionable 'evidence'.

Statistical matters

They use effect size, which does not tell us much, and statistical significance which tells us less, and effect size is frequently misused.

They often lack statistical power.

They overstate the usefulness of their currency of averages at the expense of sub-groups, outliers, distributions and variances.

Their currency of averages does not tell us what we want to know or need to know.

They understate the significances of small differences in context, people and practices.

Causality

They suggest, overstate but don't prove causality.

They don't meet the requirements for demonstrating causality.

They adopt an unrealistic, singular and naïve view of causality, mis-representing causality.

They adopt untenably simplistic views of causality and 'what works'.

They neglect the mechanisms of causality.

They misrepresent counterfactual constituents.

Generalizability

They do not generalize with sufficient certainty.

They understate and neglect factors affecting generalizability and scalability.

Utility

They do not prove beyond reasonable doubt that something 'works'.

They do not tell us much that is certain, nor do they put usable limits on how certain their findings are.

They often do not provide actionable results.

They rely on supplementary evidence in order to be useful.

They offer comparatively little for policy makers and/or practitioners.

Claims

They underdetermine the claims made for themselves yet overstate such claims.

They address simplistic questions and comparatively crude matters.

In short, RCTs encounter problems at every stage, as, indeed, happens for other types of research, and they do not live up to their promises or claims. Of course, many of these criticisms can be levelled at other kinds of research in education, and it is improper to criticize a particular type of research for something that it does not aim to do.

RCTs can contribute to the 'what works', evidence-based education agenda. Given that they are fit for some purposes but not for others, they have no privileged position or status in the overall evidence agenda; they take their place alongside or below, not above, other kinds of research evidence, teacher expertise and experience, teachers' judgement, tacit knowledge, textured accounts, fine-grained analysis, penetrating and acute observations, and context-rich scrutiny. Fitness for purpose trumps unwarranted prominence. Indeed, Jadad and Enkin (2007) question whether RCT's are an anachronism, a relic of an industrial, mechanistic age (p. 27) which should give way to innovative approaches to improving education.

As one reviewer of the present manuscript wrote: they may disprove 'the value of an intervention, as Torgerson has done with synthetic phonics', but much RCT-based work is 'sheer pointlessness', given what we already know from key reviews of evidence.

RCTs should not drive the evidence-informed practice of education. Their role is useful under certain conditions, but very modest indeed. When compared to the wealth of findings, discovery and rich veins of wisdom available from careful observation, imagination and creativity in sciences, what do many RCTs have to offer? Not much, and not as much as their prominence would suggest. As Norman (2003) remarked: it is not 'that we do not know how to do experiments; it is that we know only too well how little knowledge will emerge from all that effort' as they yield only 'marginal insights' (p. 583); placing faith in the 'supremacy' of RCTs to inform decision making in education is 'dreadfully misguided' (p. 584).

Just as with other types of research, RCTs tell us something, but far from everything. Singly and in combination, they must be viewed with the cautious eye and interrogative stance of the serious sceptic. The supremacy, indeed hegemony, currently accorded to RCTs is an arrogant siren song on an orgiastic scale; don't be seduced. We can do better than this. It is neither right nor sensible to consign other supremely legitimate and valuable research methods to the shade or to eclipse; *pace* Dylan Thomas, we have to rage against the dying of the light. The claims made for RCTs have to be tamed.

References

Agence Nouvelle des Solidarités Actives (ANSA) (2017) *British What Works Centres: What Lessons for Evidence-Based Policy in France?*Paris: Agence Nouvelle des Solidarités Actives.

Albrechtsen, T. R. S. and Qvortrup, A. (2014) Making sense of evidence in teaching. In K. B. Petersen, D. Reimer and A. Qvortrup (eds) *Evidence and Evidence-based Education in Denmark: The Current Debate.* CURSIV No. 14. Aarhus, Denmark: University of Aarhus Department of Education, 67–81. Available from: www.edu. au.dk/fileadmin/edu/Cursiv/CURSIV_14_www.pdf.

Alliance for Useful Evidence (Nesta) (2016) *Using Evidence. What Works? A Discussion Paper.* London: Alliance for Useful Evidence (Nesta).

Alt, J. (2009) Comment: conditional knowledge: an oxymoron? In C. Mantzavinos (ed.) *Philosophy of the Social Sciences.* Cambridge: Cambridge University Press, 146–153.

American Psychological Association (2010) *Publication Manual of the American Psychological Association.* Washington, DC: American Psychological Association.

Anderson, D. S. and Biddle, B. J. (eds) (1991) *Knowledge for Policy: Improving Education through Research.* London: Falmer.

Angrist, J. D. and Pischke, J.-S. (2009) *Mostly Harmless Econometrics.* Princeton, NJ: Princeton University Press.

Arnold, I. (2011) John Hattie: visible learning: a synthesis of over 800 meta-analyses relating to achievement. *International Review of Education,* 57 (1&2), 219–221. doi:10.1007/s11159-011-9198-8.

Arulampalam, W., Naylor, R. A. and Smith, J. P. (2005) Effects of in-class variation and student rank on the probability of withdrawal: cross-section and time-series analysis for UK university students. *Economics of Education Review,* 24 (3), 251–262. doi:10.1016/j.econedurev.2004.05.007.

Association of Teachers and Lecturers (2013) Using evidence to inform education policy and practice. Available from: www.atl.org.uk/Images/evidence-based-poli cy-making.03.14.pdf.

Ayres, I. (2007) *Super Crunchers.* London: John Murray Publishers.

Bachan R. (2004) Curriculum choice at A-level: why is business studies more popular than economics? Paper presented at the British Educational Research Association Annual Conference, University of Manchester, 16–18 September 2004.

Bachan, R. and Reilly, B. (2003) Evidence and warrants: a comparison of academic performance in A-level economics between two years. *International Review of Economics Education,* 2 (1), 8–24.

Bagshaw, S. M. and Bellomo, R. (2008) The need to reform our assessment of evidence from clinical trials: a commentary. *Philosophy, Ethics, and Humanities in Medicine*, 3 (23), 1–11. doi:10.1186/1747-5341-3-23.

Bak, P. (1996) *How Nature Works*. New York: Copernicus.

Bakker, A., Cai, J. F., English, L., Kaiser, G., Mesas, W. and van Dooren, W. (2019) Beyond small, medium, or large: points of consideration when interpreting effect sizes. *Educational Studies in Mathematics* 102 (1), 1–8. doi:10.1007/s10649-019-09908-4.

Bal, F., Button, K. J. and Nijkama, P. (2002) Ceteris paribus, meta-analysis and value transfer. *Socio-Economic Planning Sciences*, 36 (2), 127–138.

Banerjee, A., Chassang, S. and Snowberg, E. (2016) *Decision Theoretic Approaches to Experiment Design and External Validity*. Working Paper 22167. Cambridge, MA: National Bureau of Economic Research. Available from: www.nber.org/papers/w22167.

Bergeron, P. and Rivard, L. (2017). How to engage in pseudoscience with real data: a criticism of John Hattie's arguments in visible learning from the perspective of a statistician. *McGill Journal of Education / Revue des Sciences de l'Education de McGill*, 52 (1), 237–246. doi:10.7202/1040816ar.

Berk, R. (2011) Evidence-based versus junk-based evaluation research: some lessons from 35 years of the evaluation review. *Evaluation Review*, 35 (3), 191–203. doi:10.1177/0193841X11419281.

Bickman, L. and Reich, S. M. (2009) Randomized controlled trials: a gold standard with feet of clay? In S. I. Donaldson, C. A. Christie and M. M. Mark (eds) *What Counts as Credible Evidence in Applied Research and Evaluation Practice?* Thousand Oaks, CA: Sage, 51–77.

Biesta, G. (2007) Why 'what works' won't work: evidence-based practice and the democratic deficit in educational research. *Educational Theory*, 57 (1), 1–22. doi:10.1111/j.1741-5446.2006.00241.x.

Biesta, G. (2010) Why 'what works' still won't work: from evidence-based education to value-based education. *Studies in Philosophy and Education* 29 (5), 491–503. doi:10.1007/s11217-010-9191-x.

Biesta, G. (2014) Who knows? In K. B. Petersen et al. (eds), op cit., 19–25.

Bjerre, J. and Reimer, D. (2014) The strategic use of evidence on teacher education: investigating the research report genre. In K. B. Petersen et al. (eds), op cit., 83–104.

Borenstein, M., Hedges, L. V., Higgins, J. T. P. and Rothstein, H. R. (2009) *Introduction to Meta-analysis*. New York: John Wiley & Sons.

Boruch, R. (1997) *Randomised Experimentation for Planning and Evaluation: A Practical Guide*. London: Sage Publications.

Boruch, R., de Moya, D. and Snyder, B. (2002) The importance of randomized field trials in education and related areas. In F. Mosteller and R. Boruch (eds) *Evidence Matters: Randomized Trials in Education Research*. Washington, DC: The Brookings Institution, 50–79.

Bouguen, A. and Gurgand, M. (2012) *Randomized Controlled Experiments in Education*. EENEE Analytical Report no. 11 for the European Commission. Paris: European Commission.

Boylan, M. and Demack, S. (2018) Innovation, evaluation design and typologies of professional learning. *Educational Research*, 60 (3), 336–356. doi:10.1080/00131881.2018.1493352.

Bradford Hill, A. (1965) The environment and disease: association or causation? *Proceedings of the Royal Society of Medicine*, 58 (5), 295–300. Available from: www.edwardtufte.com/tufte/hill.

Brown, N. (2013) Book review: Visible Learning. Available from: https:academiccomputing.wordpress.com/2013/08/05/book-review-visible-learning.

Brutsaert, H. and Van Houtte, M. (2002) Girls' and boys' sense of belonging in single-sex versus co-educational schools. *Research in Education*, 68 (1), 48–56.

Buck, S. and McGee, J. (2015) *Why Government Needs More Randomized Controlled Trials: Refuting the Myths*. Houston, TX: The Laura and John Arnold Foundation. Available from: http://craftmediabucket.s3.amazonaws.com/uploads/PDFs/RCT_FINAL.pdf.

Burtless, G. (2002) Randomized field trials for policy evaluation: why not in education? In F. Mosteller and R. Boruch (eds) op cit., 179–197.

Busch, B. and Watson, E. (2019) *The Science of Learning*. Abingdon: Routledge.

Cain, T. (2019) *Becoming a Research-informed School: What? Why? How?* Abingdon: Routledge.

Campbell, D. T. and Stanley, J. C. (1963) *Experimental and Quasi-Experimental Designs for Research*. Boston, MA: Houghton Mifflin Co.

Cartwright, N. (2009) What is this thing called 'efficacy'? In C. Mantzavinos (ed.) op cit., 185–206.

Cartwright, N. (2010) In favour of laws that are not ceteris paribus after all. In J. Earman, C. Glymour and S. Mitchell (eds) *Ceteris Paribus Laws*. Dordrecht, Netherlands: Kluwer Academic Publishers, 149–163.

Cartwright, N. (2019) What is meant by 'rigour' in evidence-based educational policy and what's so good about it? *Educational Research and Evaluation*, 25 (1–2), 63–80. doi:10.1080/13803611.2019.1617990.

Cartwright, N. and Hardie, J. (2012) *Evidence-based Policy: A Practical Guide to Doing It Better*. Oxford: Oxford University Press.

Carver, R. P. (1978) The case against significance testing. *Harvard Educational Review*, 48 (3), 378–399. doi:10.17763/haer.48.3.t490261645281841.

Cheung, A. C. K. and Slavin, R. E. (2016) How methodological features affect effect sizes in education. *Educational Researcher*, 45 (5), 282–292. doi:10.3102/0013189X6656615.

Chomsky, N. (1959) Review of Skinner's Verbal Behaviour. *Language*, 35 (1), 26–58.

Cilliers, P. (2001) Boundaries, hierarchies and networks in complex systems. *International Journal of Innovation Management*, 5 (2), 135–147. doi:10.1142/S1363919601000312.

Clark, C. M. and Peterson, P. L. (1986) Teachers' thought processes. In M. C. Wittrock (ed.) *Handbook of Research on Teaching* (third edition). New York: Macmillan, 255–296.

Clarke, A. and Dawson, R. (1999) *Evaluation Research*. London: Sage Publications.

Clay, R. A. (2010) More than one way to measure. *American Psychological Association*, 41 (8), 52–55. doi:10.1177/109821401038932185.

Coe, R. (2000) What is an 'effect size'? Available from: www.cem.dur.ac.uk/ebeuk/research/effectsize/ESbrief.htm.

Coe, R. (2002) It's the effect size, stupid: what effect size is and why it is important. Paper presented at the Annual Conference of the British Educational Research

Association, University of Exeter, 12–14 September. Available from: www.leeds.ac.uk/educol/documents/00002182.htm.

Coe, R. (2018) Serious critiques of meta-analysis and effect size: researchED 2018. CEMblog, 5 September. Available from: www.cem.org/blog/serious-critiques-of-meta-analysis-and-effect-size-researched-2018.

Coe, R., Fitz-Gibbon, C. T. and Tymms, P. (2000) Promoting evidence-based education: the role of practitioners. Roundtable paper presented at the British Educational Research Association, University of Cardiff, 7–10 September.

Cohen D. K., Raudenbush, S. W. and Ball, D. L. (2002) Resources, instruction, and research. In F. Mosteller and R. Boruch (eds) op cit., 80–119.

Cohen, K. (1988) *Statistical Power for the Behavioral Sciences* (second edition). Hilsdale, NJ: Lawrence Erlbaum Publishers.

Cohen, J. and Stewart, I. (1995) *The Collapse of Chaos*. Harmondsworth: Penguin.

Cohen, L., Manion, L. and Morrison, K. R. B. (2018) *Research Methods in Education* (eighth edition). Abingdon: Routledge.

Connolly, P., Biggart, A., Miller, S., O'Hare, L. and Thurston, A. (2017) *Using Randomised Controlled Trials in Education*. London: Sage Publications.

Connolly, P., Keenan, C. and Urbanska, K. (2018) The trials of evidence-based practice in education: a systematic review of randomised controlled trials in education research 1980–2016, *Educational Research*, 60 (3), 276–291, doi:10.1080/00131881.2018.1493353.

CONSORT (2010) Checklist of information to include when reporting a randomised trial. Available from: www.consort-statement.org.

Cook, T. D. (1999) Considering the major arguments against random assignment: an analysis of the intellectual culture surrounding evaluation in American schools of education. Paper presented at the Harvard Faculty Seminar on Experiments in Education, Boston, MA, March.

Cook, T. D. (2001) A critical appraisal of the case against using experiments to assess school for community effects. Available from: www.hoover.org/publications/ednext/3399216.html.

Cook, T. D. and Payne, M. R. (2002) Objecting to the objections to using random assignment in educational research. In F. Mosteller and R. Boruch (eds) op cit., 150–178.

Cook, T. D., Cooper, H., Cordray, D. S., Hartmann, H., Hedges, L. V., Light, R. J., Louis, T. A., Mosteller, F. (1992) *Meta-analysis for Explanation*. New York: Russell Sage Foundation.

Cooper, H. and Rosenthal, R. (1980) Statistical versus traditional procedures for summarizing research findings. *Psychological Bulletin* 87 (3), 442–449. doi:10.1037/0033-2909.87.3.442.

Cowen, N. (2019) For whom does 'what works' work? The political economy of evidence-based education. *Educational Research and Evaluation*, 25 (1–2), 81–98. doi:10.1080/13803611.2019.1617991.

Cronbach, L. J. (1975) Beyond the two disciplines of scientific psychology. *American Psychologist*, 30 (2), 116–127. doi:10.1037/h0076829.

Cronbach, L. J. (1982a) Prudent aspirations for social inquiry. In W. H. Kruskal (ed.) *The Social Sciences: Their Nature and Uses*. Chicago, IL: University of Chicago Press, 61–81.

Cronbach, L. J. (1982b) *Designing Evaluations of Educational and Social Programs*. San Francisco, LA: Jossey-Bass.

Cumming, G. (2012) *Understanding the New Statistics: Effect Sizes, Confidence Intervals and Meta-Analysis*. New York: Routledge.

Curriculum Evaluation and Management Centre (2000a) A culture of evidence. Available from: http://cem.dur.ac.uk/ebeuk/culture.htm.

Curriculum Evaluation and Management Centre (2000b) Sources of evidence. Available from: http://cem.dur.ac.uk/ebeuk/sources.htm.

Curriculum Evaluation and Management Centre (2000c) Aims. Available from: http://atschool.eduweb.co.uk/e-beuk/aims/aims.html.

Curriculum Evaluation and Management Centre (2000d) Evidence-based policies. Available from: http://cem.dur.ac.uk/ebeuk/based.htm.

Dalin, P. (1978) *Limits to Educational Change*. Basingstoke: Macmillan.

Davies, H. T. O., Nutley, S. M. and Smith, P. C. (2000) Debates on the role of experimentation. In H. T. O. Davies, S. M. Nutley and P. C. Smith (eds) *What Works? Evidence-based Policy and Practice in Public Services*. Bristol: Polity Press, 251–259.

Davies, P. (1999) What is evidence-based education? *British Journal of Educational Studies*, 47 (2), 108–121. doi:10.1111/1467-8527.00106.

Deaton, A. and Cartwright, N. (2018) Understanding and misunderstanding randomized controlled trials. *Social Science and Medicine*, 208 (1), 2–21. doi:10.1016/j.socscimed.2017.12.005.

de Boer, H., Donker, A. S. and van der Werf, M. P. C. (2014) Effects on the attributes of educational interventions on students' academic performance: a meta-analysis. *Review of Educational Research*, 84 (4), 509–545. doi:10.3102/0034654314540006.

de Leon, J. (2012) Evidence-based medicine versus personalized medicine: are they enemies? *Journal of Clinical Psychopharmacology*, 32 (2), 153–164. doi:10.1097/JCP.0b013e3182491383.

Department for Education (2016) *Educational Excellence Everywhere*. London: HMSO.

Department of Education and Science (1985) *The Curriculum from 5 to16*. Curriculum Matters 2. London: Her Majesty's Stationery Office.

Didau, D. (2015) *What if Everything You Knew about Education Was Wrong?* Carmarthen: Crown House Publishing.

Donaldson, S. I. (2009) A practitioner's guide for gathering credible evidence in the evidence-based global society. In S. I. Donaldson et al. (eds), op cit., 239–251.

Donaldson, S. I., Christie, C. A. and Mark, M. M. (eds) (2009) *What Counts as Credible Evidence in Applied Research and Evaluation Practice?* Thousand Oaks, CA: Sage.

Earman, J.Glymour, C. and Mitchell, S. (eds) (2010) *Ceteris Paribus Laws*. Dordrecht, Netherlands: Kluwer Academic Publishers.

Education Endowment Foundation (2017) *Classification of the Security of Findings for EEF Evaluation*. London: Education Endowment Foundation.

Education Endowment Foundation (2018) *Evidence Strength: The EEF Padlock Rating*. London: Education Endowment Foundation. Available from: https://educationendowmentfoundation.org.uk/evidence-summaries/about-the-toolkits/evidence-strength/.

Education Endowment Foundation (2019a) *Report Template*. London: Education Endowment Foundation. Available from: https://educationendowmentfoundation.org.uk/public/files/Evaluation/Writing_a_Research_Report/EEF_evaluation_report_template_2019.docx.

Education Endowment Foundation (2019b) Teaching and learning toolkit. Available from: https://educationendowmentfoundation.org.uk/evidence-summaries/teaching-learning-toolkit/.

Einstein, A. (1941) Science, philosophy and religion: a symposium. Available from: www.update.uu.se/~fbendz/library/ae_scire.htm.

Elgin, M. and Sober, E. (2010) Cartwright on explanation and idealization. In J. Earman et al. (eds) op cit., 165–174.

Elliott, J. (2007) Making evidence-based practice educational. In M. Hammersley (ed.) *Educational Research and Evidence-based Practice*. London: Sage Publications, 66–88.

Ellis, P. D. (2010) *The Essential Guide to Effect Sizes*. Cambridge: Cambridge University Press.

European Evaluation Society (2007) EES statement: the importance of a methodologically diverse approach to impact evaluation – specifically with respect to development aid and development interventions. Available from: www.europeanevaluation.org/download/?id=11969403.

Evans, J., Sharp, C. and Benefield, P. (2000) Systematic reviews of educational research: does the medical model fit? Paper presented at the British Educational Research Association Conference, University of Cardiff, 7–10 September.

Falk, R. and Greenbaum, C. W. (1978) Significance tests die hard. *Theory and Psychology*, 5 (1), 75–98.

Faulkner, E. (2013) Real world evidence and implications for emerging technologies. Available from: www.namcp.org/journals/spring13/Faulkner%20Emerging%20Technologies.pdf (accessed June 2015).

Feinstein, A. (1995) Meta-analyses: statistical alchemy for the 21st century. *Journal of Clinical Epidemiology*, 48 (1), 71–79. doi:10.1016/0895-4356(94)00110-C.

Fisher, R. A. (1925) *Statistical Methods for Research Workers*. Edinburgh: Oliver & Boyd.

Fisher, R. A. (1966) *The Design of Experiments* (eighth edition). New York: Haffner Publishing Company.

Fitz-Gibbon, C. T. (1996) *Monitoring Education: Indicators, Quality and Effectiveness*. London: Cassell.

Fitz-Gibbon, C. T. and Morris, L. L. (1987) *How to Design a Program Evaluation*. Newbury Park, CA: Sage Publications.

Fortin, M., Dionne, J., Pinho, G., Gignac, J., Almirall, J. and Lapointe, L (2006) Randomized controlled trials: do they have external validity for patients with multiple comorbidities? *The Annals of Family Medicine*, 4 (2), 104–108; doi:10.1370/afm.516.

Frieden, T. R. (2017) Evidence for health decision making – beyond randomized, controlled trials. *New England Journal of Medicine*, 377 (5), 465–475. doi:10.1056/NEJMra1614394.

Frueh, F. W. (2009) Back to the future: why randomized controlled trials cannot be the answer to pharmacogenomics and personalized medicine. *Pharmacogenetics*, 10 (7), 1077–1081. doi:10. 2217/pgs.09.62.

Furlong, J. and Oancea, A. (2005) *Assessing Quality in Applied and Practice-based Educational Research*. Oxford: Department of Educational Studies, University of Oxford. Available from: www.birmingham.ac.uk/Documents/college-social-sciences/education/projects/esrc-2005-seminarseries5.pdf.

Garcia, A. S., Morrison, K. R. B., Tsoi, A. C. and He, J. M. (2014) *Managing Complex Change in School*. Abingdon: Routledge.

Garrahan, P. and Stewart, P. (1992) *The Nissan Enigma: Flexibility at Work in a Local Economy*. London: Mansell.

Geertz, C. (1973) *The Interpretation of Cultures*. New York: Basic Books.

Gersten, R. and Hitchcock, J. (2009) What is credible in education? The role of the What Works Clearinghouse in informing the process. In S. I. Donaldson et al. (eds) op cit., 78–95.

Gildenhuys, P. (2010) Causal equations without ceteris paribus clauses. *Philosophy of Science*, 77 (4), 608–632. doi:10.5840/jphil20121091138.

Ginsburg, A. and Smith, M. S. (2016) *Do Randomized Controlled Trials Meet the 'Gold Standard'? A Study of the Usefulness of RCTs in the What Works Clearinghouse*. Washington, DC: American Enterprise Institute.

Glass, G. V. (1976) Primary, secondary, and meta-analysis of research. *Educational Researcher*, 5 (10), 3–8. doi:10.3102/0013189X005010003.

Glass, G. V. (1977) Integrating findings: The meta-analysis of research. *Review of Research in Education*, 5 (1), 351–379.

Glass, G. V. (2000) Meta-analysis at 25. Available from: http://glass.ed.asu.edu/gene/papers/meta25.html.

Glass, G. V., McGaw, B. and Smith, M. L. (1981) *Meta-analysis in Social Research*. Beverly Hills, CA: Sage Publications.

Gleick, J. (1987) *Chaos*. London: Abacus.

Glymour, C. (2010) A semantics and methodology of ceteris paribus hypothesis. In J. Earman et al. (eds) op cit., 119–129.

Goldacre, B. (2012) *Bad Pharma: How Drug Companies Mislead Doctors and Harm*. London: Fourth Estate.

Goldacre, B. (2013) *Building Evidence into Education*. London: Department for Education.

Goldthorpe, J. H. (2007) *On Sociology, Volume One: Critique and Program* (second edition). Stanford, CA: Stanford University Press.

Goldstein, H. (2002) Designing social research for the 21st century. Inaugural professorial address, University of Bristol, 14 October.

Goodman, C. (2009) *Comparative Effectiveness Research and Personalized Medicine: From Contradiction to Synergy*. Falls Church, VA: The Lewin Group Center for Comparative Effectiveness Research.

Gorard, S. (2016) Damaging real lives through obstinacy: re-emphasising why significance testing is wrong. *Sociological Research Online*, 21 (1), 1–14. doi:10.5153/sro.3857.

Gorard, S. (2018) *Education Policy: Evidence of Equity and Effectiveness*. Bristol: Polity Press.

Gorard, S. and Torgerson, C. (2006) The ESRC Researcher Development Initiative: promise and pitfalls of pragmatic trials in education. Paper presented at the British Educational Research Association Annual Conference, University of Warwick, 6–9 September.

Gorard, S., See, B. H. and Siddiqui, N. (2017) *The Trials of Education-based Education*. Abingdon: Routledge.

Gorard, S., Griffin, S., See, B. H. and Siddiqui, N. (2018) *How Can We Get Educators to Use Research Evidence?* Durham: Durham University Evidence Centre for Education.

Gough, D, Oliver S. and Thomas J. (2013) *Learning from Research: Systematic Reviews for Informing Policy Decisions: A Quick Guide*. London: Nesta.

Greene, J. C. (2009) Evidence as 'proof' and evidence as 'inkling'. In S. I. Donaldson et al. (eds) op cit., 153–167.

Greenhalgh, T. (2016) Evidence-based medicine: A model to follow? (Or not …) PowerPoint prepared for NUT/Rethinking Schools Seminar, Teaching by Numbers: Accountability Data and Evidence-Based Practice, 13 January.

Greenhalgh, T., Howick, J. and Maskrey, N. (2014) Evidence based medicine: a movement in crisis? *British Medical Journal*, 348: g3725. doi:10.1136/bmj.g3725.

Gueron, J. M. (2002) The politics of random assignment: implementing studies in affecting policy. In F. Mosteller and R. Boruch (eds) op cit., 15–49.

Hammersley, M. (ed.) (2007) *Educational Research and Evidence-based Practice*. London: Sage Publications.

Hammersley, M. (2013) *The Myth of Research-based Policy and Practice*. London: Sage Publications.

Hassey, N. (2015) Randomised control trials and their limitations for use within educational research. Available from: www.workingoutwhatworks.com/en-GB/Magazine/2015/1/RCTs_and_their_limitations.

Hattie, J. (2009) *Visible Learning: A Synthesis of over 800 Meta-analyses Relating to Achievement*. London, Routledge.

Hattie, J. (2012) *Visible Learning for Teachers*. Abingdon: Routledge.

Hattie, J. and Clarke, S. (2018) *Visible Learning: Feedback*. Abingdon: Routledge.

Hattie, J. and Zierer, K. (2017) *10 Mindframes for Visible Learning: Teaching for Success*. Abingdon: Routledge.

Hattie, J and Yates, G. C. R. (2013) *Visible Learning and the Science of How We Learn*. Abingdon: Routledge.

Haynes, L., Service, O., Goldacre, B. and Torgerson, D. (2012) *Test, Learn, Adapt: Randomised Controlled Trials*. London: Cabinet Office Behavioural Insights Team.

Healy, D., Bechthold, K. and Tolias, P. (2014) Antidepressant-induced suicidality: how translational epidemiology incorporating pharmacogenetics into controlled trials can improve clinical care, *Personalized Medicine*, 11 (1), 79–88. doi:10.2217/pme.13.93.

Heckman, J. J. (1991) *Randomization and Social Policy Evaluation*. Technical Working Paper 107. Cambridge, MA: National Bureau of Economic Research.

Heckman, J. J. and Smith, J. A. (1995) Assessing the case for social experiments. *Journal of Economic Perspectives*, 9 (2), 85–110. doi:10.1257/jep.9.2.85.

Hedges, L. V. and Olkin, I. (1985) *Statistical Methods for Meta-analysis*. Orlando, FL: Academic Press.

Henry, G. T. (2009) When getting it right matters: the case for high-quality policy and program impact evaluations. In S. I. Donaldson et al. (eds) op cit., 32–50.

Higgins, S. (2018) *Improving Learning: Meta-analysis of Intervention Research in Education*. Cambridge: Cambridge University Press.

Higgins, S. and Simpson, A. (2011) *Visible Learning: A Synthesis of over 800 Meta-analyses Relating to Achievement* by John A. C. Hattie [book review]. *British Journal of Educational Studies*, 59 (2), 197–201. doi:10.1080/00071005.2011.584660.

Higgins, S., Kokotsaki, D. and Coe, R. (2011) *Toolkit of Strategies to Improve Learning: A Summary for the Education Endowment Foundation*. Durham: Centre for Evaluation and Monitoring, University of Durham and the Sutton Trust. Available from: www.cem.org/attachments/1toolkit-summary-final-r-2-.pdf.

Hirsch, E. D. Jr. (1997) Address to the California State Board of Education, 10 April.

HM Treasury. (2011) *The Magenta Book: Guidance for Evaluation*. London: HM Treasury.

Hogarth, S. (2012) Regulation, innovation and personalised medicine. Paper presented at the EMA workshop, London, October 2012. Available from: www.ema.europa.eu/docs/en_GB/document_library/Presentation/2012/11/WC500134985.pdf.

Holland, P. W. (1986) Statistics and causal inference. *Journal of the American Statistics Association*, 81 (396), 945–970. doi:10.1080/01621459.1986.10478354.

Houston, R. G. Jr. and Toma, E. F. (2003) Home schooling: an alternative school choice. *Southern Economic Journal*, 69 (4), 920–935. doi:10.1016/j.sbspro.2014.01.861.

Howick, J. (2011) *The Philosophy of Evidence-based Medicine*. Chichester: Wiley-Blackwell.

Hoyle, E. (1975) The creativity of the school in Britain. In A. Harris, M. Lawn and W. Prescott (eds) *Curriculum Innovation*, London: Croom Helm and the Open University Press, 329–346.

Hunter, J. E., Schmidt, F. L. and Jackson, G. B. (1982) *Meta-analysis: Cumulating Research Findings across Studies*. Beverly Hills, CA: Sage Publications.

Hutchison, D. and Styles, B. (2010) *A Guide to Running Randomised Controlled Trials for Educational Researchers*. Slough: National Foundation for Educational Research.

International Electrotechnical Commission (IEC) (2019) *Risk Management: Risk Assessment Techniques*. IEC 31010: 2019. Geneva, Switzerland: International Electrotechnical Commission.

International Organization for Standardization (ISO) (2018) *Risk Management: Guidelines*. ISO 31000: 2018. Geneva, Switzerland: International Organization for Standardization.

Ioannidis, J. P. A. (2005) Why most published research findings are false. *PLoS Medicine*, 2 (8), 696–701. doi:10.1371/journal.pmed.0020124.

Jackson, P. W. (1968) *Life in Classrooms*. New York: Holt, Rinehart & Winston.

Jadad, A. R. and Enkin, M. W. (2007) *Randomized Controlled Trials* (second edition). Oxford: Blackwell Publishing.

Jensen, N. R. and Kjeldsen, C. C. (2014) The schism between evidence-based practice, professional ethics and managerialism – exemplified by social pedagogy. In K. B. Petersen et al. (eds), op cit., 27–50.

Johnes, G. and McNabb, R. (2004) Never give up on the good times: student attrition in the UK. *Oxford Bulletin of Economics and Statistics*, 66 (1), 23–47. doi:10.1111/j.1468-0084.2004.00068.x.

Joyce, K. E. (2019) The key role of representativeness in evidence-based education. *Educational Research and Evaluation*, 25 (1&2), 43–62. doi:10.1080/13803611.2019.1617989.

Julnes, G. and Rog, D. (2009) Evaluation methods for producing actionable evidence: contextual influences on adequacy and appropriateness of method choice. In S. I. Donaldson et al. (eds) op cit., 96–131.

Kaufmann, S. (1995) *At Home in the Universe*. Harmondsworth: Penguin.

Kline, R. B. (2004) *Beyond Significance Testing: Reforming Data Analysis Methods in Behavioral Research*. Washington, DC: American Psychological Association.

Koutsouris, G. and Norwich, B. (2018) what exactly do RCT findings tell us in education research? *British Educational Research Journal*, 44 (6), 939–959. doi:10.1002/berj.3464.

Kraft, M. (2019) Interpreting effect sizes of education interventions. EdWorkingPaper 19-10. Available from: http://edworkingpapers.com/ai19-10.

Krathwohl, D. R. (1985) *Social and Behavioral Science Research: New Framework for Conceptualizing, Implementing, and Evaluating Research Studies*. San Francisco, CA: Jossey-Bass.

Krogstrup, H. K. (2011) *Kampen on Evidens. Resultatmäling, Effktevaluering og evidence*. Copenhagen: Hans Reitzelds Forlag.

Krueger, J. (2001) Null hypothesis significance testing: on the survival of a flawed method. *American Psychologist*, 56 (1), 16–26. doi:10.1037/000-066X.56.1.16.

Kvernbekk, T. (2011) The concept of evidence in evidence-based practice. *Educational Theory*, 61 (5), 515–532. doi:10.1111/j.1741-5446.2011.00418.x.

Kvernbekk, T. (2016) *Evidence-based Practice in Education*. Abingdon: Routledge.

Kvernbekk, T. (2018) Evidence-based educational practice. In *Oxford Research Encyclopedia of Education*. doi:10.1093/acrefore/9780190264093.013.187.

Kvernbekk, T. (2019) Practitioner tales: possible roles for research evidence in practice. *Educational Research and Evaluation*, 25 (1&2), 25–42. doi:10.1080/13803611.2019.1617988.

La Caze, A., Djulbegovic, B. and Senn, S. (2012) What does randomisation achieve? *Evidence-Based Medicine*, 17 (1), 1–2. doi:10.1136/ebm.2011.100061.

Lange, M. (2010) Whose afraid of ceteris paribus laws? Or: how I learned to stop worrying and love them. In J. Earman et al. (eds) op cit., 131–147.

Lehr, R. (1992) Sixteen S-squared over D-squared: a relation for crude sample size estimates. *Statistics in Medicine*, 11 (8), 1099–1102. doi:10.1002/sim.4780110811.

Levačić, R. and Glatter, R. (2000) Really good ideas: developing evidence-informed policy and practice in educational leadership and management. *Educational Management and Administration*, 29 (1), 5–25. doi:10.1177/0263211X010291001.

Levin, H.M. (1991) Why isn't educational research more useful? In D. S. Anderson and B. J. Biddle (eds) *Knowledge for Policy: Improving Education through Research*. London: Falmer, 70–78.

Lewin, R. (1993) *Complexity: Life at the Edge of Chaos*. London: Phoenix.

Li, Q. and Ma, X. (2010) A meta-analysis of the effects of computer technology on school students' mathematics learning. *Educational Psychology Review*, 22 (3), 215–243. doi:10.1007/s10648-010-9125-8.

Lipton, P. (2004) *Inference to the Best Explanation* (second edition). Abingdon: Routledge.

Liu, L., Leung, E. L-H. and Tian, X. Y. (2011) The clinical trial barriers. *Nature*, 480 (7378), S100. doi:10.1038/480S100a.

Lortie-Forgues, H. and Inglis, M. (2019a) Rigorous large-scale educational RCTs are often uninformative: should we be concerned? *Educational Researcher*, 48 (3), 158–166. doi:10.3102/0013189X19832850.

Lortie-Forgues, H. and Inglis, M. (2019b) The value of consensus prior: a response to Simpson. *Educational Researcher*, 48 (6), 385–387. doi:10.3102/0013189X19863426.

Lovell, O. (2018) Effect sizes, robust or bogus? Reflections from my discussions with Hattie and Simpson. Available from: www.ollielovell.com/on-education/effect-sizes/.

Lyman, G. H. and Hirsch, B. (2010) Comparative effectiveness research and genomic personalized medicine, *Journal of Personalized Medicine*, 7 (3), 223–227. doi:10.1634/theoncologist.2012-0445.

MacDonald, G. (1997) Social work: beyond control? In A. Maynard and I. Chalmers (eds) *Non-random Reflections on Health Service Research*. London: BMJ Publishing Group, 122–146.

MacIntyre, A. (1985) *After Virtue: A Study in Moral Theory*. London: Duckworth.

Mackie, J. L. (1993) Causes and conditions. In E. Sosa and M. Tooley (eds) *Causation*. Oxford: Oxford University Press, 33–55.

Maher, J. M., Markey, J. C. and Ebert-May D. (2013) The other half of the story: effects size analysis in quantitative research. *CBE-Life Sciences Education*, 12 (3), 345–351. doi:10.1187/cbe.13-04-0082.

Major, L. E. and Higgins, S. (2019) *What Works? Research and Evidence for Successful Teaching*. London: Bloomsbury Publishing.

Makel, M. C. and Plucker, J. A. (2014) Facts are more important than novelty: replication in the education sciences. *Educational Researcher*, 43 (5), 304–316. doi:10.3102/001389X14545513.

Malouf, D. B. and Taymans, J. M. (2016) Anatomy of an evidence base. *Educational Researcher*, 45 (8), 454–459. doi:10.3102/0013189X16678417.

Mantzavinos, C. (ed.) (2009) *Philosophy of the Social Sciences*. Cambridge: Cambridge University Press.

Manzi, J. (2012) *Uncontrollable*. New York: Basic Books.

Mark, M. M. (2009) Credible evidence: changing the terms of the debate. In S. I. Donaldson et al. (eds) op cit., 214–238.

Mason, M. (ed.) (2008) *Complexity Theory and the Philosophy of Education*. Oxford: Wiley-Blackwell.

Mathison, S. (2009) Seeing is believing: the credibility of image-based research and evaluation. In S. I. Donaldson et al. (eds) op cit., 181–196.

Mayer-Schönberger, V. and Cukier, K. (2013) *Big Data*. London: John Murray Publishers.

Maynard, A. and Chalmers, I. (eds) (1997) *Non-random Reflections on Health Service Research*. London: BMJ Publishing Group.

McKnight, L. and Morgan, A. (2019) The problem with using scientific evidence (why teachers should stop trying to be more like doctors). Available from: www.aare.edu.au/blog?p=3874.

Meinert, C. L. (1989) Meta-analysis: science or religion? *Controlled Clinical Trials*, 10 (4), 257S-263S. doi:10.1016/0197-2456(89)90064-0.

Meinert, C. L. (2011) *An Insider's Guide to Clinical Trials*. New York: Oxford University Press.

Menter, I. (2013) From interesting times to critical times? Teacher education and educational research in England, *Research in Teacher Education*, 3 (1), 38–40. Available from: http://hdl.handle.net/10552/1961.

Micklethwait, J. and Wooldridge, A. (1997) *The Witch Doctors*. London: Mandarin Paperbacks.

Mill, J. S. (2006) *A System of Logic: Ratiocinative and Inductive, Volume 7 Books I-III*. Indianapolis, IN: Liberty Fund.

Mitchell, S. D. (2009) Complexity and explanation in the social sciences. In C. Mantzavinos (ed.) op cit., 130–145.

Mitchell, S. D. (2010) Ceteris paribus – an inadequate representation for biological contingency. In J. Earman et al. (eds) op cit., 53–74.

Moher, D., Cook, D. J., Eastwood, S., Olkin, I., Rennie, D., Stroup, D. F. (1999) Improving the quality of reports of meta-analyses of randomized controlled trials: the QUOROM statement. *Lancet*, 354 (9193), 1896–1900. Available from: https://journals.plos.org/plosntds/article/file?type=supplementary&id=info:doi/10.1371/journal.pntd.0000381.s002.

Moher, D., Liberati, A., Tetzlaff, J., Altman, D. G. and The PRISMA Group (2009) Preferred reporting items for systematic reviews and meta-analyses: the PRISMA statement. *PLoS Medicine* 6 (7): e1000097. doi:10.1371/journal.pmed.1000097.

Moore, L., Graham, A. and Diamond, I. (2003) On the feasibility of conducting randomised trials in education: case study of a sex education intervention, *British Educational Research Journal*, 29 (5), 673–689. doi:10.1080/0141192032000133712.

Morrison, K. R. B. (1998) *Management Theories for Educational Change*. London: Paul Chapman Publishing.

Morrison, K. R. B. (2001) Randomised controlled trials for evidence-based education: some problems in judging 'what works'. *Evaluation and Research in Education*, 15 (2), 1–15. doi:10.1080/09500790108666984.

Morrison, K. R. B. (2002) *School Leadership and Complexity Theory*. London: Routledge Falmer.

Morrison, K. R. B. (2008) Educational philosophy and the challenge of complexity theory. In M. Mason (ed.) op cit., 33–55.

Morrison, K. R. B. (2009) *Causation in Educational Research*. Abingdon: Routledge. doi:10.1080/13645579.2011.594293.

Morrison, K. R. B. (2010) Complexity theory, school leadership and management: questions for theory and practice. *Educational Management, Administration and Leadership*, 38 (3), 374–393. doi:10.1177/1741143209359711.

Morrison, K. R. B. (2012) Searching for causality in the wrong places. *International Journal of Social Research Methodology*, 15 (1), 15–30. doi:10.1080/13645579.2011.594293.

Morrison, K. R. B. and van der Werf, M. P. C. (2014) Editorial. *Educational Research and Evaluation*, 20 (4), 251–254. doi:10.1080/13803611.2014.943471.

Morrison, K. R. B. and van der Werf, M. P. C. (2017) Discourses of diversity in evidence-based educational research and policy making. *Educational Research and Evaluation*, 23 (3&4), 75–77. doi:10.1080/13803611.2017.1400158.

Morrison, K. R. B. and van der Werf, M. P. C. (2018) Being cautious about what 'research shows'. *Educational Research and Evaluation*, 24 (1&2), 1–2. doi:10.1080/13803611.2018.1533693.

Morrison, K. R. B. and van der Werf, M. P. C. (2019) Many are the paths to understanding 'what works'. *Educational Research and Evaluation*, 25 (3&4), 143–144. doi:10.1080/13803611.2019.1701234.

Mosteller, F. and Boruch, R. (eds) (2002) *Evidence Matters: Randomized Controlled Trials in Education Research*. Washington, DC: The Brookings Institution.

Muller, J. Z. (2018) *The Tyranny of Metrics*. New Jersey, NJ: Princeton University Press.

Murphy, P. and Glover, R. (2011) *Murphy on Evidence* (twelfth edition). Oxford: Oxford University Press.

Nash, R. (1973) *Classrooms Observed*. London: Routledge and Kegan Paul.

National Center for Biotechnology Information (2018) *Randomized, Controlled Trials (RCTs) and Cohort Studies. Screening Adults for Bladder Cancer: Update of the 2004 Evidence Review for the US Preventive Services Task Force*. Bethesda, MD.: National Center for Biotechnology Information. Available from: www.ncbi.nlm.nih.gov/books/NBK47515/.

National Center for Educational Evaluation and Regional Assistance (2017) Evaluation principles and practices. Available from: https://ies.gov/ncee/projects/pdf/IESEvaluationPrinciplesandPractices_011117.pdf.

Nevill, C. (2019) EEF blog: randomised controlled trials – 3 good things, 3 bad things, and 5 top tips. 31 October. Available from: https://educationendowmentfoundation.org.uk/news/eef-blog-randomised-controlled-trials-or-how-to-train-your-dragon/.

Nietzsche, F. (1973) *Beyond Good and Evil*. Harmondsworth: Penguin.

Noble, D. (2006) *The Music of Life: Biology Beyond the Genome*. Oxford: Oxford University Press.

Norman, G. (2003) RCT = results confounded and trivial: the perils of grand educational experiments. *Medical Education*, 37 (7), 582–584. doi:10.1046/j.1365-2923.2003.01586.x.

Nuthall, G. (2007) *The Hidden Lives of Learners*. Wellington, NZ: New Zealand Council for Educational Research Press.

Nutley, S. M., Walter, I. and Davies, H. T. O. (2007) *Using Evidence: How Evidence Can Inform Public Services*. Bristol: Policy Press.

Oakley, A. (1998) Experimentation in social science: the case of health promotion. *Social Science in Health*, 4 (2), 73–89.

Oakley, A. (2000) *Experiments in Knowing: Gender and Method in the Social Sciences*. Cambridge: Polity Press.

Oakley, A. (2007) Evidence-informed policy and practice. In M. Hammersley (ed.) op cit., 91–105.

Oancea, A. and Pring, R. (2008) The importance of being thorough: on systematic accumulations of 'what works' in education research. *Journal of Philosophy of Education*, 41 (1), 15–39. doi:10.1111/j.1467-9752.2008.00633.x.

Paterson, T. A., Harms, P. D., Streel, P. and Credé, M. (2016) An assessment the magnitude of effects sizes: evidence from 30 years of meta-analysis in management. *Journal of Leadership & Organizational Studies*, 23 (1), 66–81. doi:10.1177/1548051815614321.

Pawson, R. (2006) *Evidence-based Policy: A Realist Perspective*. London: Sage Publications.

Pawson, R. (2013) *The Science of Evaluation: A Realist Manifesto*. London: Sage Publications.

Pawson, R. and Tilley, N. (1993) OXO, Tie, brand X and new improved evaluation. Paper presented to the British Sociological Association Annual Conference, University of Essex.

Pearce, W. and Raman, S. (2014) The new randomized controlled trials (RCT) movement in public policy: challenges of epistemic governance, *Policy Sciences*, 47 (4), 387–402. doi:10.1007/s11077-014-9208-3.

Pearl, J. (2009) *Causality: Models, Reasoning and Inference* (second edition). Cambridge: Cambridge University Press.

Peile, E. (2004) Reflections from medical practice: balancing evidence-based practice with practice-based evidence. In G. Thomas and R. Pring (eds) *Evidence-based Practice in Education*. Maidenhead: Open University Press, 102–115.

Petersen, K. B. (2014) Danish language and citizenship tests: is what is measured what matters? In K. B. Petersen et al. (eds), op cit., 123–145.

Petersen, K. B., Reimer, D. and Qvortrup, A. (2014) Introduction. In K. B. Petersen et al. (eds), op cit., 7–17.

Phillips, D. C. (2019) Evidence of confusion about evidence of causes: comments on the debate about EBP in education. *Educational Research in Education*, 25 (1), 7–24. doi:10.1080/13803611.2019.1617980.

Poulsen, S. C. (2014) John Hattie: a revolutionary educational researcher? *Adult Education*, 108 (March), 13–18.

President's Council of Advisers on Science and Technology (2008) *Priorities for Personalized Medicine*. Washington, DC: Executive Office of the President of the United States. Available from: https://bigdatawg.nist.gov/PCAST_Personalized_Medicine_Priorities.pdf.

Prigogine, I. and Stengers, I. (1985) *Order out of Chaos*. London: Flamingo.

Pring, R. (2015) *Philosophy of Educational Research* (third edition). London: Bloomsbury Academic.

Puttick, R. (2018) *Mapping the Standards of Evidence Used in UK Social Policy*. London: Alliance for Useful Evidence. Available from: www.alliance4usefulevidence.org/assets/2018/05/Mapping-Standards-of-Evidence-A4UE-final.pdf.

Puttick, R. and Ludlow, J. (2013) *Standards of Evidence: An Approach that Balances the Need for Evidence with Innovation*. London: Nesta. Available from: https://media.nesta.org.uk/documents/standards_of_evidence.pdf.

Rallis, S. F. (2009) Reasoning with rigor and probity: ethical premises for credible evidence. In S. I. Donaldson et al. (eds) op cit., 168–180.

Rickinson, M. (2005) *Practitioners' Use of Research*. Working Paper 7.5. London: National Education Research Forum. Available from: https://studylib.net/doc/7634496/how-do-practitioners-use-research%3F.

Robinson, D. H. (2004) An interview with Gene V. Glass. *Educational Researcher*, 33 (3), 26–30. doi:10.3102/0013189X033003026.

Rochat, D. and Demeulemeester, J-L. (2001) Rational choice under unequal constraints: the example of Belgian higher education. *Economics of Education Review*, 20 (1), 15–26. doi:10.1016/S0272-7757(99)00046-1.

Rømer, T. A. (2014) The relationship between education and evidence. In K. B. Petersen et al. (eds), op cit., 105–121.

Rosenthal, R. (1991). Effect sizes: Pearson's correlation, its display via the BESD, and alternative indices. *American Psychologist*, 46 (10), 1086–1087. doi:10.1037/0003-066X.46.10.1086.

Roses, A. D. (2000) Pharmacogenetics and the practice of medicine. *Nature*, 405 (6788), 857–865. doi:10.1038/35015728.

Rossi, P. H. and Freeman, H. E. (1993) *Evaluation: A Systematic Approach*. Beverly Hills, CA: Sage Publications.

Russell, B. (1959) *The Problems of Philosophy*. Oxford: Oxford University Press.

Sacks, P. (1999) *Standardized Minds*. Cambridge, MA: Perseus Books.

St Pierre, E. A. (2002) 'Science' rejects postmodernism. *Educational Researcher*, 31 (8), 25–27. doi:10.3102/0013189X031008025.

Sanders, M. and Chonaire, A. N. (2015) *'Powered to Detect Small Effect Sizes': You Keep Saying That. I Do Not Think it Means What You Think it Means*. Working paper No. 15/337. Bristol: University of Bristol Centre for Market and Public Organization.

Sanderson, I. (2010) Is it 'what works' that matters? Evaluation and evidence-based policy-making. *Research Papers in Education*, 18 (4), 331–345. doi:10.1080/0267152032000176846.

Schofield, J. W. (2007) Increasing the generalizability of qualitative research. In M. Hammersley (ed.) op cit., 181–203.

Schulmeister, R. and Loviscach, J. (2014) Errors in John Hattie's Visible Learning. Available from: https://j3l7h.de/publications/MetaSchulmeisterLoviscach.pdf.

Schurz, G. (2010) Ceteris paribus laws: classification and deconstruction. In J. Earman et al. (eds) op cit., 75–96.

Schwandt, T. A. (2009) Toward a practical theory of evidence for evaluation. In S. I. Donaldson et al. (eds) op cit., 197–212.

Scriven, M. (2009) Demythologizing causation and evidence. In S. I. Donaldson et al. (eds) op cit., 134–152.

See, B. H. (2018) Evaluating the evidence in evidence-based policy and practice: examples from systematic reviews of literature. *Research in Education*, 102 (1), 37–61. doi:10.1177/0034523717741915.

Shadish, W. R., Cook, T. D. and Campbell, D. T. (2002) *Experimental and Quasi-experimental Designs for Generalized Causal Inference*. Boston, MA: Houghton Mifflin Company.

Shanahan, T. (2017) Why you need to be careful about visible learning. *The Reading Teacher*, 70 (6), 749–752. doi:10.1002/trtr.1570.

Sheffield Hallam University (2015) Can randomised controlled trials revolutionise educational research? Available from: www.shu.ac.uk/research/ceir/randomised-controlled-trials-1.

Sheldon, B. and Chilvers, R. (2000) *Evidence-based Social Care: A Study of Prospects and Problems*. Lyme Regis: Russell House.

Sheldon, J. (2016) 'What works' doesn't work: the problem with the call for evidence based practices in the classroom. Available from: https://files.eric.ed.gov/fulltext/ED574817.pdf.

Sheldon, T. and Chalmers, I. (1994) The UK Cochrane Centre and the NHS Centre for Reviews and Dissemination: respective roles within the Information Systems Strategy of the NHS R & D Programme, coordination and principles underlying collaboration. *Health Economics*, 3 (3), 201–203. doi:10.1002/hec.4730030308.

Siddiqui, N., Gorard, S. and See, B. H. (2018) The importance of process evaluation for randomised controlled trials in education. *Educational Research*, 60 (3), 357–370. doi:10.1080/00131881.2018.1493349.

Simpson, A. (2017) The misdirection of public policy: Comparing and combining standardised effect sizes. *Journal of Education Policy*, 32 (4), 450–466. doi:10.1080/02680939.2017.1280183.

Simpson, A. (2018a) Unmasking the unasked: correcting the record about assessor masking as an explanation for effect size differences. *Educational Research and Evaluation*, 24 (1&2), 3–12. doi:10.1080/13803611.2018.1520131.

Simpson, A. (2018b) Princesses are bigger than elephants: effect size as a category error in evidence-based education. *British Educational Research Journal*, 44 (5), 897–913. doi:10.1002/berj.3474.

Simpson, A. (2019a) The evidential basis of 'evidence-based education': an introduction to the special issue. *Educational Research and Evaluation*, 25 (1&2), 1–6. doi:10/1080/13803611.2019.1617979.

Simpson, A. (2019b) Separating arguments from conclusions: the mistaken role of effect size in educational policy research. *Educational Research and Evaluation*, 25 (1&2), 99–109. doi:10.1080/13803611.2019.1617170.

Simpson, A. (2019c) Whose priori is it anyway? A note on 'rigorous large-scale educational RCTs are often uninformative'. *Educational Researcher*, 48 (6), 382–384. doi:10.3102/0013189X19855076.

Simpson, A. (2020) On the misinterpretation of effect size. *Educational Studies in Mathematics*, 103 (1), 125–133. doi:10.1007s10649-019-09924-4.

Slavin, R. E. (1986) Best-evidence synthesis: an alternative to meta-analytic and traditional reviews. *Educational Researcher*, 15 (9), 5–11. doi:10.3102/0013189X015009005.

Slavin, R. E. (1995) Best evidence synthesis: an intelligent alternative to meta-analysis. *Journal of Clinical Epidemiology*, 48 (1), 9–18. doi:10.1016/0895-4356(94)00097-a.

Slavin, R. E. (2008) What works? Issues in synthesizing educational program evaluations. *Educational Researcher*, 37 (1), 5–14. doi:10.3102/0013189X08314117.

Slavin, R. E. (2016) Education policy in the age of unproven school and classroom approaches. Available from: https://robertslavinsblog.wordpress.com/2016/12/08/education-policy-in-the-age-of-proven-school-and-classroom-approaches/.

Slavin, R. E. (2018a) John Hattie is wrong. 21 June. Available from: https://robertsla vinsblog.wordpress.com/2018/06/21/john-hattie-is-wrong.

Slavin, R. E (2018b) Meta-analysis and its discontents. Available from: https://robert slavinsblog.wordpress.com/2018/06/07/meta-analysis-and-its-discontents.

Slavin, R. E. and Smith, D. (2009) The relationship between sample sizes and effect sizes in systematic review in education. *Educational Evaluation and Policy Analysis*, 31 (4), 500–506. doi:10.3102/0162373709352369.

Smith, J. and Naylor, R. (2001) Determinants of degree performance in UK universities: a statistical analysis of the 1993 student cohort. *Oxford Bulletin of Economics and Statistics*, 63 (1), 29–60. doi:10.1111/1468-0084.00208.

Smith, M. (2013) Evidence-based education: is it really that straightforward? *The Guardian*, 26 March. Available from: www.theguardian.com/teacher-network/2013/mar/26/teachers-research-evidence-based-education.

Smith, M. L. and Glass, G. V. (1977) Meta-analysis of psychotherapy outcome studies. *American Psychologist*, 32 (9), 752–760. doi:10.1037//0003-066X.32.9.752.

Snook, I., Clark, J., Harker, J., O'Neill, A., O'Neill, J. and Openshaw, R. (2009) Invisible learnings? A commentary on John Hattie's book *Visible Learning: A Synthesis of over 800 Meta-analyses Relating to Achievement*. New Zealand Journal of Educational Studies, 44 (1), 93–106.

Spencer, M. and Spencer, J. (2013) *Evidence*. Oxford: Oxford University Press.

Spohn, W. (2010) Laws, ceteris paribus conditions and the dynamics of belief. In J. Earman et al. (eds) op cit., 97–118.

Sternberg. R. J. (1995) Theory and measurement of tacit knowledge as a part of practical intelligence. *Zeitschrift für Psychologie*, 203 (4), 319–334.

Stone, R. (1993) The assumptions on which causal inferences rest. *Journal of the Royal Statistical Society, Series B (Methodological)*, 55 (2), 455–466. doi:10.1111/j.2517-6161.1993.tb01915.x.

Strevens, M. (2012) Ceteris paribus hedges: causal voodoo that works. *Journal of Philosophy* 109 (11), 652–675. doi:10.5840/jphil20121091138.

Styles, B. and Torgerson, C. (2018) Randomized controlled trials (RCTs) in education research – methodological debates, questions, challenges. *Educational Research*, 60 (3), 255–264. doi:10.1080/00131881.2018.1500194.

Sullivan, G. M. (2011) Getting off the 'gold standard': randomized controlled trials and education research, *Journal of Graduate Medical Education*, 3 (3), 285–298. doi:10.4300/JGME-D-11-00147.1.

Suri, H. (2018) Meta-analysis, systematic reviews and research syntheses. In L. Cohen et al. (eds) op cit., 427–439.

Thomas, G. (2004) Introduction: evidence and practice. In G. Thomas and R. Pring (eds) op cit., 1–18.

Thomas, G. (2012) Changing our landscape of inquiry for a new science of education. *Harvard Educational Review*, 82 (1), 26–51. doi:10.17763/haer.82.1.6t2r0891715x3377.

Thomas, G. (2016) After the gold rush: questioning the 'gold standard' and reappraising the status of experiment and randomized controlled trials in education. *Harvard Educational Review*, 86 (3), 390–411. doi:10.17763/1943-5045-86.3.390.

Thomas, G. and Pring, R. (eds) (2004) *Evidence-based Practice in Education*. Maidenhead: Open University Press.

Thompson, B. (2001) Significance, effect sizes, stepwise methods, and other issues: strong arguments more the field. *Journal of Experimental Education* 70 (1), 80–93. doi:10.1080/00220970109599499.

Thompson, B. (2002) What future quantitative social science research could look like: confidence intervals for effect sizes. *Educational Researcher*, 31 (3), 25–32. doi:10.3102/0013189X031003025.

Thompson, B. and Snyder, P. A. (1997) Statistical significance testing practices in the Journal of Experimental Education. *Journal of Experimental Education*, 66 (1), 75–83. doi:10.1080/00220979709601396.

Tilley, N. (1993) *After Kirkholt: Theory, Methods and Results of Replication Evaluation*. London: Home Office Police Department, Police Research Group.

Todd, P. E. and Wolpin, K. I. (2003) On the specification and estimation of the production function for cognitive achievement. *The Economic Journal* 113 (485), F3-F33. doi:10.1111/1468-0297.00097.

Torgerson, C. J. and Torgerson, D. J. (2001) The need for randomised controlled trials in educational research, *British Journal of Educational Studies*, 49 (3), 316–328. doi:10.1111/1467-8527.t01-1-00178.

Torgerson, C. J. and Torgerson, D. J. (2003) The design and conduct of randomised controlled trials in education: lessons from health care. *Oxford Review of Education*, 29 (1), 67–80. doi:10.1080/0305498032000045368.

Torgerson, C. J. and Torgerson, D. J. (2008) *Designing Randomised Trials in Health, Education and the Social Sciences*. Basingstoke: Palgrave Macmillan.

Torgerson, C. J. and Torgerson, D. J. (2013) *Randomised Trials in Education: An Introductory Handbook*. London: Education Endowment Foundation. Available from: http://educationendowmentfoundation.org.uk/uploads/pdf/Randomised_trials_in_education_revised.pdf (accessed June 2015).

Toulmin, S. E. (2003) *The Uses of Argument*. Updated edition. Cambridge: Cambridge University Press.

Tymms, P. B. (1996) Theories, models and simulations: school effectiveness at an impasse. In J. Gray, D. Reynolds, C. T. Fitz-Gibbon and D. Jesson (eds) *Merging Traditions: The Future of Research on School Effectiveness and School Improvement*. London: Cassell, 121–135.

Tymms, P. B. (1999) *Baseline Assessment and Monitoring in the Primary Schools*. London: David Fulton Publishers.

Upshur, R. E. G. (2000) Seven characteristics of medical evidence. *Journal of Evaluation in Clinical Practice*, 6 (2), 93–97. doi:10.1023/A:1026006801902.

Upshur, R. E. G., van den Kerkhof, E. G. and Goel, V. (2001) Meaning and measurement: an inclusive model of evidence in health care. *Journal of Evaluation in Clinical Practice*, 7 (2), 91–96. doi:10.1046/j.1365-2753.2001.00279.x.

US Department of Education (2003) *Identifying and Implementing Educational Practices Supported by Rigorous Evidence: A User Friendly Guide.* Washington, DC: Coalition for Evidence-Based Policy. Available from: www2.ed.gov/rschstat/research/pubs/rigorousevid.pdf.

US Department of Education (2018) *Reporting Guide for Study Authors: Group Design Studies.* Washington, DC: Department of Education, Institute of Education Sciences, National Center for Education Evaluation and Regional Assistance, What Works Clearinghouse.

Vaidyanathan, G. (2012) Redefining clinical trials: the age of personalized medicine. *Cell*, 148 (6), 1079–1080. doi:10.1016/j.cell.2012.02.041.

Waldrop, M. M. (1992) *Complexity: The Emerging Science at the Edge of Order and Chaos.* Harmondsworth: Penguin.

Weiss, C. H. (2002) What to do until the random assigner comes. In F. Mosteller and R. Boruch (eds) op cit., 198–224.

What Works Clearinghouse (2017) *Procedures Handbook.* Washington, DC: What Works Clearinghouse. Available from: https://ies.ed.gov/ncee/wwc/Docs/ReferenceResources/wwc_procedures_handbook_v4_draft.pdf.

Whyte, W. F. (1955) *Street Corner Society: The Social Structure of an Italian Slum* (second edition). Chicago, IL: University of Chicago Press.

Wiberg, M. (2014) Evidence-based methods and conforming judgment. In K. B. Petersen et al. (eds), op cit., 51–65.

Wickens, P. (1987) *The Road to Nissan: Flexibility, Quality, Teamwork.* Basingstoke: Macmillan.

Wiliam, D. (2016) *Leadership for Teacher Learning: Creating a Culture Where All Teachers Improve So That All Students Succeed.* West Palm Beach, FL: Learning Sciences International.

Wiliam, D. (2019) Some reflections on the role of evidence in improving education. *Educational Research and Evaluation*, 25 (5), 127–139. doi:10.1080/13803611.2019.1617993.

Wilkinson, L. and the Task Force on Statistical Inference (1999) Statistical methods in psychology journals: guidelines and explanations. *American Psychologist*, 54 (8), 594–604. doi:10.1037/0003-066X.54.8.594.

Willis, J and Saunders, M (2007) Research in a post-colonial world: the example of Australian Aborigines. In M. Pitt and A. Smith (eds) *Researching the Margins.* London: Palgrave Macmillan, 96–114.

Winch, C., Oancea, A. and Orchard, J. (2015) The contribution of educational research to teachers' professional learning: philosophical understandings. *Oxford Review of Education*, 4 (2), 202–216. doi:10.1080/03054985.2015.1017406.

Wolf, F. M. (1986) *Meta-Analysis: Quantitative Methods for Methods for Research Synthesis.* Newbury Park, CA: Sage.

Wood, P. (1995) Meta-analysis. In G. M. Breakwell, S. Hammond and C. Fife-Shaw (eds) *Research Methods in Psychology.* London: Sage, 396–399.

Woodcock, J. (2007) The prospects for 'personalized medicine' drug development and drug therapy, *Clinical Pharmacology and Therapeutics*, 81 (2), 164–169. doi:10.1038/sj.clpt.6100063.

Woodward, J. (2010) There is no such thing as a ceteris paribus law. In J. Earman et al. (eds) op cit., 27–52.

Worrall J. (2004) *Why there's no cause to randomize.* Technical Report 24/04. London: Centre for Philosophy of Natural and Social Science, London School of Economics.

Worrall J. (2007) Why there's no cause to randomize. *The British Journal for the Philosophy of Science,* 58 (3), 451–488. doi:10.1093/bjps/axm024.

Wright, D. B. (2003) Making friends with your data: improving how statistics are conducted and reported. *British Journal of Educational Psychology,* 73 (1), 123–136. doi:10.1348/00070990376289950.

Wrigley, T. (2015) Bullying by numbers. *Primary First,* 12, 10–13. Available from: https://issuu.com/synergyprint/docs/primary_first_12.

Wrigley, T. (2018) The power of 'evidence': reliable science of a set of blunt tools? *British Educational Research Journal,* 4 (3), 359–376. doi:10.1002/berj.3338.

Wrigley, T. (2019) The problem of reductionism in educational theory: complexity, causality, values. *Power and Education,* 11 (2), 145–162. doi:10.1177/1757743819845121.

Wrigley, T. and McCusker, S. (2019) Evidence-based teaching: a simple view of 'science'. *Educational Research and Evaluation,* 25 (1&2), 110–126. doi:10.1080/13803611.2019.1617992.

Zeuli, J. S. (1994) How do teachers understand research when they read it. *Teaching and Teacher Education,* 10 (1), 39–55. doi:10.1016/0742-0051X(94)90039-90036.

Zhao, Y. (2014) *Who's Afraid of the Big Bad Dragon?* San Francisco, CA: Jossey-Bass.

Zhao, Y. (2017) What works may hurt: side effects in education. *Journal of Educational Change,* 18 (1), 1–19. doi:10.1007/s10833-016-9294-4.

Ziliak, S. T. and McCloskey, D. N. (2008) *The Cult of Statistical Significance.* Ann Arbor, MI: University of Michigan Press.

Index

access 117, 152
agency 34, 50, 60, 65, 77, 93, 100, 102, 174, 212
attrition 30, 72, 76, 116, 130, 141, 173, 187, 188
averages 63, 64, 80–1, 110–11, 150–9, 186, 189–90, 194–5, 197, 211

bias 48, 78, 80, 82, 133–4, 139, 141–2, 162, 184–5, 197, 199, 200, 205
blinding 82, 104, 139–40, 152, 174
Bradford Hill, A. 51, 52

Cartwright, N. 12, 48, 59, 74, 75, 99, 120, 134, 138, 143, 179, 181
Cartwright, N. and Hardie, J. 20, 24, 36, 41–4, 50, 52–4, 74, 92, 100, 178, 179
'causal cakes' 37, 39, 41–2, 79, 92, 100, 143, 179, 181
causal mechanisms 44, 79, 84, 90, 122, 214
causality 17, 23, 39–61, 66, 68–9, 74, 79, 84, 87–92, 98, 100, 104, 105, 115, 121–2, 138, 142–3, 146–7, 174, 179, 181, 187, 214
ceteris paribus 39, 46, 56–60, 141–3, 146–7
chaos theory 95–6, 116
clinical trials 78, 103–18, 138,139, 178, 190, 194, 212
comparison groups 47, 87, 159, 162, 164, 170–1, 187, 195 *see also* control group
complexity theory 95–102, 121, 147
CONSORT 167–8
contamination 82, 130, 139–40, 143, 174
context 9, 11, 12, 21, 24, 28, 34–7, 39, 44, 50–6, 59–60, 66, 82, 84, 109, 119–25, 135, 160, 162, 173, 178–81, 195, 204

control group 46, 60, 63–4, 72, 73, 75, 76, 79, 87, 90–1, 102, 103, 105, 127, 128, 129, 131–2, 139, 142–3, 146–7, 154–7, 160–1, 165, 173, 174
controls 28, 47–8, 63, 65, 71, 76, 81, 87–8, 98–100, 119, 120–3, 173, 188, 197, 200, 213
counterfactuals 23, 28, 46–7, 59, 60, 68, 73, 76, 79, 87–8, 105, 147, 173, 187

data analysis 30, 44–5, 115, 149–66, 174–5, 187, 188
Deaton, A. and Cartwright, N. 71, 88, 138, 140, 144, 145, 152, 154, 178, 179–80, 181
distributions 80, 138, 152, 154–7, 159, 163, 174, 175
dose-response 78, 104, 107–11
'dredging' 115, 124, 139, 186

Education Endowment Foundation 49, 70, 108, 116, 117, 118, 168–9, 179, 182–3, 184, 191, 192, 207, 211
effect size 23, 51, 78, 82, 104, 105, 150, 159–66, 175, 182, 183–6, 188–90, 192, 194–5, 197
effectiveness 12, 92, 106, 117, 159, 160, 165, 179, 189
effects *see* causality; outcome measures; outcomes
efficacy 12, 37, 83, 92, 103, 106, 116–7, 165, 179, 181
emergence 20, 57, 81, 93, 96, 97, 98, 101, 118, 121, 146, 213
epistemology 35, 44, 77–9, 86, 90, 213
ethics 9, 22, 29, 34, 65, 75, 77, 114, 116–8, 124, 125, 127–9, 140, 152, 169, 173

Printed in Great Britain
by Amazon